Praise for the Book
Endorsements & Reviews

Pastoral Endorsement
"...Full of Practical Help"

Miranda has written an excellent book full of practical help for people who find themselves married to someone of a different belief structure. The issues are real and have lots of consequences if not handled well. I love Miranda's personal stories of her journey. She has navigated this journey with dignity and grace. It is my privilege to know Miranda and to see her excel with this book!

—*Steve Long, Senior Leader, Catch the Fire Toronto. Author of "My Healing Belongs to Me," "On the Run," "The Faith Zone" and several other books.*

Pastoral Endorsement:
"The journey...is very real..."

...I know the author and can testify that the journey she has walked is very real. ...Her description of a marriage between a believer and unbeliever is extremely realistic and well portrayed...there is a responsibility on both partners to...continue the journey of first love. I commend you Miranda for being so brave and inviting others to invest in your own individual journey with...tenacity...

—*Pastor Cheryl Davies, Heaven's Place Ministries, Phoenix, Arizona*

A Unique Resource for Issues Often Endured in Silence

All marriages have differences, but one of the most difficult challenges...is the existence of a spiritual wedge between partners. In this book, Miranda J. Chivers meets a need that is much needed in the body of Christ, by providing a resource to turn to for those who find themselves in an unequally yoked union.

She breaks the silence and addresses issues and questions that are often endured by many in silence. Beyond the title of the book, Miranda over-delivers...in this extremely well written book.

Miranda offers a perspective on how to find rest for a shriveled spirit and water for a thirsty soul from a God who feeds us with supernal manna! Great resource, Highly recommended!

—*Elenah Kangara, Christian Literary Prestigious Henri Award Winner and Author of Amazon Bestseller "Supernal Grace"*

A Real How-To Kit for Anyone in a Similar Situation

This is a powerful book! The author shares her very personal story of challenge and victory in her own marriage, and the hard-won lessons she learned along the way. This book will be a blessing and a real how-to kit for anyone in a similar situation. The keys I discovered in reading this book are to keep faith, love and serve, practice proven relationship skills, forgive, persevere, and keep hope alive each day knowing that a loving God is with you every step of the way. I highly recommend this book.

—*Bento C. Leal III, Author of Amazon Bestseller "4 Essential Keys to Effective Communication in Love, Life, Work--Anywhere!"*

A helpful book that covers a sensitive topic

When I first heard that this book was coming out, I immediately thought, "Now THAT is a topic that needs to be discussed more." You just don't hear much about unequally yoked marriages and it needs to be talked about more...Chivers has written this book thoroughly, brilliantly, and in a very sensitive manner. It doesn't come across as preachy...you will feel like a good friend is talking with you about this sometimes painful subject. I highly recommend this book to any Christian who is in an unequally yoked marriage or to any Christian who has a friend who is in an unequally yoked marriage. I personally didn't understand what it would be like...but at least now I know...enough to help someone who is in one. Read it today and have your eyes opened.

—*Ashley Emma, Bestselling Author of "Undercover Amish"*

Thoughtful, intelligent understanding of how to thrive in one's personal beliefs when the marriage partner is on another track...

Intelligently written, Ms. Chivers' words offer guidance to not only those in an unequally yoked Christian marriage, but those in any marriage in which...beliefs are not matching. Written from a compassionate and loving viewpoint, Ms. Chivers work deserves a place in marriage counseling offices everywhere!

—*Katharine Elliott, Bestselling Author of "A Camino of the Soul: Learning to Listen When the Universe Whispers."*

All Marriages are Unequally Yoked in Different Ways at Different Times—HIS Plan Saved this Marriage

Miranda J. Chivers has put her heart into writing UNEQUALLY YOKED. She has intimately shared her journey of leading her marriage through changes and challenging viewpoints, working through all of it by keeping God's WORD in her heart and implementing God's PLAN in her marriage...

She weaves the beautiful relationship that God intended the marital union to provide...oneness with your spouse, yourself and God—in the trilogy of marriage.

...an excellent resource for all marriages...spousal relationships are forever evolving...to keep our love relationships moving in a positive direction, combining objective assessment with Miranda's example...can bring resolution and peace to our marriages, our hearts, and our minds.

—Virginia Ritterbusch, Author of "Reframe Your Viewpoints: Harness Stress & Anxiety—Transform It Into Peace & Confidence"

Very Helpful!

Unequally Yoked is a helpful book for anyone who finds him-or herself in the situation of believer married to unbeliever. Miranda speaks from her own experience in a way that makes you not feel alone and helps you recognize the situation for what it is. She understands, educates and encourages...

—Kristen Tiber, Author of "At the Well: Discovering God's Plan for Finding True Love"

Inspiring and thought provoking

The depth of topics and issues covered within this book was amazing...She shares the thoughts and struggles the believing spouse may have, the need of a good support system, and impresses on the reader the importance of one's personal faith walk...and consistency within it...I found this book to be very eye opening...it...has enabled me to see ways I can be part of their support system.

—Tina Pocernich, Author of "Open Doors Open Hearts: Change Lives with Generosity, Love, and Compassion"

Perfect for anyone married to an unbeliever!

This book is exactly what I need right now... It's very supportive and encouraging and so reassuring to know I'm not alone!

—Chris Lambert, Author of "Brother James: Growing Up With the Messiah."

Wisdom, encouragement, and practical answers for living with and loving an unbelieving spouse

Miranda tackles the multi-faceted challenges faced by a believer who is married to an unbeliever with candor, helpful suggestions, and Scripture. She shares from her own experience, holding up a high standard for the believing spouse... If you're looking for wisdom, encouragement, and answers about living with and loving an unbelieving spouse, this book is for you.

—*Ruth L. Snyder, Author of Twitter Decoded: Tips & Tools for Authors.*

The book that can change your marriage and your family's destiny—for the better.

Grab this excellently researched and well-written guide... If you have an unbeliever for a life partner, do you allow that to break your faith or grow it?...a crystal clear guide, infused with contagious love....This is no spiritual only woo-woo guide, it goes right down to how to have sex with your spouse...not the 50 shades variety but the Song of Solomon type...how God means you have a great time in the bedroom...how to harness this power. The combination of practical steps and guidance from the Bible, with quality writing that sparkles with joy and clarity makes this book unique. Don't hesitate to grab this, whether or not you have an unbelieving spouse.

—*Susan Jagannath, Bestselling Author of The Camino Ingles:6 days (or less) to Santiago*

Unequally Yoked is a book that could benefit anyone

Unequally Yoked is a book that could benefit anyone...encouragement, inspiration, and resources...an honest picture... Friends and family...will come to better understand what their loved one is going through and how they can support them.

...I felt uplifted and better informed...not only information...a glimpse into the author's heart...Ms. Chivers has a very successful career ahead, sharing her experiences in a compassionate way and helping others along the path she has already walked.

—*Marie Clapsaddle, Author of "Become a Tech-Active Senior: Defeat Your Fears, Get Connected, Expand Your World."*

So Much Useful Information.

...it is about looking at your own life and the role you play in taking responsibility for your own life...valuable if you want to help others who are married to a non-believer too...

—*Lisha Lender, Author of Breaking the Silence: A Call to the Church to Help Victims of Child Abuse*

Are you Unequally Yoked and looking for answers?

How do you stay in a committed, covenant relationship when the other spouse does not believe like you do? Miranda J. Chivers addresses this question with the depth of biblical as well as personal understanding.

—Susan B. Mead, Award-winning Author of Dance with Jesus: From Grief to Grace and Don't Go Through Life Naked: How to Clothe Yourself in God's Power

Not by "religious rules."

...I am in a strong Christian marriage...applying most of the principles to our family and friends...We...agonize how to...witness... stand strong while...the world ...is...against us...influence them to the love of Jesus without any of those "religious rules." Thanks Miranda, you...made ...principles come alive. God bless you as you continue your journey.

—Kate Sanderson, Musician, The Sandersons Gospel Music.

If This is An Issue in Your Marriage ... You Need This Book!

Written with clarity and compassion and packed with practical and specific approaches to strengthen your faith and relationship. The author...encourages the reader to view things through the lens of their spouse, i.e. their level of understanding, their upbringing, interest, level of faith or non-faith...I've already recommended this to a friend of mine who's dealing with this very issue.

—Glenda Gabriel, Life Coach

Practical and clear approach to a tough topic

...I was deeply pleased with the practical, clear approach that the author has taken to address this real-life issue...As someone in ministry, I was pleased with...so many doctrinal topics...recommending to (those) seeking support...help many people...to be faithful in an unequally yoked marriage.

—Nancy Braun, Community Life Director, Winnipeg, Canada

As a pastor for many years, I run across...

As a pastor for many years, I run across the issues that many people deal with in unequally yoked marriages. I am so thankful that Miranda has decided to speak out and share what God has shown her. I will use this book as a reference for others in my ministerial counseling. It is going to help so many people!

—Amazon reader "LM"

A Great Must Read!

...a must read for anyone that has...questions ...re...Marriage of Christians and Non-Christians...encourages the reader to ponder the unanswered questions...(of) their...understanding and belief systems...will equip the reader with knowledge and keys to help...discern what the Bible actually teaches about Marriage.

—Donna M. Garth

Practical and inspiring

While I am a Christian, I willingly chose to marry a man that is a nonbeliever...I fall into the category of..."spiritually immature," assuming that our love could overcome any religious differences. What I was searching for, and found in this book, are practical suggestions that I could apply to everyday situations in my home. This book, most importantly, brings me back to an examination of my own heart and actions... I feel like I have hope that I can be the wife I need to be and know how to pray for my husband.

—Amazon verified Reader: Amanda

Leads to understanding

This book is well-written and thought provoking...provides helpful insights for navigating the effects of different belief systems within a marriage...This is good guidance...to understanding and personal peace.

—Amazon verified Reader CE

Offers Insight and a path to peace

This is an excellent book about how to deal with an unbelieving spouse. Instead of looking at your situation as being hopeless, it offers insight and shows you a path to peace I would highly recommend it to anyone who is in an unequally yoked marriage.

—Amazon verified Reader masper

Good to hear other experiences

This was a surprise as it was not only well written and clear, which I expected, it was also non-judgmental. I was interested because I also live a marriage to a non-believer. I don't consider myself an expert because I am still struggling...But...as Miranda said, we have to listen. My experience didn't even get to the first step she has in this book...I tried my best to show them what a Christian is by how I behaved and what I believed.... I will not know until this life is over if I did the right thing. All I know is I did my best...

—Amazon verified reader Christine

UNEQUALLY YOKED

**Staying Committed to Jesus and
Your Unbelieving Spouse**

UNEQUALLY YOKED

Staying Committed to Jesus and Your Unbelieving Spouse

MIRANDA J. CHIVERS

UNEQUALLY YOKED:
Staying Committed to Jesus and Your Unbelieving Spouse.

Copyright © 2018—Miranda J. Chivers.
Published by: Sanctified Hearts Publishing
ISBN: E-book 978-1-7751895-2-7
ISBN: Print: 978-1-775-1895-0-3

Scripture quotations marked NKJV are taken from the Holy Bible, NEW KING JAMES VERSION®. Copyright © 1982 by Thomas Nelson. Used by permission. All rights reserved. Scripture quotations marked NIV are taken from the Holy Bible, NEW INTERNATIONAL VERSION. Copyright © 1973, 1978, 1984, 2011 by Biblica, Inc. Used by permission of Zondervan. All rights reserved worldwide. (www.zondervan.com) Scripture quotations marked NLT are taken from the Holy Bible, NEW LIVING TRANSLATION. Copyright © 1996, 2004, 2007 by Tyndale House Foundation. Used by permission of Tyndale House Publishers, Inc., Carol Stream, Illinois 60188. All rights reserved. Scripture quotations marked NLV are taken from the Holy Bible, NEW LIFE VERSION. Copyright © 1969 by Christian Literature International, Oregon City, Oregon 97045. Scripture quotations marked MSG are taken from THE MESSAGE. Copyright © 1993, 1994, 1995, 1996, 2000, 2001, 2002. Used by permission of NavPress Publishing Group. Scripture quotations marked VOICE are taken from THE VOICE™. Copyright © 2008 by Ecclesia Bible Society. Thomas Nelson Publishers. Used by permission. All rights reserved. Scripture quotations marked ESV are taken from The ESV® Bible (The Holy Bible, English Standard Version®) copyright © 2001 by Crossway, a publishing ministry of Good News Publishers. ESV® Text Edition: 2011. The ESV® text has been reproduced in cooperation with and by permission of Good News Publishers. All rights reserved. Scripture quotations marked AMP taken from the Amplified® Bible (AMP), Copyright © 2015 by The Lockman Foundation. Used by permission. www.Lockman.org Scripture quotations marked AMPC taken from the Amplified® Bible (AMPC), Copyright © 1954, 1958, 1962, 1964, 1965, 1987 by The Lockman Foundation. Used by permission. www.Lockman.org

Cover Design and Formatting:
Happy Self-Publishing

Disclaimer

The advice given within this book are the author's personal thoughts. They are not intended to be a definitive or expert set of instructions. You may discover there are other methods and resources more applicable to your personal situation. This book is not intended to be a substitute for professional help. The author is not a medical or spiritual professional, nor a marriage counselor. This book is not intended to diagnose, treat or cure any physical, medical or spiritual disorders or conditions. The reader is responsible for his or her own actions, as well as his or her own interpretations of the material found within this publication. The reader is urged to consult a pastoral advisor, professional marital therapist or other professional for further support. The author shall not be held liable for any damages resulting from the use of this book. Any perceived slight of any individual or organization is purely unintentional.

At the time of publication, all external website links mentioned in this publication were correct. However, due to fluid nature of the internet, it is possible that they may change in the future. The author bears no responsibility for any errors in this regard. The author is not responsible for any damages that result to the reader's computer that may result from clicking on these links. The author reserves the right to update this information in future editions.

"One of the biggest religious divides cuts across religious traditions rather than between them. It is the difference between those who treat religion as a magnifying glass to help expose and oppose the sins of others more effectively, and those who treat it as a mirror to help one's own spiritual and moral life by fostering introspection and personal repentance and transformation."

— James F. McGrath[1]

[1] Exploring our Matrix, The Great Religious Divide, October 25, 2015 http://www.patheos.com/blogs/exploringourmatrix/2015/10/the-great-religious-divide.html Used with permission.

Dedication

This book is dedicated to all the brave soldiers at the front lines of the Christian faith in unequally yoked marriages who are fighting the good fight with quiet and valiant suffering. If you wonder if you are winning or losing the war, if you feel discouraged or question your ability to continue in this battle, I want you to know this: God has heard your cries for help and has seen your pain. I encourage you to stand tall and continue in the fight so that one day you may be able to say:

> *I have fought the good fight, I have finished the race, I have kept the faith. Finally, there is laid up for me the crown of righteousness, which the Lord, the righteous Judge, will give to me on that Day, and not to me only but also to all who have loved His appearing.*
> — 2 Timothy 4:7–8 NKJV

Table of Contents

Links:

Do you want the free workbook?

Click the link on my website: https://mirandajchivers.com

Learn how to hear from God. Check out the courses at the Christian Leadership University.

Here is the link: https://www.cluschoolofthespirit.com?affiliates=84

Discover how you can write and self-publish your own book:

Go here: https://xe172.isrefer.com/go/curcust/mchivers

Introduction

All marriages have differences, but faith differences are unique. When one person discovers that Jesus is the way, the truth and the life and they commit their life to Him, a giant shift occurs in the relationship. Suddenly two people who were in sync prior to this change are no longer so. A spiritual wedge has come between them.

The unbelieving spouse may perceive this shift as an emotional affair, and may react accordingly. This puts the believer in a difficult dilemma. The most important human being in their life refuses to join with them and share in this personal and pivotal experience. Can such a marriage be healthy and grow if two people have such divergent beliefs?

If we—as the believing spouse—are unable to speak openly about faith in our homes, we feel both shut-down and torn between our spiritual and physical loves—pressured to choose one over the other. We want spiritual harmony in our homes, but this seems unattainable.

Our new or renewed spiritual life can seem like an earthquake, threatening our marriage. We worry, is everything about to come tumbling down? Can we avoid these rock slides that force us to take different paths from other Christians? Is there a secret that we haven't discovered?

How can we nurture our connection with God while living in an environment where God is not welcome?

Persevering in our faith while married to an unsaved spouse is a very lonely and difficult journey. Some of us may be in a marriage that also struggles with workaholism, substance abuse, adultery or other chronic sins. The unique support we need isn't readily available in the church, nor in the secular world.

However, we are not alone. God sees our trials and struggles and He sends us the answers that we need when we need them. We may question why we are on this difficult path, but His ways are always higher than our ways (Isaiah 55:9). We need only trust.

The Bible gives us encouraging examples that show us that we are not the first ones to carry this burden. Our journey is not as unique as we might think. We can capture strength from the story of Abigail in 1 Samuel 25. A marriage to an abusive drunkard is a hard life and we can imagine the trials that she endured. Nonetheless, God's plan for her was freedom from that despairing life. 2 Samuel 11 tells us of the affair between Bathsheba and King David. She was married to a workaholic husband who refused to visit his lonely wife because his job was more important.

The book of Hosea portrays a dysfunctional, unequally yoked marriage that seems to fit right into our sexually crazed society. Hosea was a prophet of God specifically instructed by God to marry a prostitute and to have children with her, as a message to the people of Israel. We read this disturbing story of Hosea's difficult life and shake our heads at the shame that he had to endure. But we sometimes miss the fact that God loved the prostitute so much that He offered her sanctification and redemption in a marriage with a husband who would never give up on her. She only had to embrace the new life being offered.

In the New Testament, we learn of women who received the Good News, such as Timothy's mother Eunice and his grandmother Lois, and there is no mention of their husbands doing the same. We read of Joanna, the wealthy wife of Herod Antipas' household manager, an unbeliever. She helped to finance the apostles' work.

In Acts 16:14–15, the businesswoman Lydia led her entire family to the Lord.

These biblical examples show us that even if your spouse has not accepted Jesus into their heart and life yet, you can still serve God effectively and continue to grow in your faith. You don't have to sit alone in the back row of the church and feel sorry for yourself. However difficult, God has a purpose for you and your marriage. These stories in the Bible prove that God *can* and *does* use anyone, at any time, and in any place. We just need to be willing to be that instrument.

For my part, I am not a theologian, pastor, or Sunday school teacher—neither has my Christian life been a shining example of what to do. I've lived more than two-thirds of my life in unequally yoked marriages—and I've learned many of my lessons the hard way—through trial and error. My searches for helpful resources— both in the marketplace and in the church—have proved frustrating. Jesus' final command was to spread the Gospel to the world. I've wondered...how can I do that when my own home seems closed to the receptivity of the Good News? Is there a formula that I can crack open?

We use guidebooks for so many things in our lives—whether it is a recipe for our favorite dessert or for raising our children. There are plenty of self-improvement books and marriage books on the market—but very few address the distinct problems faced by those living with an unsaved spouse. If we are going to succeed and thrive in our unequally yoked marriages, we need a guidebook. I didn't have one when I needed it. I decided to write one to help both you and me.

This book is not about my life, but to get the most out of it, and it may help to know a little bit about my journey.

In 1997, my husband and I left the big city and moved to one of the most beautiful areas of Canada, in Northern Ontario. In the multicolored granite hills of the Canadian Shield, our mid-century scribed log home was tucked into the dense mixed forest overlooking a sparkling quiet lake. Included with our purchase was a tiny rundown cottage resort. With my husband's income as an airline pilot and a lot of hard work, we were certain we could turn it into a viable venture. My career as a social worker helped me to assess and prioritize the heavy physical and mental demands of running a complicated tourism business. Life was challenging, but the haunting beauty of the wilderness captured my soul.

Four years later I became ill with an unknown disease and doctors feared the worst. The eventual diagnosis of Sarcoidosis and other autoimmune diseases predicted a painful and unknown future. This caused me to re-evaluate my life.

Spiritually, I knew that I needed supernatural strength to get through this—strength that I did not have within myself. Reluctantly, I turned to The One that I had once followed. My gradual return to faith was encouraged as I pleaded for the restoration of my health.

The first step to physical healing required complete rest. Seemingly overnight, my ambitious businesswoman status changed to "no longer employed." My formerly busy mind grasped for a new purpose. Perilously, I threw myself into over-parenting our two intellectually challenged adult daughters. My life, controlled by anxiety and fear, continued to spiral downward.

Desperately overwhelmed, I cried for something to shift. *I needed healing.* In 2007, we made a pivotal decision to purchase a winter vacation home in Arizona, hoping that the sunny, dry desert climate would improve my health.

A new home, even a part-time winter home—brings both anxiety and the joy of making new friends and exploring new activities. While my husband continued to commute in his job as an airline pilot, I spent many weeks alone, slowly attempting to regain my physical strength in the warm Arizona sunshine. That solitary time gave me plenty of opportunity to explore the diverse churches that thrive in the Phoenix East Valley. Since my husband was not an avid churchgoer, my search for spiritual growth targeted only my own needs and entailed a search for mutual Christian friendship and understanding.

My time alone with my Heavenly Father became my sacred time in the desert. The northern wilderness had left me physically and mentally exhausted, and aching with loneliness. In the desert, I found answers for my shriveled spirit and water for my thirsty soul. My spiritual needs changed rapidly as my Heavenly Father reached down and fed me supernal manna. The more I grew in my faith, the more I hungered. Lengthy times of introspection led me deeper into the Word of God. As I grew in my faith, I felt my spirit expand and the light of Heaven seemed to shine right through my tired body, bringing it back to life.

Although I had grown up in a Christian home, I abandoned my faith when my first marriage failed. When I remarried, my new husband had no religious upbringing and despite having a vague belief in God, he had no interest in "religion." My rediscovery of faith was confusing to him. As far as he was concerned, he had not married a Christian, so why was it that I felt the need to change my life?

While he questioned my obsession with Christianity, I could not understand why he wasn't interested in learning about the Lord and growing with me. I tried everything I could think of to push him into accepting my beliefs. I prayed, I coerced him into attending church, I begged him to read scriptural literature, I played Christian music both at home and in the car, I left the TV on Christian channels, I talked about my faith incessantly, I even threatened him with hellfire. All to no avail. I became frustrated. Clearly, I was missing something.

The atmosphere in our home shifted unpleasantly. He seemed suspicious of Christians, mocked worship music and sneered at faith-related media. His coldness to the subject of Christianity created unwelcome boundaries with my Christian friends. I had to find creative ways to socialize with them outside my own home. His words and actions implied that he was not interested in attending church or learning about my faith. Eventually, I stopped asking him to join me. But my concern for his salvation was overwhelming.

Winter after winter in Arizona, summer after summer in my isolated northern home, I searched church after church for answers, but I came up empty.

In the winter of 2015, I discovered Fountain of Life Christian Fellowship in Mesa, Arizona. The energy in this church lifted my spirits, restoring my hope. It was here that I found many answers, but I also came face to face with the limits of my own understanding. While I prayed for God to change me to be a better wife, I also begged and pleaded for ways to witness to my husband.

Then one day, He opened my eyes and showed me something I needed to see. The reality of my life smacked me head-on into a new awareness. This revelation spurred me into understanding the missing piece in our marriage, while questioning the missing pieces in my own life. I felt like I had been climbing a mountain for years and then abruptly there I was—on the mountaintop looking down at the big picture, seeing the missing piece.

My "lightbulb moment" happened during a regular church service on January 17, 2016.

The energy level of this charismatic church was always vibrant and that day was no exception. Shortly after the worship started, I felt an odd stirring of the Holy Spirit. My attention was captured by the chemistry between a middle-aged married couple on the worship team. This couple frequently sang on Sunday mornings, and I had watched their delightful, high-energy worship on many occasions. Today, however, I noticed something different. As they sang and led worship in beautiful harmony, their eyes met and their faces lit up. Something deeply spiritual exploded between them. Suddenly, I knew what I was seeing. It was the Holy Spirit manifesting in their union. I felt the sharp stab of jealousy. Jealous, because I soberly realized that I did not have that same level of intimacy in my marriage.

I wondered...what is it like to have a marriage in which both people are walking in complete harmony with the Lord...what is it like to experience that kind of love? What is it like for two souls to be bonded so completely—body, soul and spirit? The Holy Spirit was showing me that here was an intimacy so enmeshed that only God could tell the two souls apart.

I turned to the Lord, and my heart cried out, "I want that!"

I heard the Lord reply to me, "Pray for your unsaved spouses. Pray for each other and their unsaved spouses. Pray together corporately, all you who have unsaved spouses. Come together and pray."

My understanding of that word from the Lord was the answer to the cry of my heart. If I truly wanted a spirit-filled relationship, I needed to join with others who were in unequally yoked marriages...those who were also crying out to the Lord for answers. I realized that together, through prayer and mutual support, we could help each other.

If this is also the cry of your heart, then this book is for you. It's time to come together and mutually pray for one another. It's time to reach out and pray, "Dear God, it's time! It's time for the Holy Spirit to sweep into our homes and save our spouses."

As we pray, we must also examine the actions we take within our homes. When we discover Jesus, but our spouse does not, we walk on eggshells. We want to keep our marriage healthy and intact while living out and strengthening our faith—without our faith becoming a source of miscommunication and discord.

We need to join together to answer these difficult questions:

- How do we find joy while living in difficult circumstances?
- How do we strengthen our marriage and be the example to our spouses that God has called us to be?
- How do we lead them to Christ by our example?
- How do we follow Christ and model our lives for them to follow?
- How do we make sure that we are not an excuse for them to refuse to accept a personal relationship with Jesus Christ?

Can we learn to live as the Apostle Peter commands?

> *Wives, in the same way submit yourselves to your own husbands so that, if any of them do not believe the word, they may be won over without words by the behavior of their wives, when they see the purity and reverence of your lives.*
> — 1 Peter 3:1–2 NIV

How can we do this when there are so many divisive issues that threaten to tear our families apart?

If you have asked any of these questions, I want you to know that you can find joy in your circumstances. Your faith can thrive while married to the non-believer. Your loving example and devotion to Christ demonstrates His love and redemption. As we love those who don't love Him, we can shine His light everyday through our words and actions.

We cannot do this alone. We need one another. Instead of imprisoning ourselves in isolation, we can find support and acceptance in our Christian community. United in conversation and prayer, we can explore ways to strengthen our marriages, without sacrificing our faith in the process. In this book, we will learn how to do that while becoming an encouraging spiritual and physical family for one another.

As we come together, we can rejoice in God's promise—that we will bear fruit, even if takes our entire lifetime.

> *Those who are planted in the house of the LORD shall flourish in the courts of our God. They shall still bear fruit in old age; they shall be fresh and flourishing, to declare that the LORD is upright; He is my rock, and there is no unrighteousness in Him.*
> — Psalm 92:13–15 NKJV

Whether you are looking for help in your own marriage or for someone else who is suffering, I pray that as you read along with me, you will gain perspective, hope, help, and comfort in navigating the turbulent waters of your unequally yoked marriage.

Understanding Your Unequally Yoked Marriage

There's an old saying—you can't fix what's broken if you don't know what's wrong. Staying committed to Jesus while living in an unequally yoked marriage is challenging. You may feel defeated at times. But take heart. You can grow your faith and have a healthy, happy marriage too. Understanding the problem is half the solution. You can't get rid of weeds if you don't kill the roots. If we want to dig in and remove the obstacles that are preventing us from growing, we need to know what we are dealing with. In this section, we explore the root of our dilemma so that we can gain the understanding that we need to propel us forward in our Christian growth.

Let's start at the beginning.

CHAPTER ONE

Living on Different Levels

And it shall come to pass in the last days, says God, That I will pour out of My Spirit on all flesh; Your sons and your daughters shall prophesy, Your young men shall see visions, Your old men shall dream dreams.
— Acts 2:17 NKJV

In my dream, my husband and I are going on a trip. We arrive at our pre-flight hotel with a car full of luggage, but there are no trolleys available, nor anyone to help us. We drag our bags into the hotel with great effort. As we check-in, we notice a busy lobby filled with hundreds of other people who are also trying to check-in at the same time, making for a very noisy and crowded environment. We must take the elevator to get to our rooms, but they are blocked by this large crowd. A moving mountain of suitcases clutters the floor, further obstructing our passage.

Rather than fight the crowds, I decide to do some shopping and wait for things to calm down. My husband takes the stairs and finds another way to our room. Eventually, the crowd thins out and I can access the elevator. Once inside, I realize that I have forgotten the room number. I press what I think is the right button, but when the doors open, I know I am on the wrong floor. I feel lost. I start to panic.

I pick up the white hotel phone and try to call him, but the noise in the lobby prevents me from hearing the operator. Then, I realize that I've forgotten the room number. I don't know where he is or how to reach him. I go floor to floor looking for him, knocking on doors. All this time, I'm dragging our bags with me.

Eventually, I find him. He laughs at me, scoffing, "What took you so long?" His sarcastic reaction upsets me. I believe that he deliberately abandoned me, knowing that I would become confused and lost. I am both perplexed and furious.

I fret, "Why did he abandon me with all this luggage? Why didn't he come looking for me?"

I angrily reply, "I didn't know the room number. I had to go floor to floor to try to find you. Plus, you left the bags behind. I had to do all the work lugging them from floor to floor. Do you have any idea how much work that was?"

If you are interested in dream interpretation, you can probably pull many threads out of this one. For me, this dream painted a vivid picture of my emotional state and our relationship at the time. The baggage in the dream represented emotional baggage that I felt I needed to carry with me everywhere. This slowed me down, hindering me from getting to my destination, as well as impairing my relationship with my husband. His approach to dealing with the problem was to dump the baggage, push through and reach the end goal as quickly as possible. My approach was to procrastinate (shopping) and wait for the stress to pass before dealing with the work ahead of me—waiting for an easier way to carry not only my bags, but his as well.

The background noise from the crowds and my stressed state made it impossible to "hear" the conversation on the telephone. This inability to hear represented a difficulty in communication.

At the time, in real life, I felt that we were at an impasse in our communication—unable to get our points across to each other. However, I didn't understand why. It wasn't until months later that I re-evaluated the dream and realized the message that God was trying to convey to me. I was carrying around too much emotional baggage and it was interfering in our communication. I needed to simplify things.

It's true—I tend to complicate matters. In a way, this dream pointed out that I needed to put more effort into our marriage and learn to "take the stairs with him," instead of being lazy by "taking the elevator without him." I also needed to stop thinking that I was responsible to look after his emotional baggage, as well as my own.

Have you ever wondered whether God is trying to tell you something in your dreams? There is a saying that a picture is worth a thousand words. When God gives us a dream, He is painting a picture for us that gives us the message that we can see without hearing the words. Dreams are one of God's more fascinating communication tools. They can point out with clarity the very thing that we are having difficulty with in our day-to-day waking life, and sometimes, they provide us with the answers that we need to fix our problems.

Unfortunately, even though the solution to our dilemma may be in our dreams, bringing that solution to functional reality can be a challenge. The barrier is often communication.

From time to time, every couple experiences communication difficulties. Under normal circumstances, a few conversations usually clarify the problem or misunderstanding. However, when we carry our emotional baggage of past hurts, resentments and unforgiveness into our marriage, we often feel disconnected from our mates. You may know something is wrong, but you can't quite put your finger on it. You might feel frustrated, confused, or even angry.

You've probably experienced something like this when—in the middle of a conversation—you've discovered that your partner's understanding of the "facts" are vastly different from yours. When faith differences are added into the mix, communication can become bizarre.

Try to imagine someone who has never had any religious education of any kind, hearing that the blood of a man who died two thousand years ago will forgive our sins, and because of His sacrifice, we can go to Heaven. Then they hear about the Jewish roots of our faith and the story of the Israelites painting animal blood on their doorposts to keep the angel of death away from their homes. The story of Abraham preparing to sacrifice his only son Isaac on an altar only to be stopped by a voice from Heaven may have a nice ending, but what kind of father deliberately sets out to murder his only son? Now, add in our communion elements...when we "drink the blood of Christ and eat His flesh."

Someone who hears this for the first time might think: "A religion that believes in human sacrifice, eating human flesh, drinking human blood, and covering themselves with that blood to redeem themselves is cannibalistic, superstitious, and downright crazy. Of course, I don't want to believe that!" Let's remember then, that to an outsider, Christianity does indeed look strange.

Our emotional baggage is the result of doing things our own way, without God. We may call it sin, but many people do not believe in the concept of sin (as in sinning against God). If your unbelieving spouse was never educated in the Christian faith, they may have difficulty understanding our tenets of sin and salvation.

Our western society has been educated with a psychological interpretation on self-reliance and independence. This implies that our only responsibility is for our closest loved ones and ourselves. We elevate ourselves on man-made pedestals and push for success in whatever we define as valuable. Sometimes this comes at the expense of our relationships.

Many people see themselves and others as self-made, whether as a success or as a failure. When a person fails in their life, they believe that if they admit they have messed up, they can overcome their feelings of guilt and shame by changing their ways and attitudes. They can redeem themselves. They may or may not admit the need to confess to those that they have hurt and to ask for forgiveness.

Self-help programs are often good at pushing people to understand and change their behavior. But only those truly following Christ will call sin what it is and encourage us to repent to an almighty God and accept the forgiveness that awaits us under the banner of the cross. It is only here that we can truly drop our baggage of guilt and shame.

Because so many people view the word 'sin' as an old-fashioned term that no longer belongs in modern society, we need to understand how our spouse interprets the concept of sin and the process of redemption from sin. This is one step up the irregular staircase of understanding from where they are standing. We are the ones that need to take the initiative to start the flow of information. It is very unlikely that they will walk in our direction without any movement on our part.

This brings us to three imperative steps. First, we need to understand our faith well enough that we can carry on a clear and open-minded conversation with others. Second, we must recognize that our unbelieving spouse may have difficulty comprehending our Christian beliefs. Third, we need to be aware that our thinking and our language are colored by Christian concepts that we have learned through our many years of church involvement. Someone who has not lived as I have will not understand what I am trying to communicate, unless I first learn how to speak on their level in a way that invites them to step into my world.

When we find a way to help our loved one comprehend our Christian language and concepts, then they will begin to understand how we see and interpret the world through a Christian lens. The work of communicating our faith in our marriages, our families, and our communities takes patience, persistence, plenty of prayer, and vigilance. We must be prepared to give an answer for the hope that is in us, but to do this with gentleness and respect (1 Peter 3:15).

If we try to impose our faith on others without understanding their humanity first, we are like colonialists dominating foreign lands, refusing self-government to the native born. This causes strife and eventually civil war. People must be free and feel free to make their own decisions.

In marriage, we want love to govern everything we do. We want our partners to desire the Jesus within us, not resent Him. At the same time, we must not be passive bystanders. To be like Jesus, we must be as "wise as serpents and as innocent as doves" (Matthew 10:16). The virtue of patience needs to thrive in our life, while we wait for the Holy Spirit's strategic guidance to direct our words and actions. As Christians married to non-believers, we will never be truly in sync with our spouse, and we should not strive to be. After all the Bible tells us that:

> *Do not be unequally yoked together with unbelievers. For what fellowship has righteousness with lawlessness? And what communion has light with darkness?*
> — 2 Corinthians 6:14 NKJV

There will always be a void in our relationship if there is no commonality of faith. Although we must learn to accept this fact, we can pray for it to change. Change may require that we look inward at our own thoughts, motivations, desires, and beliefs. As we prepare to examine ourselves, we must ask the Holy Spirit to clarify what in us needs to change, and how we should do this.

Objectivity is one change that we can strive to make. This helps us to better understand the unbeliever's belief system, their spiritual desires and their motivations. Objective questions may include— what do they believe and what are those beliefs based upon? How do they view Christianity?

An understanding of Christian language requires a level of cultural education. Without that education, our language and figures of speech are hard to understand, and easy to misinterpret. If your spouse was raised in a different faith—it will complicate things even more. Christians, Jews and Muslims may share the books of Moses, but our interpretations of those books are quite different.

A person's ability to evaluate religious ideology also requires a degree of inner awareness and general spiritual intuitiveness. If your spouse operates with a logical scientific mind, they may have little comprehension of a creative, loving God whom they cannot see, feel or even imagine. Such a person may have difficulty tapping into the emotional elements of our faith. Inner awareness and spiritual understanding are concepts foreign to many people. If this subject only mildly interests them, the non-believer may dismiss the topic simply because of the commitment of time and the effort required to truly focus on their relationship to God.

Many of us Christians aren't much better. Our daily lives can be overwhelming, as we try to balance our jobs, family activities, childcare, housework and paying the bills. As one week blurs into the next, the years fly by. Going to church on our busy weekends is often an unwelcome intrusion on any private time that we might have. If we are truly honest with ourselves, some of us don't want to make the time for God either. It's so easy to procrastinate having those very important spiritual discussions in our homes. Ask me next week, next month, or on my vacation.

When that vacation eventually arrives, we struggle between pouncing on our unsuspecting spouse with the thought, "It's time to have a talk about your eternal salvation!" Or, avoiding that thought in favor of, "Let's just have fun and be together. I'll just ignore all those snide comments about Christians or the obscene jokes or the excess of everything that is going on around us."

We arrive home from our vacation to the same problems, the same routines, and the same feeling of emptiness in our marriages and in our homes. Once again, we find the same thoughts running through our minds: "If only I could get him to come to church," or "Why didn't I talk to him when I had the chance?" or "Why doesn't he ask me about my faith?"

We go round and round like a hamster on a wheel—desperately seeking answers—but unwilling to make the changes in ourselves or in doing the work required to make the changes in our home that would facilitate an answer to those very questions.

If we want change to happen, we must start with ourselves. As we work to make those changes in ourselves, we can begin to examine the differences between our belief system and that of our spouse. When we can understand what they think, how they think, and how they interpret our faith from the outside in, we can begin the process of education so that our spouse can understand how we see our faith and what we believe. We do not need a degree in apologetics to be able to defend our faith, but it helps to be able to see things from a different perspective.

In the book, *The Advancing Kingdom* by Dr. Jonathan Welton[2], he describes a scene in which a boy tried to watch a baseball game through a knothole in a wooden fence. All he could see were men running back and forth. To him, the game appeared quite boring and he could not understand why the crowd of people in the stands were so noisy, screaming and cheering, while alternating between sitting and standing. Why were people so excited? Then one day, he climbed a tree and observed the game from a higher perspective. At that point, he realized what he had been missing.

This is a great picture of how we walk through life. We all look through our own knotholes at our faith and think we have the entire picture. Our perception is not always reality.

The filters of our life experiences act like sunglasses to our soul that color our perception and reception of truth. Added to this, is

---

[2] Welton, Jonathan: Normal Christianity, Destiny Image Publishers; 2011

the incredible enigma of God. Our triune God is mysterious, never revealing all of Himself at once or to one person. Each of us sees one aspect of who He is and we have the privilege of connecting with, and sharing our diverse perceptions with others. By doing this, we deepen our faith and strengthen our human ties.

Love can only grow through relationship. The Song of Solomon is a beautiful, artistic portrayal of the perfect love story. It is frequently used as an allegory for the love that Christ has for His church. It shows how our relationship can grow if we continue to seek Him. He wants us to keep chasing Him, searching for greater truth. In searching for greater truth, we gain intimacy with Him. This is what He really wants—a deep intimate and personal relationship that we cannot get through any other source. If we close off our desire for intimacy and only focus on obtaining knowledge, we will not grow. Instead, we will become "religious" like the Pharisees that Jesus condemned in Matthew 23.

The Pharisees studied the Torah and the rabbinical writings, memorizing every dot and tittle. They believed that by doing so, God would see them as righteous, and welcome them into paradise after death. However, Jesus condemned them because they had lost the true meaning of the Scripture—God's desire for intimate relationship between God and humanity, and intimacy between humans.

As Christians, we seek harmony both in our relationship with our spouse, and in our relationship with God. In this marriage, harmony seems almost unattainable. We feel caught between two worlds—either living in a world of darkness and struggling to bring the light of Jesus into it, or finding ourselves in a constant position of warfare, fighting the darkness. Both positions are exhausting—potentially threatening our spiritual, mental and physical health. Somehow, we must learn to *be* the light in the darkness.

The steps and strategies we each need to take are relationship specific. Every person comes to their marriage with their own baggage, thoughts, ideals and spiritual belief systems. There is no set answer for every situation. However, in examining some of the commonalities that we face in our unequally yoked marriages, we can come together, knowing that we are not alone in our journey.

Bonding with others that struggle as we do, gives us the opportunity to share our challenges, joys and sorrows. Finding a community of believers who face the same trials as we do, is a step in the right direction to knowing that we are not isolated in our difficult journey. The following verse expresses the importance of community and not trying to do this all alone:

> *Let us consider how to inspire each other to greater love and to righteous deeds, not forgetting to gather as a community, as some have forgotten, but encouraging each other, especially as the day of His return approaches.*
> — Hebrews 10:24–25 VOICE

In inspiring and encouraging each other, we need to respect and honor the different levels of the perceptions of faith, both in our marriages and in our community of believers. When it comes to ourselves, we need to understand:

- What is it that we believe and why do we believe it?
- What are the underlying faith issues that are preventing our spouses from coming to know the Lord?
- How do we define salvation?
- How do we interpret and explain salvation to others?

Before we can answer those questions, we need to clarify whether our loved one is an uncommitted Christian or truly a non-believer. Knowing what they believe or don't believe will greatly affect how we discuss or deal with faith-related conversations.

CHAPTER TWO

Married to the Uncommitted Christian

*For by grace you have been saved through faith, and that
not of yourselves; it is the gift of God, not of works, lest
anyone should boast.*
— Ephesians 2:8–9 NKJV

This chapter is for those of you who are confused about what
your spouse believes. Maybe you are married to someone who
says they're a believer, but their lifestyle doesn't match their
words. Perhaps your spouse goes to church with you and rubs
shoulders with other believers, but you feel that they have not fully
committed themselves to Jesus.

Possibly they see you as the religious zealot in your marriage, and
they see themselves as more down-to-earth and realistic. Do they
view your enthusiasm for the Lord as "over the top"? Do they scoff
at your zealousness and argue over Scriptures and doctrine?

If you suspect that your spouse is only playing the Christian game,
you may have questioned if there is anything that you can do to
encourage them to fully commit their life to Jesus. Where do you
start...what do you say? Do you know what they believe and what
they do not believe?

It's very difficult to burn wet, green wood. It requires a lot of
preparation and attention. Until it lights, you will see more smoke
than flame. Likewise, the fire of the Spirit only lights the wood that
is ready to be burned. In the book of Revelation, the apostle John

quotes Jesus as warning the lukewarm churches of Sardis (Revelation 3:1–3) and Laodicea (Revelation 3:14–21).

> *I know your works, that you are neither cold nor hot. I could wish you were cold or hot. So then, because you are lukewarm, and neither cold nor hot, I will vomit you out of My mouth.*
> — Revelation 3:15–16 NKJV

This warning applies to us as well. It is so easy to slip into that lukewarm climate and be sucked into the world's attitude of "live and let live." We must always be vigilant of our conduct, attitude, and words—both in and outside of our homes.

God knows we are not perfect. We all have slip-ups, negative moments (or days), lose our temper, or commit other sins. We will never get it right, no matter how hard we try. Perfection doesn't happen in our physical lifetime. Thankfully, if we see where we have gone wrong, we can repent and make it right. I try to keep in mind the three "P's"—Persistence, Patience and Prayer.[3] These three words help me to keep my mouth shut and my attitude right. Many times, of course, I still lose my temper and my impatience takes center stage. Thankfully, with God's help, I am slowly becoming more like Jesus and losing my selfish and self-centered ways.

While we work on our imperfections and strive to become more like Jesus, we often wonder about our spouse. If they say they believe, but we are questioning their lives, then there must be something that can give us evidence that we are both on the same path. Jesus said:

---

[3] "The 3P's: Persistence, Patience, Prayer."
http://iambusiness.weebly.com/good-vibes/the-3-ps-persistence-patience-prayer.
April 23, 2012.

Enter by the narrow gate; for wide is the gate and broad is the way that leads to destruction, and there are many who go in by it. Because narrow is the gate and difficult is the way which leads to life, and there are few who find it.
— Matthew 7:13–14 NKJV

How narrow is the narrow gate of salvation? If someone is saved, shouldn't there be some evidence in their life? What about my own life? Does my light shine, or am I hiding it under a "bushel" of excuses?

What is that evidence? What does the Bible say?

Salvation Basics

Before we can talk about how faith demonstrates itself in the committed Christian's life, we need to clarify what we mean by "salvation." The Christian church encompasses some varying views about the salvation process. I take an Evangelical approach in this book, so if you come from an Anglo-Catholic background, your understanding may be slightly different.

The Evangelical approach to salvation requires an acceptance that we are born into a world contaminated with sin. We are physically and spiritually the descendants of Adam and Eve, the first humans to rebel against God. This seed of sin has been inherited by us, causing us to repeatedly transgress God's perfect laws. Although it is impossible for us to achieve perfection, God, in His perfect love, made a way for us to become perfect in His sight through the blood sacrifice of His son, Jesus Christ.

For by one sacrifice He has made perfect forever those who are being made holy.
— Hebrews 10:14 NIV

To start our new life with Christ at the helm, the pilot of our life, we must first surrender our pride and admit that we are sinners. Repentance is the key to surrender. Repentance means starting over. It is a complete turning away from our sin and changing our thinking. This may include making significant changes in our lives. This cannot fully happen without a belief in the true Son of God and in His ability to take away our sins and wipe the slate clean.

Acceptance of Jesus Christ as the Son of God includes the belief that:

- Jesus was born of a virgin.
- He lived a sinless life.
- He was crucified and died.
- He physically rose from the grave, evidenced by witnesses who saw Him after the fact.
- He ascended to Heaven in full view of hundreds of His followers.
- He will return to this earth one day as He promises in Revelation 22:20.

Accepting Jesus as the Savior of the world is not simply a nod to His divinity, it is a complete unabashed belief that He is in fact a member of the trinity—Father, Son, and Holy Spirit. Although He is God, He came to earth as a human being. His physicality shows us that He truly understands everything that we experience. His bloody death was a sacrifice of horrific proportions to take the punishment upon Himself that was deservedly ours. He suffered and died so that we don't have to.

Finally, His resurrection proves His immortality. Without a resurrection, Christianity would be meaningless. Our belief in the physical resurrection of Jesus makes Christianity different from other religions. Without the resurrection, we would only be following the path of another prophet. Jesus Christ was no ordinary prophet, He was the physical embodiment of the one true God.

When we bend our knee in repentance, we ask Jesus to forgive our sins as we accept His true divinity. Our commitment to follow

Jesus Christ requires that we submit our lives—body, soul and spirit. He is not only our Savior, but also our Lord—the master of our lives. By following Jesus, we are relieved of our spiritual burdens and fears. We receive the amazing gift of love, joy and peace in this life, and the promise of eternal life in Heaven after we die.

These are the first steps of becoming a part of the Christian family. We must recognize that we are saved by faith, and faith alone. Without Jesus, we are simply trying to save ourselves by our own strength. Any change that we make on our own is an ongoing struggle with our basic sinful nature and is likely to fail. None of us are righteous and we cannot make ourselves righteous by our own efforts. The Bible says:

> *For all have sinned and fall short of the glory of God, and all are justified freely by His grace through the redemption that came by Christ Jesus.*
> — Romans 3:23–24 NIV

You can live as righteously as you want to, but still never be good enough to stand in the presence of the Almighty. Jesus was the perfect lamb that took away the sins of the world (John 1:29), and it is in Him that we live and move and have our being (Acts 17:28 NIV). It is in Him that we put our trust and our faith. It is because of Him that we have eternal life.

God wants to bless us with the joy available in His Kingdom, not just in the afterlife, but also in this life. This cannot happen if our focus is not on Him and Him alone. When we divide our loyalty to God with our desires of the flesh, we short-change ourselves of the good things that He offers us. Becoming part of the family of God requires total commitment.

The Works Dilemma

If it is by faith alone that we are saved, is there a way that you can tell if someone is saved? Strictly speaking, the answer is no, because we cannot see into someone's heart. Only God can do that. If someone is living a righteous life, attends church and participates with all things Christian, is he or she a Christian? Maybe—maybe not. Churches are filled with people who grew up in the church, adopted a religious lifestyle, but never made a heart connection with Jesus. A person can be nice, doing all the right things, but still not be a Christian. It is all about having a humble and repentant heart wanting to connect with the heart of God.

A second type of uncommitted Christian are those we call "seat warmers"—people that attend church on the weekend but live like the devil during the week. Church is a habit, it's not a lifestyle. It does not change the way they run their business, how they talk to their family at home, how they treat others, the language they use, or the entertainment they choose.

These people see themselves as saved because they prayed the prayer of salvation once. They have missed the point of Christianity. A true relationship with Jesus changes a person from the inside out. A true Christian wants to change and become more and more like Jesus.

Some people will argue that you can tell when someone is saved because true faith is demonstrated by works. Many churches emphasize the importance of living Christianity out through good deeds. Whether it's helping inside the church building, or feeding the homeless, or being politically active for righteous accountability in our government, there are many ways that a person can do good deeds. The Apostle James sums up the works versus faith dilemma:

> *Thus, also faith by itself, if it does not have works, is dead.*
> — James 2:17 NKJV

For as the body without the spirit is dead, so faith without works is dead also.
— James 2:26 NKJV

To be clear, good deeds alone will not save you. You are only saved by grace through faith (Ephesians 2:8–9; Galatians 2:16). The change that Christ makes in your life after you have accepted Him into your heart, is observable in your life as righteous living and good works. A person that has genuinely repented and invited the Lord into their life will have measurable works verifiable by others.

Is Your Spouse Saved?

If you've had the salvation discussion with your spouse, perhaps they told you that they said the prayer of repentance once, so therefore they are saved. If you feel that there is a lack of righteous living or they have no hunger for the things of God, then you may question their sincerity. In this case, you want peace of mind in knowing that there has been a change of heart. Conversely, perhaps you want to have a sit-down talk to confront them about the lack of clarity in their lives. After all, the Bible does say that those who are filled with the Spirit will bear fruit.

But the fruit of the Spirit is love, joy, peace, forbearance, kindness, goodness, faithfulness, gentleness and self-control.
— Galatians 5:22–23 NIV

Those who love the Lord hunger for more of Him, as the Psalmist declares:

For He satisfies the longing soul, And fills the hungry soul with goodness.
— Psalm 107:9 NKJV

Being hungry for God means that you want to move more into His light and love. You want to attract the good things from God into your life. Moreover, since He's your Heavenly Father, you want

29

Him to be proud of you. God says He wants to give us good gifts (Matthew 7:11), and of course we want to receive them.

Just as we can be on different spiritual levels with our spouse, so too can believers be on different faith levels with one another. What your faith experience has been to date and how you interpret the Bible will all be reflected in your Christian lifestyle.

It's easy to look at someone and say, "You're not a Christian because..." but bear in mind it's what is in the heart that matters. We all show our faith differently through our unique personalities and God-given talents. But not everyone is anointed to be an apostle, prophet, evangelist, a teacher, or a preacher (Ephesians 4:11). Some of us are called to the mountain of business, and some to clean restrooms. Everyone has helping hands, but everyone helps differently. It's important that we don't judge someone's faith by what he or she does or doesn't do. It is God who judges the heart.

"But I need to know," you might say. This concern is understandable.

This is a tricky area to discuss, but I believe that you can spot a true Christian within a few conversations. Bear in mind that this is my personal belief, and the checklist I use is far from foolproof, so please do hold this loosely. It is extremely important that you do not judge someone because their life or conversation doesn't match up to the questions and answers listed here. Put all of this in your knowledge base and then look at your own life. Use this information to better understand what spiritual level your spouse is on, as well as what level you are on. I hope this will help you with some of your discussions or clarify that missing piece for you.

1. Can they point to a time or event when they decided to follow Jesus?

All the disciples and apostles made conscious decisions to follow the Lord. Jesus talked about being "born again" and differentiated between being born of the flesh and being born of the Spirit.

> *Jesus answered, "Most assuredly, I say to you, unless one is born of water and the Spirit, he cannot enter the kingdom of God. That which is born of the flesh is flesh, and that which is born of the Spirit is spirit. Do not marvel that I said to you, 'You must be born again.'"*
> — John 3:5–7 NKJV

At the age of seven, I recognized that I was a sinner and asked Jesus for forgiveness. However, I struggled with following the faith for most of my life. Many times, I repeated the cycle of falling away and coming back, without following through with a total commitment. My awakening to the truth happened during a health crisis four decades later. You could say that I slowly woke up and knew what I needed to do. I can't point to an exact date on the calendar, but I can point to a time when I made that decision. I began to study the Bible in earnest, repented for my wasted years, and vowed to serve the Lord for the rest of my life. Later in my faith, I received the baptism of the Holy Spirit, which triggered a deep hunger within me for greater intimacy with Jesus.

I was an on-again–off-again Christian for three-quarters of my life, never fully understanding my Christian faith, and never being fully committed to it. In those days, I was double-minded, exactly like the Bible warns us not be, in James 1:5–8.

When I fell away from the Lord, was I still saved according to Evangelical doctrine? Good question. It depends who you ask. The parable of the prodigal son is a good study for this subject (Luke 15:11–32).

2. Do they base their salvation on the fact that they attend church?

> *For God so loved the world that He gave His only begotten Son, that whoever believes in Him should not perish but have everlasting life.*
> — *John 3:16 NKJV*

> *He who has the Son has life; he who does not have the Son of God does not have life.*
> — *1 John 5:12 NKJV*

Salvation is found only in Jesus. No amount of church attendance will give you salvation. While people may judge on outward appearances, God sees the heart (1 Samuel 16:7). Standing in a kitchen does not make you a chef. Likewise going to church does not make you a Christian.

3. Where do they spend their money? Do they understand the need to support the local church and other Christian organizations? Do they willingly give to support the spread of the Gospel? Are they a charitable person by nature, or do they give grudgingly?

As the popular saying goes "follow the money." If you watch how a person saves and spends their money, you can tell where their priorities lie. A charitable attitude is a demonstration of a compassionate heart. We'll look at money more closely later.

> *Remember this: Whoever sows sparingly will also reap sparingly, and whoever sows generously will also reap generously. Each of you should give what you have decided in your heart to give, not reluctantly or under compulsion, for God loves a cheerful giver.*
> — *2 Corinthians 9:6–7 NIV*

Religion that God our Father accepts as pure and faultless is this: to look after orphans and widows in their distress and to keep oneself from being polluted by the world.
— James 1:27 NIV

4. Are they interested in, and do they enjoy learning about, the faith? Do they take the initiative in Christian activities? Do they read and listen to the Bible?

People who are serious about searching for and growing in their faith will usually be interested in faith-based discussions and will want to read and grow their knowledge. The Bible is very clear about the need to study and meditate on it daily.

Keep this Book of the Law always on your lips; meditate on it day and night, so that you may be careful to do everything written in it. Then you will be prosperous and successful.
— Joshua 1:8 NIV

5. Do they pray and petition the Lord during times of difficulty? Do they ask the Lord for strength and wisdom?

We all need supernatural strength during difficult times. Relying only on our own strength and wisdom often gets us into trouble.

But the salvation of the righteous is from the Lord; He is their strength in the time of trouble.
— Psalm 37:39 NKJV

Call to Me, and I will answer you, and show you great and mighty things, which you do not know.
— Jeremiah 33:3 NKJV

6. Does their lifestyle and attitude reflect one of praise and thanksgiving? Is there real joy that is attributable to their faith?

The Bible tells us to be joyful always. It is important to maintain an attitude of gratitude. Joy is one of the defining characteristics of the Christian life.

> *Rejoice always, pray without ceasing, in everything give thanks; for this is the will of God in Christ Jesus for you.*
> — 1 Thessalonians 5:16–18 NKJV

> *Yet I will rejoice in the Lord, I will joy in the God of my salvation.*
> — Habakkuk 3:18 NKJV

> *Dear brothers and sisters, when troubles of any kind come your way, consider it an opportunity for great joy.*
> — James 1:2 NLT

7. What is their general attitude toward life?

People that are grateful and happy exude a positive personality. When life is tough, they look for the silver linings in their difficulties. They are not afraid to ask for help, and are usually thankful for any help received. Other people want to be around them. Positive-minded people search for positive friends.

People that lean toward negativity find fault in others, gossip, complain about their lives, and generally display critical attitudes. They often refuse offers of help, but then complain that no one ever helps them. They are quick to negate solutions to problems, preferring to sit in a stew of their own making. Negative people usually gravitate to having negative friends.

Jesus said that what is inside one's heart comes out of the mouth.

> *But whatever [word] comes out of the mouth comes from the heart, and this is what defiles and dishonors the man.*
> — Matthew 15:18 AMP

Paul explained this further in his writings:

Let there be no filthiness and silly talk, or coarse [obscene or vulgar] joking, because such things are not appropriate [for believers]; but instead speak of your thankfulness [to God].
— Ephesians 5:4 AMP

Regardless of how bad life is, our attitudes should always reflect the strength and joy that comes with being filled with the Holy Spirit.

8. What is their attitude toward church involvement and worship?

A person that loves the Lord will generally want to worship and fellowship with like-minded believers. Appreciation for the style of worship will vary from person to person, and no one style of worship is more right or wrong than another.

For example, one of the disagreements in our marriage has been differences in the music we enjoy. My husband dislikes modern worship music and considers it no different than modern rock music. He prefers the traditional hymns— he sees them as more reverent. I see all Christian music as acceptable forms of worship. To me, it's the intent of the person and the spirit of the heart during worship that's important.

I particularly enjoy modern music. Some of my greatest breakthroughs happened when I learned to praise God during my most difficult battles. To me, music and dance are a victorious celebration of God's love and power. Praise and worship are integral weapons in our spiritual arsenal.

Regardless of our worship styles—church attendance, praise, and worship are a fundamental part of a spirit-filled believer's life.

The LORD is my strength and song, and He has become my salvation; He is my God, and I will praise Him.
— Exodus 15:2 NKJV

9. Do they talk about their faith and salvation with others?

Our speech either confirms or denies our association with Jesus Christ. A true Christian will acknowledge their faith when asked. Someone who isn't sure of their faith might shrug it off or be deliberately vague. A non-believer will never claim to be a believer unless it's to their advantage in a specific social circumstance (i.e., church functions or socializing with other Christians).

Sharing our faith is tough. Living it out at home is even harder. One of the biggest displays of our faith happens when we go through trials. It is during these times that the world can see how we cope with stress. Our honest reactions and attitudes toward stress can often open the door to others who want to ask us questions about our faith.

> *I have not hidden Your righteousness within my heart; I have declared Your faithfulness and Your salvation; I have not concealed Your lovingkindness and Your truth from the great assembly.*
> — Psalm 40:10 NKJV

> *For with the heart one believes unto righteousness, and with the mouth confession is made unto salvation.*
> — Romans 10:10 NKJV

> *Therefore, whoever confesses Me before men, him I will also confess before My Father who is in heaven.*
> — Matthew 10:32 NKJV

10. Do they acknowledge that there is only one path to salvation?

This is one of the toughest things for non-Christians to accept. Some Christians also struggle with this belief. It can be difficult to comprehend why God only made one path to Himself. After all, there are so many choices to everything else in this life.

Nor is there salvation in any other, for there is no other name under heaven given among men by which we must be saved.
— Acts 4:12 NKJV

Jesus said to him, "I am the way, the truth, and the life. No one comes to the Father except through Me."
— John 14:6 NKJV

Jesus declared that He is the only Way. We can only respond one of three ways. Either:

He was a liar...but the Bible's response to that is:

He committed no sin, and no deceit was found in His mouth.
— 1 Peter 2:22 NIV

He was a lunatic...but the Bible's response to that is:

All the people were astonished and said, "Could this be the Son of David?" But when the Pharisees heard this, they said, "It is only by Beelzebul, the prince of demons, that this fellow drives out demons." Jesus knew their thoughts and said to them, "Every kingdom divided against itself will be ruined, and every city or household divided against itself will not stand."
— Matthew 12:23–25 NIV

or...He was telling the truth.

11. Do they admit when they are wrong, and do they ask for prayer?

Humility is one of the key hallmarks of a true believer. Repentance goes hand-in-hand with humility. Certainly, one can be humble and repentant without being a Christian, but the Word declares this as an important marker of our spiritual status.

Confess your trespasses to one another, and pray for one another, that you may be healed. The effective, fervent prayer of a righteous man avails much.
— James 5:16 NKJV

12. Have they repented of their unbelief, or only for the wrong things they have done?

There is a big difference between repentance and simply saying sorry. Too often, we hurt or offend people and just say "Sorry," but true repentance is heartfelt and produces a change in the person's character and lifestyle.

> *For godly sorrow produces repentance leading to salvation, not to be regretted; but the sorrow of the world produces death.*
> — 2 Corinthians 7:10 NKJV

> *And to whom was God speaking when He took an oath that they would never enter His rest? Wasn't it the people who disobeyed Him? So we see that because of their unbelief they were not able to enter His rest.*
> — Hebrews 3:18–19 NLT

13. Which of these fruits are more evident in their lives?

> *The acts of the flesh are obvious: sexual immorality, impurity and debauchery; idolatry and witchcraft; hatred, discord, jealousy, fits of rage, selfish ambition, dissensions, factions and envy; drunkenness, orgies, and the like. I warn you, as I did before, that those who live like this will not inherit the kingdom of God. But the fruit of the Spirit is love, joy, peace, forbearance, kindness, goodness, faithfulness, gentleness, and self-control. Against such things, there is no law. Those who belong to Christ Jesus have crucified the flesh with its passions and desires. Since we live by the Spirit, let us keep in step with the Spirit. Let us not become conceited, provoking and envying each other.*
> — Galatians 5:19–26 NIV

Many people live good, moral lives and do not necessarily exhibit the "acts of the flesh" as Paul wrote here. However, these are common struggles for everyone, whether Christian or not, whether simply in our thought-life or in everyday living. Who has never struggled with envy or jealousy, or reacted in unjust anger? The difference between a Christian and a good moral person is that we, as Christians, are not relying on our own strength. We are to admit our shortcomings and ask the Lord to keep molding us into better human beings. We have the power of the Holy Spirit to give us the strength to live better lives.

14. Do they rest their salvation on infant baptism?

Therefore we were buried with Him through baptism into death, that just as Christ was raised from the dead by the glory of the Father, even so we also should walk in newness of life.
— Romans 6:4 NKJV

He who believes and is baptized will be saved; but he who does not believe will be condemned.
— Mark 16:16 NKJV

Unfortunately, in my searches regarding infant baptism, there is no reference anywhere in Scripture regarding the baptizing of infants or children. Every reference involves adults who are making a conscious decision to follow Jesus. After they repent, they demonstrate their faith through baptism. When I read Mark 16:16 above, it implies that if a person who is baptized does not believe, they are still condemned. Therefore, baptism alone does not save someone.

There are some excellent websites that explore the origins of infant baptism, the historical practices, and the twists and turns that the church has taken over the centuries. If you question this practice, the website bible.org has some great information.[4]

---

[4] "Lesson 35: Why We Do Not Baptize Infants (Genesis 17 and Other Scriptures)." Steven J. Cole https://bible.org/seriespage/lesson-35

15. Is baptism required for salvation?

Then one of the criminals who were hanged blasphemed
Him, saying, "If You are the Christ, save Yourself and us."
But the other, answering, rebuked him, saying, "Do you not
even fear God, seeing you are under the same condemnation?
And we indeed justly, for we receive the due reward of our
deeds; but this Man has done nothing wrong." Then he said
to Jesus, "Lord, remember me when You come into Your
kingdom." And Jesus said to him, "Assuredly, I say to you,
today you will be with Me in Paradise."
— Luke 23:39–43 NKJV

Clearly, the thief on the cross was never baptized. Yet Jesus
brought him into Paradise with Him that very day.

How often have you heard stories about a person accepting Christ
on their deathbed, but there is never enough time to be baptized?
Baptism neither saves one, nor is it required by one to be saved.

Baptism is a symbol of Christ's death and resurrection. When we
are baptized, we declare to the world that we are a follower of
Christ.

Therefore we were buried with Him through baptism into
death, that just as Christ was raised from the dead by the
glory of the Father, even so we also should walk in newness
of life.
— Romans 6:4 NKJV

The uncommitted Christian is reluctant to give all of themselves to
Jesus. This includes those Christians that rely on their salvation
experience as a type of fire insurance to keep them out of hell.
They may be afraid of giving up something in their lifestyle that
they know is ungodly, thinking that their loving Father would deny
them what they consider fun. Or perhaps they fear being seen by
their peers as religious.

Some struggle with past hurts that stop them from trusting the message of love and acceptance. They are afraid to believe that God truly wants to give them good gifts and a better life. They seem to miss Jesus' heartfelt plea:

> *If you then, being evil, know how to give good gifts to your children, HOW MUCH MORE will your Father who is in heaven give good things to those who ask Him!*
> — Matthew 7:11 NKJV

We must keep in mind that a full dedication to the Lord is a lifetime process. Everyone grows uniquely in their understanding of the Christian faith and the Lord works in all of us in different ways at the various stepping-stones of our lives.

I feel the need to repeat this again: Never judge someone's salvation. Everyone is at a different stage in their spiritual journey. We are to encourage one another in the growth of our faith. People who are not committed to a daily diet of the Word of God are going to progress at a much slower rate in their understanding than someone who is eager and desperate to fill their lives with more of Jesus.

If you believe that your spouse is on this lukewarm path and you see yourself as the zealous one in your marriage, take heart. Kindly encourage them and support them as they walk through tight spaces until they see the truth again. Encouragement is one of the greatest things one spouse can do for the other.

> *So encourage each other and build each other up, just as you are already doing.*
> — 1 Thessalonians 5:11 NLT

Please allow me to ask you a personal question: While you were reflecting on the above questions and Scriptures, did you ask yourself, "What is *my* conversion experience based on?"

If your relationship with Jesus is based on a fire escape plan, you might want to rethink your own salvation. Is your relationship with the Creator of the Universe built on pure, unadulterated love? Before we start pushing our faith on others, we should make sure our own heart is in the right place.

Right now, take a few moments for some "Holy Spirit house cleaning" in your soul. Ask the Lord to show you where you need to clean up your act. Reflection and repentance never go out of style.

CHAPTER THREE

---◆———◆———◆---

Married to the Unbeliever

Wives, in the same way submit yourselves to your own husbands so that, if any of them do not believe the word, they may be won over without words by the behavior of their wives, when they see the purity and reverence of your lives.
— 1 Peter 3:1–2 NIV

In the last chapter, I discussed the signs that indicate whether a person has truly committed themselves to Christ. We looked at the person who might claim to be a Christian, but seems to have one foot in the church and one foot in the world.

Sometimes our differences in faith may simply be denominational, linguistic or cultural misunderstandings. It's difficult to know that without asking the right questions. If we want to understand our spouse's spiritual beliefs, then we must initiate opening the door of conversation. Clarifying those differences is the first step to knowing upon which staircase of faith we are each standing. Moving to a different staircase of understanding encourages conversation and connection.

It's discouraging to discover that we don't share similar beliefs, but the Holy Spirit is all-powerful and all-knowing. Prayer can do amazing things in seemingly hopeless situations. Never give up.

Is your spouse an unbeliever in all things spiritual?

This chapter is about marriage to the unbeliever. To clarify here, I'm talking about the person who does not know very much about Christianity and may not be interested in learning about it either. We might refer to them as agnostics or atheists, or simply non-Christian. They may classify themselves as spiritual, but not religious. Their background may be spiritually irreverent, new age, or religiously different. Our Christian words and concepts can be as odd to them as their beliefs are to us. We must pause, listen and learn about these differences. We should never take for granted that everyone understands our terminology.

Maybe your spouse does not label themselves an unbeliever, but will not commit to calling themselves a believer either. Maybe they believe in something spiritual, but it's not the Christian definition of spirituality. If you can't talk meaningfully about Christianity with your spouse, you may feel isolated in your faith. This is when connecting with like-minded believers is so helpful. There are many options for connecting with others, and we will discuss this more fully later.

When you give your heart over to Jesus, the unbelieving spouse will typically react one of four ways:

- Assume that this is a fad. They are dismissive when you want to talk about your faith.
- Fear that you have lost your mind or joined some cult. They will try to convince you to go back to the person you used to be.
- Are offended or indifferent. They may say that your religion is your business and their beliefs are none of your business.
- Be curious and ask questions.

In any of the first three scenarios—when you get saved—the atmosphere in your home begins to change, sometimes drastically. The formerly level playing field has suddenly turned into two or more dramatically different levels, with a variety of spiritual and secular collisions occurring.

The unbelieving spouse who decides that they want nothing to do with your "religion" may become avoidant, sullen, even belligerent. Spoken or unspoken boundaries are placed around conversation and activities, sometimes involving family and friends. Communication becomes strained and confusing. Simple everyday misunderstandings seem difficult to rectify, and often turn into full-blown arguments. There is an emptiness in your relationship that you didn't feel before. The joy that should be there is replaced with tension and apprehension. You might question whether you were truly happy in this marriage before you were saved.

Your marriage now feels unstable, like the unsteady feeling of walking on a narrow suspension bridge over a deep canyon. You worry that you might lose your balance and fall. You may be willing to step across that shaky bridge, but your spouse might prefer the slippery descent to the bottom of the chasm. You hope that they will find their way to that scenic waterfall on the other side where you will be waiting. Many people do have to go down before they can come up. Let's face it; the view from whatever level you are at isn't necessarily wrong, it's just different. Whatever your scenario, the journey to get back on the same level can be turbulent, and filled with many rocky obstacles.

This wilderness is full of mental warfare designed to discourage you and push you into depression and despair. Instead of trusting God to lead you through this, you sink into negative thoughts that start with "what if", and "why." It's easy to focus inward and blame yourself for the confusion, miscommunication or shift in atmosphere. Don't fall into the dysfunctional "blame game."

When you think that you are in this alone, it's tempting to self-isolate. You presume that other Christians have no idea what it's like to be married to someone who isn't interested in learning about, or joining with you in your passion. That feeling of disconnection can interfere in your desire to attend church services or interact with other Christians.

Perhaps you make judgments about church lingo and assume that everyone grew up either in the church, or at least in a Christian environment. Surely, no one else has experienced being married to an unbeliever who has no faith background or Christian language database to draw from. You try to explain your situation to other Christians, but you are met with blank stares and empty words of sympathy. Consequently, without practical encouragement, you might believe that you are living in somewhat of a no-man's land. It's easy to conclude that staying home and watching church on television is emotionally safer than interacting with other believers.

As you try to find a way to make your marriage more workable, you reach for biblical guidance. In your search, you come across this verse:

> *Do not be unequally yoked together with unbelievers. For what fellowship has righteousness with lawlessness? And what communion has light with darkness?*
> — 2 Corinthians 6:14 NKJV

This verse is regularly used by pastors to explain to Christian singles that they should not date someone who is a non-believer. The rationale is obvious—dating eventually leads to marriage and marrying a non-Christian is an invitation to a lifetime of problems. However, *you* are not in the dating field anymore. You *are* unequally yoked. You can't go back, you can only go forward. After reading this passage, you may be asking yourself, "If light and darkness cannot co-exist, how can my marriage survive?"

First, few things are as dark as they seem. Moreover, we are not as "enlightened" as we might think we are. Accepting Jesus as our Lord and Savior is the first step to eternal salvation. There is much more work to be done. Every one of us is on a journey of progressive sanctification. We do not achieve full sanctification until we die. If there is life, there is hope!

Consider this: We all came to Jesus as sinners and even while we were still sinners, Christ died for us (Romans 5:8 NKJV). That speaks not only of us who are saved, but of all people who are still unsaved.

If all the people on earth started as a thought in the mind of God (Jeremiah 1:5), were given life by His spirit (Ecclesiastes 12:7), and are written on the palm of His hand (Isaiah 49:16)—this declares that every person on the planet, even the worst of the worst, were given the light of God at conception. Therefore, if the breath of life remains—everyone must, to some degree, contain some light. The light is not extinguished until death. That means there is hope for everyone.

If God planted His seed in every heart at conception (Ecclesiastes 3:11; Romans 2:15; Genesis 1:26–27) and made us in His image, that means every person, whether they recognize it or not, has the capacity to know God. It is only the soil of the heart that determines whether that seed will grow. (See Jesus' parable in Matthew 13:3–9.) It is our job to keep watering that seed with the water and method shown to us by the Holy Spirit.

When a gardener plants a new seed, he nurtures it with the right food and the right amount of water. He can't see the life burst forth under the ground, but he trusts the process. When that sprout becomes visible, he monitors it to ascertain health and growth, and feeds it accordingly. He protects it from thieves, bad weather and disease. A plant needs help to grow healthily. That help comes from a gardener that has knowledge, wisdom and discernment.

Just like being able to discern the needs of a plant's growth, so too must we be able to encourage the spiritual growth in ourselves, and recognize spiritual growth in our mates. Our own spiritual growth requires continual study and spiritual discernment. Spiritual discernment means learning to tell the difference between your head, the enemy's voice, and the Lord's voice. That takes time and diligent practice. There are courses online to help you to learn this.[5]

Part of discernment in the unequally yoked marriage is compassionately understanding that every person is at a different level of spiritual growth. Culture, language, social background, and environment all play a role in our interactions with others. And just as cultural and social differences slant our interpretive lenses, faith differences also alter our perceptions.

Words mean different things to different people. We think our spouse understands what we are saying, but how often do we stop to ask, "What does this word mean to you?" The varied definitions of the language and lingo of our faith can create a type of cultural dissonance in our conversations.

Although Christianity is appreciated as a religion or ideology, most unbelievers cannot grasp the concept of Christianity as a genuine relationship with the person of Jesus Christ. Jesus is usually recognized by secular society as a historical or mythical human being. In many religious circles, He is known as a wise man and a prophet, while His virgin birth and physical resurrection are considered myths.

God the Father is generally seen as separate from Jesus the Son. God is perceived to be the invisible creative cosmic force, a type of universal energy or a higher power. The Holy Spirit...well, that just might conjure up some ghost-like mental images. Put these three together and now we have "The Trinity."

Christians learn that each of these three are simply different aspects of God, but together they are one and the same God. We

---

[5] A resource I highly recommend is called Communion with God / The School of the Spirit, with Dr. Mark Virkler. Visit www.cluschoolofthespirit.com?affiliates=84

worship one God who presents in three persons. This is a confusing concept to many people...even to some Christians.

The belief that this invisible being is real and can be felt and experienced is often at odds with our scientific, logical world. When you add in the belief that one is eternally damned if they do not accept Jesus as their Lord and Savior, you end up losing your audience very quickly. That one and only path to salvation is met with a great guffaw that labels you as intolerant or bigoted.

Our reputation as being intolerant and bigoted may be partly due to an unbeliever's previous experience with Christians, or watching fundamentalist televangelists preach hate and doom, prosperity gospel preachers begging for money, or hearing stories about right-winged intolerance.

Sadly, there are some Christians that are indeed intolerant of other faiths or belief systems and refuse to step outside of their comfort zone. If you're concerned that this describes you, I invite you to consider how you can become more compassionate and understanding without compromising your beliefs.

How can we deliver the true Gospel message to our unbelieving spouse? How do we "wear our faith on our sleeves" in our homes without putting up walls and barriers?

Evangelical history in the past century has been through some dramatic changes in its approach to delivering the Gospel message. Just like the political spectrum from the extreme right-wing Conservative to the far left Liberal, the Christian church still varies in its inclusivity of unbelievers and new believers. Most often it feels like you are either "in the club," or you're not.

I grew up in an era where fire and brimstone were preached from the pulpit. The pervading thought at the time was that scaring a person out of hell was the best way to get them into Heaven. Fear replaced the message of the love, grace and compassion of Christ.

This theology didn't win very many enthusiastic believers. They came to church, but often under a blanket of fear. Eventually, churches began to realize that they were producing a generation of apathetic, Sunday morning seat warmers. Thankfully, many churches today have changed their approach. They have come to realize that most people have enough inferiority and rejection issues to deal with, and that the last thing they need is to be hit over the head with more scare tactics. The message from the pulpit increasingly today is grace, compassion and acceptance.

This move toward a focus on grace has also taken place in the wider secular society, and most Western nations now embrace a culture in which almost anything goes. The message of hell-fire seems to be disappearing. The result is confusion and apathy— with many Christians standing at the sidelines, not taking a stand for or against anything. As the general public watches the lives and speech of some Christians, they can't tell the difference between a Christian and an unbeliever. This adds to the struggle for the believer married to an unbeliever. Where exactly should we be drawing the line between grace and non-acceptance of sin in our homes?

As you struggle to find creative ways to deliver your message of hope, you need to allow the Holy Spirit to do His work. Believe me, I understand that you are living under a constant dark cloud of opposition to your faith, and are feeling terribly discouraged. Some days you may want to walk away from your marriage or compromise by suppressing your faith. I know how that feels...I've been there too.

Has your spouse been dismissive or belligerent about your faith, or accused you of intolerance?

If I can encourage you at all, I want you to know that opposition is frequently based on fear and ignorance. You can't save them, but you can subtly educate them. Only the Holy Spirit can bring them to the point where they will be curious enough to ask questions. In the meantime, be mindful of your own attitudes and actions so that you do not behave in a way that is hypocritical to the words you speak.

Being married to the non-believer requires us to fine-tune our spiritual radar to the signals of the Holy Spirit. We do that by reading the Bible, prayer, keeping our spiritual eyes and ears open to the leading of the Holy Spirit, listening to good, sound Christian teaching, and staying connected with other believers. As we learn to hear from the Holy Spirit, we also become more aware of our own need for repentance. Repentance opens the door to greater understanding. It begins with a willingness to look inside yourself, seeing yourself as imperfect, and asking for help. If we want to guide others along this path, we must start with ourselves.

In Section Three of this book, I talk more about some of the boundaries that we need to create to help shift the atmosphere in our home, ways to increase the receptivity to Jesus, and how to grow our faith without creating chaos. Before we get to that, let's take a closer look at ourselves. Let's examine how we got to where we are now, and discover what we need to learn to create a positive pathway in our journey with our unsaved spouse.

CHAPTER FOUR

---◆---

How Did I Get Here?

*You are the salt of the earth. But if the salt loses its
saltiness, how can it be made salty again? It is no longer
good for anything, except to be thrown out and trampled
underfoot. You are the light of the world. A town built on a
hill cannot be hidden. Neither do people light a lamp and
put it under a bowl. Instead they put it on its stand, and it
gives light to everyone in the house. In the same way, let
your light shine before others, that they may see your good
deeds and glorify your Father in heaven.*
— Matthew 5:13–16 NIV

In the previous chapters, we discussed how one's receptivity to
the Christian faith may be positively or negatively affected by
their previous knowledge of Christianity, interpretation of
Christian language or church customs, or experience with
believers. I've also tried to help you to clarify whether your spouse
is an uncommitted Christian or truly a non-believer. Now it's time
to look at ourselves and try to understand why and where we are in
this situation.

The dynamics within the unequally yoked marriage are often
frustrating, stressful and confusing for both parties to this
relationship. Have you ever asked yourself some of these
questions?

- Why does my marriage seem to be so stressful and
  confusing?

- Is my marriage falling apart, or is everything I am experiencing typical for an unequally yoked marriage?
- How can I serve God effectively when my spouse doesn't know God?
- Why am I staying? Am I really honoring God by staying married? Is this really where God wants me to be?

Before you can answer these questions, you need to go back to the beginning of where you started in your journey of faith.

Let's assume your spouse has been observing your faith journey from the beginning, and has been watching you in the ups and downs of your daily trials. Your maturity level in the Christian faith may affect their acceptance or non-acceptance of the new ideals that you try to implement in your daily routine. Your journey in your faith may be at a different stage than your Christian sister or brother who is also experiencing different spiritual levels in their marriage. We all grow at various rates and we all have different obstacles to overcome. It's helpful to think back to our starting point and review our journey and progress.

Does your starting point for your relationship fit into one of the following categories?

Spiritually Immature: At the time you got married, you were both so in love that your religious differences didn't seem to matter. Maybe each of you had a contrasting concept of God, or you came from dissimilar faiths, but you both assumed that your differences were minimal. Now, as you have grown in your Christian life, you have discovered that your differences are huge, and those differences are interfering in your relationship. You seem to be growing apart in your marriage, even though you still love each other.

Backslidden: You were saved at one time, but then fell away and returned to the Lord after you were already married to a non-believer. Now, you are feeling torn between your love for Jesus and your love for your spouse. You know it isn't a competition, yet you sense your spouse is feeling left out or rejected because your time is spent with Christian people and Christian activities. You are not sure how to interpret those angry outbursts, and you seem to be fighting about everything. You question if it's abuse, persecution, or something else.

New Believer: You got saved after you were married, but your spouse didn't. You are finding yourself walking in new, uncharted territory, and your spouse is completely disinterested in your new-found faith. You seem to be getting a ton of advice from people who have never been in your situation. Every time you try out a new piece of advice, it seems to backfire. You feel lost and alone.

Backslidden Spouse: You were both following the Lord when you married. Somewhere over the years, they drifted away from the Lord. You want to help them return to the faith. You are worried and frustrated.

By reviewing the starting point in your journey of faith, you can answer the question: "Why does my marriage seem to be so stressful and confusing?" Now you can see how and when the feeling of living on different spiritual levels, or in being caught between two worlds began, and where your feelings of growing apart have validity. Living on different spiritual levels isn't just a perception—it's your reality.

You continually interact with your spouse on both a physical and a spiritual dimension. We are usually not aware of the spiritual dimension, but we are always immersed in it and surrounded by it. When our loved ones are unsaved and we are saved, we interact on a physical level, but mentally we bounce back and forth between two different spiritual levels. Think of it as two different dimensions—because spiritually, that is what it is.

It's no surprise that we feel stressed, confused and exhausted! Your spouse probably does too! Bear in mind that they likely don't know how to communicate on our spiritual plane, so they may feel lost and confused interacting with us. However, they do not know why that is happening. They only know that we have changed, and somewhere, somehow the rules in our relationship have changed as well. Chances are we've been right where they are, so we should be able to (metaphorically speaking) reach over, communicate what we need to and then step back—while never losing our spiritual foothold.

Although there may be other types of spiritually unequal marriages that I didn't mention, and there are many marriages in which the partners successfully live on different spiritual levels all the time—those differences may not be as great as those listed above, or, possibly not as important to one or both spouses. More frequently, significant spiritual differences play havoc with one's sense of stability or security within the union.

You might be asking, "Is my marriage falling apart?" Or "Is everything I am experiencing typical for an unequally yoked marriage?"

Friends, family, social activities, parenting, even how you spend your money—are all impacted by your faith decisions. Finding Jesus means you are suddenly plunked down into a new peculiar dynamic that causes conflict in all areas of your life. Before you came to faith, you probably never thought about spiritual differences, and it may never have been a topic of conversation. In this area of your marriage, you probably felt stable and secure.

How we view the differences of the belief systems in our relationship changes how we view the stability of our marriage. If we are becoming less confident and less satisfied, it may be due to the spiritual growth in your relationship with Christ in contrast to your spouse's lack of interest in spiritual things or their rate of spiritual growth. If you feel that your relationship is becoming stronger and you are becoming more confident in your ability to see things on the same level, it may point to the growth your spouse is making in the forward direction that will eventually propel them into a decision for Christ. Remember, darkness flees from light (John 1:5). Therefore, the more light we shine in our homes, the less darkness will remain.

The winds in the darkness are felt, but not seen. Those winds create turbulence that shift the direction of our projected intention. Our intentions may be good, but they aren't always received as such. A crosswind blows across our path and suddenly we feel very unstable. We may feel that we are losing control of our marriage or ourselves.

If you were saved at one time, but fell away from the Lord, and then came back later in life, you might have a greater appreciation for the spiritual differences between the two of you. You will have insight into how easily one can slip into the dark abyss, and how difficult it can be to climb back up the walls of that chasm. However, you also know that even though things may seem impossible right now, with God all things are possible (Matthew 19:26). We need to keep praying and keep believing. Good pilots know how to steer the airplane, and when to hit the rudder during a crosswind so that they don't lose control. So too, in our marriages, timing and discernment are extremely important.

If you are new to Christ, focus intentionally on strengthening your faith, and trust that God will give you the answers as you need them. Let me clarify that—as you need them, when you need them—not before you need them. Read and soak in the Word and every Christian resource that you can find to keep your faith strong, and keep your spirit receptive to messages from the Lord.

Allow me to share a vision that I had about trusting God, which affected me powerfully.

In the vision, I was standing by a small bonfire and Jesus was standing across the fire from me. Around the fire were several other people (disciples), but they all had their backs to me and I couldn't see their faces. My position allowed me to focus directly on Jesus as he was speaking. I felt that He was only looking at me, even though there were others present. He held a small fish in His hands. As I watched, He broke open the fish exposing the whole skeleton. He tore off a piece of the fish and handed it to me across the fire. I took the fish and ate. It was the sweetest tasting fish I had ever eaten. When I looked up the fish was whole again. I asked Him for another piece. Jesus repeated the action of breaking open the fish, exposing the skeleton, and giving it to me. Again, when I looked up, the fish was whole. This sequence of events repeated four times until I understood the message: "When you need strength, I will provide it; when you need nourishment, I will provide it. I will provide what you need when you need it. I (Jesus) hold the backbone and the food. You need only ask. What I give you will be sweet and nourishing." It reminded me of this verse:

> *For everyone who asks receives, and he who seeks finds, and to him who knocks it will be opened. Or what man is there among you who, if his son asks for bread, will give him a stone? Or if he asks for a fish, will he give him a serpent? If you then, being evil, know how to give good gifts to your children, how much more will your Father who is in heaven give good things to those who ask Him!*
> — Matthew 7:8–11 NKJV

If we are open to the Spirit, He will provide us what we need, when we need it. We simply need to nourish our faith and exercise trust. Even though these paths may feel like new and uncharted territory (and they may be), we are never alone. Jesus always walks beside us and He sends angels to comfort and encourage us (Matthew 4:11). If God sent the angels to minister to Jesus, they are also available to minister to us (Psalm 91:11–12).

Asking for help can be tough. We all have times when we don't recognize that we need help until it's too late. Often, we are too stubborn and insist on plowing through the storm in our own way. Then we wonder why we are stressed and exhausted! It's difficult to plow through a snowstorm without a snowplow! Sometimes, even though we may be trying to follow the snowplow as closely as possible through the difficult and dangerous conditions, it feels like the storm will never end. That's when we get discouraged. Sometimes we want to give up.

You might be asking, "How can I be happy, and how can my marriage be happy, when everything that is going on in my home seems in conflict with the Word of God?"

When the reality of this conflicting situation hits you, sadness creeps in. Then the comparison game begins. You start to notice how different your life is from those families where God is front and center. You start to notice Christian marriages where both husband and wife flow together like a finely tuned violin. You compare your marriage to those relationships and see frayed strings and rusty keys. You see happy families engaged in celebrations centered around church activities, and other people's children seem to be so well-behaved compared to yours.

Overall, your life isn't what you want it to be. You are probably wondering, "Can I change it? If so, how can I change it? How can I serve God effectively when my spouse doesn't know God?"

I will get to those answers in time. Right now, I want to give you some encouragement. God is inviting you to be an influence in this very difficult situation. Think of yourself as a missionary to your own family. Most missionaries face tremendous loneliness and persecution, and question whether they are making a difference. However, you don't have to travel to strange countries for your mission field. It's right here, at home. You can make a difference, and you probably are making a difference. You are one light in a dark world.

Let's think about this influence for a minute. Not only are we bringing light to a dark world, we also bring salt and seasoning to a flavorless world (Matthew 5:13). If every Christian on the planet took these verses to heart and we lived out the truth of this, we would change many lives. If we changed only one life in our lifetime, and that person changed one, two or more lives, eventually the entire world would be covered with light. Jesus said the Kingdom of God is within us (Luke 17:21), we need only reach inside and reveal it to others (Romans 14:17). This is our task, given to us by Jesus.

> *Then Jesus came to them and said, "All authority in heaven and on earth has been given to me. Therefore go and make disciples of all nations, baptizing them in the name of the Father and of the Son and of the Holy Spirit, and teaching them to obey everything I have commanded you. And surely, I am with you always, to the very end of the age."*
> — Matthew 28:18–20 NIV

When we take on the evangelical task, but see no fruit from our labor, we can feel hopeless. We may feel like the Apostle Paul when he says:

> *"We are hard-pressed on every side, yet not crushed; we are perplexed, but not in despair; persecuted, but not forsaken; struck down, but not destroyed."*
> — 2 Corinthians 4:8–9 NKJV

If conflict seems to happen frequently in our relationship, we can get to the point where we want to quit. We ask, "Why am I staying? Am I really honoring God by staying married? Is this really where God wants me to be? Should I leave or should I stay?"

This is when we need to remind ourselves that not only are we to be salt and light to the world, but the Bible is very clear about how we are to conduct ourselves in our homes—being an example to those around us by living pure and reverent lives:

> *In the same way, you wives must accept the authority of your husbands. Then, even if some refuse to obey the Good News, your godly lives will speak to them without any words. They will be won over by observing your pure and reverent lives.*
> — 1 Peter 3:1–2 NLT

If you are a woman reading this, you will notice here that the Apostle Paul says you must accept the authority of your husband, even though he doesn't believe. That can be very difficult, especially if you don't agree with some of the decisions he makes. I believe that this means we are to honor our husbands in their decision-making process, regardless if it is right or wrong. This is part of respect. There is a way to agree to disagree without conflict, and maintain respect in the process. (I will go into this further, later.) How we conduct ourselves during these difficult times sets a Christian example and brings godliness into our home.

As we honor God and our families with our chaste lives, by speaking words of life into those around us, encouraging others, and completing whatever tasks God puts in our path—we are not only being a model to our spouses and others in our homes, but we are also encouraging ourselves in our faith. Sometimes we need to remind ourselves that we are on a progressive journey too. We don't have all the answers. If we did, we would be like Jesus already. We're not. This is the reason we continue to study and learn about our faith—to grow and become more and more like Him.

> *For now, we see in a mirror, dimly, but then face to face. Now I know in part, but then I shall know just as I also am known.*
> — 1 Corinthians 13:12 NKJV

We may be justified by faith, but we are not yet fully sanctified. We are in a process called "progressive sanctification." Every human being on the planet is given the opportunity to go through this process. God reveals Himself to everyone at different times and in different ways.

> *For since the creation of the world God's invisible qualities— his eternal power and divine nature—have been clearly seen, being understood from what has been made, so that people are without excuse.*
> — Romans 1:20 NIV

Not everyone recognizes the glory that is surrounding them (Psalm 19). This requires that spiritual eyes be opened. As we pray for the Holy Spirit to move, we also pray that our lives will not be a hindrance.

CHAPTER FIVE

Sanctification and Justification

For the unbelieving husband has been sanctified through his wife, and the unbelieving wife has been sanctified through her believing husband. Otherwise, your children would be unclean, but as it is, they are holy.
— 1 Corinthians 7:14 NIV

This verse regarding sanctification has been a topic of discussion in many Christian Bible studies. It is often poorly explained and poorly understood. It has left many of us scratching our heads, trying to understand how that applies to our unequally yoked marriage. If you have wrestled in your mind about the questionable state of your loved one's soul and you feel that it comes up wanting, then keep reading. This is a very important topic to understand.

What exactly is sanctification? How does it apply to the unequally yoked marriage?

As I mentioned previously, I am not a theologian and I don't pretend to be. So, when I heard that when one person in a family is saved, the rest are sanctified, I pondered, "What does that mean? What's the correlation between sanctification and justification?" I was further baffled when I heard the term "progressive sanctification."

First, let's define sanctification.

The word *'sanctify'* as used in the New Testament is listed in *Strong's KJV Dictionary* (#G37) as the Greek verb *hagiazo* or (#G38) as the noun *hagiasmos*. It appears to be used differently from the Old Testament, where the word *'qodesh'* (#H6944) or *'qadosh'* (#H6918) are used to describe the word 'sanctification.'[6]

Vine's Concise Dictionary of the Bible defines the Old Testament terms for sanctification as "to be made holy," or "to be set aside for God," or "the process of making something holy."[7]

However, in the New Testament, the noun for sanctification is different with a slightly different meaning. The Greek noun *hagiasmos* is defined by this source as: a separation unto God, or a separation of the believer from evil. The Greek verb *hagiazo*, as used in 1 Corinthians 7:14, seems to refer more to a sacrificial type of setting apart, or laying something on the altar, or a ceremonial cleansing.

Both *Vine's* and *Strong's* have exhaustive explanations of how these words are used in various places in the Bible. Other resources define these terms in similar fashion. For the sake of conciseness, it's not possible to go through these lengthy definitions here. If you want to review them in more detail, I suggest reading through various biblical and non-biblical resources to gain a fuller understanding. I will do my best to summarize this information for you.

The differences between the Old Testament terms and the New Testament appear subtle and can be confusing.

To interpret the Word from the Old Testament definition—we can say that if something is made holy, it must be set aside from objects that are not holy. There also must be a reason why that item is set aside, such as it must have a purpose for holiness.

---

[6] Two good resources to study these terms in more depth are https://www.bibletools.org and http://biblehub.com/strongs/g.htm

[7] W.E.Vine, Vine's Concise Dictionary of the Bible, Thomas Nelson Inc. Publishers 2005.

As Christians, we are set aside or separated from the world for God's exclusive purpose. Part of that purpose is the process of sanctification itself, or the process of becoming holy. During our Christian life, we go through a process of sanctification gradually, that is, we are continually being purified as we mature in the faith. If we look at the New Testament definition, we are not only being made holy, we are separated from evil and we could say that we have laid ourselves on the altar to be cleansed by God. However, as human beings, we can never be completely holy. Therefore, we are not fully sanctified until death.

This explanation helps us to understand the process of becoming more righteous after salvation, but it still leaves us questioning the verse in 1 Corinthians 7:14, where the Apostle Paul says our unsaved spouses and children are already sanctified because we are saved. How is this possible? How do we make them holy while they are unsaved?

This is where the New Testament Greek definition of the verb helps us to understand this better. According to *Vine's*, the word *'hagiazo'* which the Apostle Paul uses is referring to setting something apart, or to lay something on the altar, or a type of cleansing. Initially, our loved ones enter the sanctification process as we lay them on the altar of prayer. At this point, God sets them aside for His future purpose, but they still need to make that final decision. Every person is responsible for their own salvation. This is where justification comes in.

What does "justify" mean? Romans 5:1 says we are justified by faith. *Vine's* dictionary quotes *Strongs #G1344* as the verb *dikaioo*, meaning "to deem to be right, or righteous."

When we accept Jesus as our Lord and Savior in a conscious act— we are saved from eternal death and saved to eternal life. That action has included repentance of our sins, belief in the death and resurrection of Jesus Christ, and accepting that the blood of Jesus Christ that was shed on the cross covers all our sins, granting us eternal life (see Romans 8:33–34 and 1 Corinthians 6:11). When we make this decision, we are justified through our action of faith, and declared righteous and worthy of salvation by God.

Justification has a starting point. Sanctification carries on after we have been justified. In a believer's life, we are justified while continuing to be sanctified (since we do not achieve perfection until we die).

But what about before a person is saved? Can we interpret the word used in 1 Corinthians 7:14 to say that Paul is referring to a type of ceremonial cleansing? Can sanctification refer to a type of cleansing that happens gradually before justification happens? Perhaps we can think of it this way: In a non-believer's life, sanctification is the preparation work for the future act of justification.

Let's take the example of planting a seed. A farmer needs to till the soil before he can plant a seed. Once the seed is planted, it must be nourished appropriately so that it can grow. Without the right temperature, soil and moisture...it will not sprout. Too much moisture...it will rot. If there is no soil for nourishment...it will die. If the temperature is too cold or too hot...it will either be stunted (defective or subject to illness) or it will die.

Growth begins slowly in the belly of the seed. This sprouting process is not visible to the naked eye until a tiny green shoot breaks forth from the seed. Once it begins, the action cannot be undone except by death. It continues to need nourishment for its entire life as it continues to grow and produce fruit. It stops needing nourishment only when it dies.

Just like the planting process, sanctification is a two-pronged approach—before salvation (justification) and after. Like the sprouting of a seed, justification happens once.

One author explains it as follows:

"Sanctification differs from justification in several ways. Justification is a one-time work of God, resulting in a declaration of "not guilty" before Him because of the work of Christ on the cross. Sanctification is a process, beginning with justification and continuing throughout life. Justification is the starting point of the line that represents one's Christian life; sanctification is the line itself."[8]

As believers, when we consciously make the decision to accept salvation, we are justified into right standing with God. At that point, sanctification begins, but the job is not complete. There is much more work to be done. A child does not graduate with a high school diploma the day they enter kindergarten. They first need to begin the process of learning. At a certain age, we assume that they have completed this initial learning process when we "knight them" with the designated title of "adult." So too, is our job in the Kingdom. Sanctification begins when we enter the "School of the Kingdom of Heaven," but we do not graduate until the day we die. Therefore, sanctification is a progressive process that takes a lifetime to complete.

The difference between sanctification and progressive sanctification is explained more clearly as follows:

"Progressive sanctification is a daily dealing with our sins and growth in holiness. This progressive sanctification will culminate in perfect sanctification when we see Jesus and become eternally like Him. Growth in holiness should follow conversion (Ephesians 1:4; Philippians 3:12).

The Christian life begins with regeneration, whereby the Holy Spirit implants spiritual life in the believer. Sanctification begins at that same moment of the new birth, and God progressively separates the new believer from sin unto Himself. He transforms the whole life toward holiness and purity.

---

[8] See http://www.gotquestions.org/progressive-sanctification.html

This process of sanctification never ends during this earthly life.... Believers have been "set apart"—sanctified, once-for-all by the perfect offering of Christ's body for our sins. All believers are sanctified positionally. It is our new standing with God as Christians. Our standing is what God has done for us in Christ. Progressive sanctification, on the other hand, refers to sanctification as experienced in the daily life of the believer. Daily victory over sin is itself a separation unto God and is, therefore, sanctification. This should be an ever-increasing growth experience."[9]

The above text explains that initially, we are justified into right standing with God through repentance, followed by a conscious decision of our faith in Jesus and allowing the Holy Spirit to guide us into a holy lifestyle. True and final justification happens only when we stand before God at our final judgment, and He determines whether we are "not guilty" by our acceptance of the cleansing blood of Jesus.

Sanctification progresses as the Holy Spirit makes Himself known in the new believer's life. Since we are always learning, always growing until the day we die—we are continually being sanctified, set aside to be part of God's Kingdom and to do His work—growing in holiness. As we accept Jesus' lordship and allow the Holy Spirit to work in us, we deliberately set aside our own selfish and worldly desires to become more and more like Jesus.

This explanation of sanctification and progressive sanctification helps us in understanding the salvation process after we accept Jesus as our Savior. However, it still leaves open questions regarding the point of our family being sanctified because of us.

We know that the Holy Spirit works to make Himself known to the unbeliever, but the unbeliever cannot understand the Holy Spirit until he invites Jesus to become a part of his life (1 Corinthians 2:14–16). Your family's spiritual eyes are still closed, and they have not yet learned how to step out in faith.

---

[9] See http://www.abideinchrist.com/keys/sanctification-progressive.html

When we looked at the definition of the word 'sanctify' earlier, one of the definitions was to "make something holy." In any religious ceremony, the process of making something holy requires that it be set aside for a specific and religious purpose. Is it possible that our loved ones are "set aside" to serve God, even though they don't know Him yet?

Another author explains this more fully:

> "In this sense sanctify does not refer to salvation; otherwise, the spouse would not be spoken of as unbelieving. It refers to being set apart, the basic meaning of sanctify and holy, terms that are from the same Greek root. The sanctification is matrimonial and familial, not personal or spiritual. In God's eyes, a home is set apart for Himself when the husband, wife, or, by implication, any other family member, is a Christian. Such a home is not Christian in the full sense, but it is immeasurably superior to one that is totally unbelieving. Even if the Christian is ridiculed and persecuted, unbelievers in the family are blessed because of that believer. One Christian in a home graces the entire home. God's indwelling that believer and all the blessings and graces that flow into the believer's life from heaven will spill over to enrich all who are near. In addition, although the believer's faith cannot suffice for the salvation of anyone but himself, he is often the means of other family members coming to the Lord by the power of his testimony."[10]

This was my "Aha!" moment. The "setting aside," or sanctification of our unsaved spouse and other unsaved family members doesn't guarantee that they will be saved. That eternal decision is still theirs to make. Rather, they are set side to be influenced by whatever person or method the Holy Spirit brings across their path. That, in a large part, is us. It is *our* influence that is the salt and light in our household. This is what makes our home different from those who have no Christian influence. Everyone in our household knows that we believe. Everyone who enters our home

---

[10] "A Sanctified Spouse" Grace to You Resources.
https://www.gty.org/resources/print/bible-qna/BQ102612

is quickly informed (either by words or by our actions) that we are Christians. This means our home is now "set apart," or sanctified. This helps to prepare the ground for the planting of the seed. Spiritual growth happens as we water those seeds with truth, love and grace. Growth takes time. Conversion is the fruit that we pray for.

When it comes to children in the home, the Apostle Paul says in 1 Corinthians 7:14 that if our children did not have our Christian influence, they would be considered "unclean, but as it is, they are holy." This again refers to the incredible spiritual influence that we have in our home. Regardless of whether our spouse agrees to continue to live with us, our children are influenced by what we teach them. If we teach Christian principles and doctrine, they too are more likely to have a conversion at some point in their life. The word 'holy' in this verse again refers to a "setting aside" to be influenced for the Gospel of Christ through us.

In summary, we are justified by our faith in Christ, and we are progressively sanctified by our daily dealing with our sins and growing in our faith. As we place our loved ones on the altar of prayer, they become sanctified (set apart) to be influenced for Christ. We are the most consistent Christian influence in their lives. As we live out our faith, our homes undergo a type of spiritual cleansing. This cleansing process affects the way life is conducted in our home. Our home becomes purified, or in a sense, decontaminated from the influences of sin. This continual influence will, at some point, take our loved ones down the path of decision where they will hopefully accept Jesus as their Savior.

The promise that our spouse and children are sanctified is an encouragement that we need to hold close to our heart. This also places on us an awesome responsibility of consciously honoring the Lord in our daily walk. Since we live in a marriage that is functioning spiritually on different levels, we must bear in mind that everyone learns things in various ways. Our influence in our home may not be clear to us, and we may not see the fruit of our endeavors during our lifetime. That is not guaranteed to us. But we continue to live in faith that this will happen.

The process of progressive sanctification also means that as we grow in holiness, our own understanding of our faith may look very different ten or twenty years down the road from what we understand today. The more time we spend with the Lord—the more is revealed to us. At the same time, while we are learning— God is also revealing Himself to those in our household at different times and in diverse ways—sometimes even through us! We may always be spiritually out of sync with our spouse throughout our marriage simply because of our different rates of growth. This should not impede our levels of happiness. There is a saying that things always look darkest before the dawn. The sun is always shining, even when it's hiding behind dark clouds.

Remember, God is always working in the past, present, and future—at the same time. There is no time in God's world. Although we don't know what's going to happen in our future or in the future of our loved ones, God knows the decisions that will be made, have been made, or are being made without our knowledge. The Holy Spirit is *always* at work. Never second guess what God is doing. We can remain encouraged that God's Word tells us that our spouse and family are sanctified, simply because of our witness. This means our prayers are being heard and answered, though possibly not in the way we think or expect.

It's easy to feel discouraged when we don't see progress. But good fruit doesn't grow on a tree with bad roots. We may need to dig a little deeper to see where the problem lies. Understanding what our loved ones believe might help us communicate our faith more effectively.

CHAPTER SIX

Understanding Belief Systems

When Jesus came into the region of Caesarea Philippi, He asked His disciples, saying, "Who do men say that I, the Son of Man, am?" Simon Peter answered and said, "You are the Christ, the Son of the living God."
— Matthew 16:13,16 NKJV

Understanding the process of sanctification is helpful, as we communicate our faith in our home. But to communicate effectively, we need insight into what it is that they believe. If our goal is to influence our spouse toward a decision for Christ, then we need to be able to explain salvation and Christianity in a way that they can understand. If they are not interested in our faith, then the problem may simply be that they don't understand Christian concepts or our language.

When a person hears a foreign language for the first time, it often sounds like gobbledygook. To understand this strange tongue, one must be motivated by a reason or a desire to learn it. If a person is unschooled in Christianity or religious concepts, it really is analogous to a foreign language. Clarifying language or conceptual differences is essential before you can begin to talk about Christianity as a faith and of God's provision for salvation. This is only one of the hurdles to jump through as you struggle through what to say and how to say it.

Once you have clarified whether there are language or conceptual misunderstandings, you can progress to comparing your different belief systems.

We tend to assume a lot, especially in marriage. We think we can read each other's minds because when we first got married we were able to finish each other's sentences. Maybe we still do. Since we live together, we know each other's favorite foods, enjoy the same movies, and participate in many of the same activities. We just assume that we know each other so incredibly well.

But without asking the right questions or giving our opinion on what we like or don't like, we end up buying chocolate ice cream to please our spouses when they would rather have vanilla. And they don't tell us...because they don't want to hurt our feelings. They buy theatre tickets to a play that they really don't want to see, while not knowing that we really had no interest in it either. They question why we aren't more excited or grateful, but we don't tell them...because we don't want to hurt their feelings.

Too often, we make excuses or lie about how we feel. We carry on our lives in a façade of honesty, calling it love—when truthfully, we are terrified of causing conflict because of differences. We don't want to take the chance of losing what we have or disrupting our bubble of happiness. Unfortunately, you can't fix a problem by hiding from reality.

Belief systems are often so deeply ingrained in our psyche and so rarely discussed in any depth, that without frank discussion, we have no idea what our partner really believes. Your spouse's perception of what they think you believe, and your perception about what you think they believe or understand, may be partly skewed or totally false.

Awareness of the similarities or differences in each other's understanding begins with asking the right questions. Discovering that we are on different levels in our belief systems is a starting point in opening the door to further discussions of faith. When that door begins to open, then and only then, can we truly have a discussion of clarifying possible misperceptions of our Christian faith or misinterpretations of our Christian language. This can be a huge key in encouraging our loved ones toward a decision of faith.

If I want my husband to understand what I believe, then it's my responsibility to present the Gospel in such a way that he can comprehend what I am saying. Part of that responsibility is to uncover the intellectual barriers to faith that are preventing that understanding. At the same time, I need to know what I believe, and why I believe it. After all, if I start asking questions, he is undoubtedly going to respond with questions of his own. He will expect me to have the answers. Naturally, I won't have *all* the answers—none of us do—but we should not be afraid to confess our own lack of knowledge. We can always find the answer to those questions and come back to the conversation later.

When we live on different faith levels, we often crash into other people's perceptions of the definitions of spirituality, Christianity and the concepts of morality. However, we cannot be bulldozing our own views into our homes or the lives of others, dumping our opinions in the middle of the floor and demanding that everyone think like us. That style is not compassionate or understanding. Honoring people may require that we have some difficult conversations, bite our tongues on words that we would like to say, or go to some questionable places.

When Jesus had dinner at the tax collector's house, it was considered highly improper (Matthew 9:10–11). His scandalous conversation with the adulterous woman at the well shocked even His own disciples (John 4:27). How, where and when we interact with people can often have more impact than the words we speak.

Jesus ate and drank with the lowest of sinners in some questionable environments (for that day), but He did it in a way that won their respect, love and loyalty. He validated each person as valuable, regardless of social, religious, or economic status. He always held relationship over principle, and always displayed an attitude of humility. Even in His confrontations, He drew attention to sin without demeaning the individual. His biggest battles were with the system of religion and those who enforced it—the "know-it-all" religious leaders, the Pharisees.

A "Pharisaical attitude" is a form of judgment and condemnation. This type of attitude lacks compassion, invalidates the other person's belief system, and disallows them the ability to gradually digest new information. No one truly comes to Jesus through having Him stuffed down their throat. That type of religion results in regurgitation without digestion. Not a pretty picture or experience.

I was raised under the religion of guilt, shame and fear, with "hell-fire and brimstone" pouring down from the pulpit twice on Sundays, once on Wednesdays, and daily at home. This message shouted that we were not good enough, and implied that our value was determined by our conduct. We were discouraged from asking questions, disagreeing with "experts", or relying on the Holy Spirit to personalize the scriptures for us. We rarely heard messages about love, grace or forgiveness. This negative approach to the gospel turned many away from the faith, including my three brothers and myself.

Thankfully, three of us eventually came back to serve the Lord, but today each one attends different denominations from one another. Sadly, one sibling claims to be an atheist. All of us have struggled with our beliefs. I often wonder how different our lives would be today if we had been encouraged to ask questions and test the doctrines of our faith. I believe that healthy questions answered with knowledgeable and understanding advice will bring a person to their knees faster than being hit over the head with a hammer of guilt.

This is not to say that guilt over one's sins should be ignored. Repentance is all about acknowledging our sins and turning our lives around. We cannot accept Jesus as our Lord and Savior without repentance. I am only saying that guilt is not the recommended method to encourage someone to discover Jesus. If we prioritize approaching salvation from the point of guilt, we negate the more important reason we live this life—to experience the joy and fulfillment that Christ brings into every believer's life. We are to attract people to Jesus and to the Christian life, not push them away. The spirits of guilt and shame are already very effective in pushing people away from one another.

Part of repentance from sin often includes human-to-human confession. Most people are terrified at disclosing their sins, yet they still feel a need to be absolved. In marriage, certain sins command a very expensive price...sometimes the union itself. We often don't tell each other everything, even if we wish we could. Many of us look elsewhere for a way or a place to confess.

The booming business of psychology shows the desperate need that people feel to unburden themselves. They want to be told that they are OK in a world that is not. In this respect, psychology has successfully become a religion in its own rite. Guilt and shame are dismissed as psychological diseases or failures of poor parenting. If we stop feeling ashamed of our past, our sins, or our feelings, and become more "me-centered"—we will conquer the guilt and shame and save ourselves from our own damnation. In this thinking, it is perfectly acceptable for each of us to create our own spiritual reality. Essentially, we become our own god. This belief declares that your truth is your truth, and my truth is my truth, and there are no absolutes. This dangerous thinking leads people down a self-centered, and eventually, a self-destructive path.

When truth becomes elusive, society slides down a slippery slope of relativity. When there are no absolutes in truth, then there are no absolutes in right and wrong. However, we will all eventually meet our Maker. When the reality of eternity commands our attention on our deathbed, the guilt and shame of everything that we have done or not done rises to overwhelm us. Fighting for one's right to believe what you want to believe, and do what you want to do, pales in the face of death. In those final moments, thoughts about God and eternity do overshadow the pain of the past. It is there that psychology loses in the battle of faith.

Although psychology might help us feel better about ourselves, and provide a useful framework for counseling, there is still a deep human need for absolution that is not resolved through introspection. Everyone wants to feel loved, valued and accepted, but guilt and shame get in the way and overwhelm even the most confident. We all want to be absolved of our sins and rescued from our pits of despair. This desire for absolution provides a confirming foundation for the need of salvation. This information can help to answer the question, "Why do I need to be saved?"

Helping our loved ones get to the place where they can understand their need for salvation is our quest. The human desire to be absolved of guilt and shame is, in itself, proof that every person has a spiritual belief system. Even atheists have faith in their own ability to solve problems, although many won't call it faith. Some people claim to be spiritual simply because they believe in good moral values and living a good moral life. Religion to them is a bunch of defined rules that are dictated to us by people who think they are closer to God than the rest of us. And they're not far wrong, to be honest. Sadly, by rejecting religion, they reject Christianity as simply being another religion. We can scream and shout that "Christianity is not a religion—it's a relationship," but most people don't stick around long enough in a conversation to let us explain.

Some people claim to believe in a god, or a universal entity, or an energetic cosmic force, or just a "higher power." Some don't believe in any power outside of themselves, that there is no eternity. They may say we are composed of energy and matter that dies when we die. Many perceive that we are spiritual beings connected to something greater than ourselves. But just what that something is, they say, is debatable and unknowable. Countless people will say that no one knows the real truth—after all, there are numerous religions in the world, and every religion thinks that they are right. Almost every religion believes they are the only true path to God. Some religions believe in multiple gods and many paths to God.

When it comes to Christianity, the agnostic/atheist often points to the presumed hypocrisy of thousands of different Christian churches that have varying theological differences. Yes, every major denomination has a slightly different interpretation of certain aspects of the Bible, and this is portrayed in their doctrine and practice of their faith. Even Christians walk on different spiritual levels. Every denomination, and each church within those denominations, and even the people inside those congregations— may see certain life or faith issues from different angles.

We are human beings working out the sanctification aspect of our salvation with "fear and trembling" (Philippians 2:12). Although we are justified by faith, we desire to grow to become more and more like Jesus. Part of that growing process is learning from each other. As we learn more about what we believe, and what our Christian family around us accepts as truth, our beliefs may shift or change. This is normal. If we did not grow, we would become like stagnant ponds. If we want to avoid becoming stagnant and full of stinking sameness, we must learn to embrace growth and change.

Over the millennia, the Christian church has carried the same message of love, forgiveness, grace, and redemption. However, the way this message is understood and delivered has changed dramatically since Jesus walked this earth. Part of this has been the consequence of cultural differences, political control over the message, as well as misinterpretations due to a lack of access to written Scriptures. (The average person has only had easy access to the written word for the past few centuries.)

When the first disciples began to carry the message of Christ to the world, they encountered cultural conflicts in perceptions of faith. Many of the epistles discuss some of the cultural misinterpretations happening at that time. The entire book of Hebrews explains Jesus through the lens of Judaism to the new Jewish believer. The other epistles were written to the various churches in the diverse geographical areas that we describe as the modern-day Mediterranean and Middle Eastern world.

It is interesting to note that our "progressive" society today still struggles with many of the same problems that those early churches faced. The sin of selfishness still causes the plagues of envy, jealousy, anger, resentment, sexual idolatry, and other ungodly behaviors. These sins still plague us today just like they did then. If we can look at ways that the early church dealt with those conflicts, we can discover keys to solving the problems that confront our lives today. But the way those biblical answers are interpreted may change over time. As our cultural lens changes, or as we grow in faith...our understanding of Scripture may also change.

The many Christian denominations that exist today, developed because of a unique interpretation of the Christian faith. That occurred either as the result of a cultural viewpoint, or a significant event that happened because one person, or a group of people, received a revelation of Scripture that was outside the norm of the standard church view at the time. Leaders, such as John Wycliffe, Martin Luther, Menno Simons, John Calvin, John Wesley, and Smith Wigglesworth, all received revelation that opened the Scriptures to people in new ways within their present contexts.

This continues today. Pentecostal and Charismatic churches are currently in a season of significant shifts of belief, partly because of the work of Bill Johnson and Bethel Church in Redding, California. Ripples from this movement are reaching beyond the Charismatic world, and we can assume that the Christian faith is once again going through a growth spurt that will predictably shift our faith into a new and greater dimension of belief that will impact the future. Christianity will continue to carry the same message in succeeding generations, but the way in which it will be delivered may look very different from how it looks today.

It's quite normal to feel confused or embarrassed when a non-believer cries "hypocrisy" about what appears to be conflicting differences in beliefs within the countless Christian denominations. Don't let yourself get caught in this trap designed to attack your faith! It's easy to think that all Christian churches should be unified in all things simply because we are (or are supposed to be) delivering the same message of love, grace and redemption. But cultural differences in perceptions and applications are huge.

Our human instinct is to focus on our differences. This impacts the ease and quality of our conversations. If your spouse tries to use Christian disagreement as an argument against your faith, it is more helpful to focus on our common beliefs—the deity of Jesus, the death and resurrection of our Lord and Savior, and the message of love and redemption that Jesus brought to this world. Many of our doctrinal differences need to be left to the explanations of those more educated in these areas. That doesn't mean you shouldn't talk about theological differences. We all need to understand what we believe and why. Educating ourselves in what makes other churches different gives us a framework of understanding when these topics arise in a conversation.

Understanding differences also helps us to be more compassionate and patient with our unsaved loved ones, while they struggle with finding the meaning in our faith that makes sense to them. We should not live in ignorance. The fact that we all have a desire to be absolved from our guilt and shame, can help our unbelieving spouse understand that we are all human and are all flawed. The fact that we are all flawed and each congregation delivers their understanding of Christianity in slightly different ways, shows the humanity of the Christian faith. We can admit that none of us have all the answers. Each church has a piece of the truth. No church has all the truth.

When you are talking about faith to the outside world, you can often choose your location and timing, and plan what you want to say. This rarely happens in marriage. Living under the same roof results in many spontaneous conversations, which sometimes consist of only a few words. This is one reason why you need to be diligent and pray always, without ceasing (1 Thessalonians 5:17). Wait for that prompting from the Holy Spirit as to when and what to say. Learn discernment. Ask the Holy Spirit to teach you how to be discerning. While you wait for an open door to start (or continue) in this conversation, do your homework—study the Word and ask for revelation.

Whether you are asking questions to understand your spouse's belief system, or trying to give answers to the questions they ask you, keep an attitude of humility and walk in grace and love. Remember that you are a child of God, the Creator and King of the Universe—you are royalty! Act like it. Be knowledgeable, but be respectful of others' unbelief and theological differences. The Bible says to be ready to give a defense of your faith whenever asked.

> *But in your hearts revere Christ as Lord. Always be prepared to give an answer to everyone who asks you to give the reason for the hope that you have. But do this with gentleness and respect, keeping a clear conscience, so that those who speak maliciously against your good behavior in Christ may be ashamed of their slander.*
> —1 Peter 3:15–16 NIV

Arguing about belief systems is fruitless. Whether we are right or wrong, arguing hurts relationships. Be kind. Be wise. Learn to listen. Begin with a point of agreement, not a point of disagreement. Follow the example of the Apostle Paul with the Greeks (see Acts 17:17–33). State your belief and then be quiet. Let them think about it—change rarely happens overnight. Let the

Holy Spirit do His work. When you don't know the answer to that important question being asked, trust that God will come along and surprise you.

> *Do not worry about how or what you should answer, or what you should say. For the Holy Spirit will teach you in that very hour what you ought to say.*
> — Luke 12:11b–12 NKJV

Here are a few points in closing this chapter:

- Living on different spiritual levels with an unsaved or uncommitted spouse requires that we assess where our differences lie. It may be as simple as Christian language or concept misunderstandings. If the difference is a genuine disparity in beliefs, then we need to find an area of common ground to begin a conversation of faith.
- Pray for the Holy Spirit to help you when you are faced with giving an answer for your faith or defending your situation. If no words come to you, perhaps you need to stay silent and walk away.
- Read the Bible diligently. You can't talk about your faith if you don't understand it yourself. You need to know the Bible so that when the time comes, you can quote it intelligently.
- Remember this: The enemy will whisper in your ear that you aren't good enough (or don't know enough) to witness to someone. Choose to listen to God's voice and wait for his leading. Studying the Bible daily helps to silence the accuser (Revelation 12:10–11). We need to be prepared for an attack. The Bible is our spiritual sword. The Holy Spirit and the angels are our partners in battle. We need to learn how to use the Word and how to ask for supernatural help. Don't despair and don't worry about failure. The Holy Spirit will always bring the right words or Scriptures to your mind when you need them. Learn to trust in Him. He will never let you down.

Despite your best efforts to sharpen your sword and follow the Holy Spirit's leadings, there will be times when you will feel persecuted. This may come in the form of mocking, avoidance, frequent arguing, lies, manipulation, or public scorning. Every one of Jesus' disciples endured great persecution and most died for their faith. It is part of the price that we pay for living our faith the way Jesus asks us to live.

> *In fact, everyone who wants to live a godly life in Christ Jesus will be persecuted.*
> — 2 Timothy 3:12 NIV

Trials and tribulations are almost guaranteed. But you can handle the valleys of trouble better if you understand your faith. You can only do that by meditating on the Word, learning from those who know the Word, and practicing what you preach.

CHAPTER SEVEN

Abuse or Persecution?

For God has not given us a spirit of fear, but of power and of love and of a sound mind.
— 2 Timothy 1:7 NKJV

Fear is the dominant emotion that is present in an abusive situation. Frequent exposure to fearful situations can result in multiple psychological problems, including depression and post-traumatic stress syndrome. Constant stress as the result of fear can also cause physical problems, such as chronic pain disorders or autoimmune issues.[11] This information is well-known in the medical community, but doctors seldom take the time to find the root cause of the stress. Instead, the easier fix is to reach for the prescription pad. Consequently, many victims of abuse never get a proper diagnosis, treatment, or the help that they need.

God does not want us to live in fear. He wants us to live in peace and harmony with one another.

When abuse happens in a home, quite often the victims of that abuse become so numb to the fear that they no longer recognize the abuse as the dysfunctional enemy that it is. It's difficult to be at peace with God or others when you live in fear. It can also be difficult to feel that personal connection with God. God may appear distant and prayers for help can feel like they are hitting a ceiling. Halting fear in its tracks requires deliberate action.

---

[11] See https://www.stress.org/stress-effects/

Stopping abuse requires a strategy that usually includes the help of a third party.

Abuse is not unknown to Christians. Unfortunately, the church has done a poor job of understanding the topic of abuse, and has too often turned a blind eye to abusive relationships. Turning a blind eye may be the result of ignorance of the dangers of the goings-on behind closed doors, or simply not knowing what to do or what to say. It takes courage to confront an abusive situation.

The adage that "a man's home is his castle," dominated society for many years, and seemed to give license for a man to run his home any way he wanted. This included controlling his wife and children in the way he felt was correct. This thinking is still dominant in some cultures.

License to ignore abusive situations was also received through misunderstandings of certain biblical passages, such as Ephesians 5:22–23. These verses, which tell women to submit to their husbands, have sometimes been interpreted to say that women should do whatever their husband requests and bow completely to his authority. Men used these Scriptures to excuse their demeaning or violent behavior to not only their wives, but other women as well. Women were not only subjected to violence at home, but also at their workplace.

Thankfully, in North America we now have laws that protect people who may be experiencing harassment or abuse in the workplace. The home, however, is still subject to laws of privacy, and terror still happens behind closed doors. Although the church seems to have gotten better at understanding the need for intervention when someone reaches for help—some churches still teach the belief that men are superior to women.

This sanctioning of old definitions, and refusal to accept modern reinterpretations of the biblical text, still dominates the mindsets of many. Churches that hold to this thinking inadvertently encourage abuse. Telling a man to "be a man," without helping him understand the tender heart of his wife and children, can result in a misunderstanding by the man that he can run his home and his family as he sees fit.

Until this demon has been exorcised from society, it will have the tendency to raise its ugly head in our homes. We must do what we can to help those who are in such vulnerable situations. Part of doing what we can, means we need to understand what it is that we are dealing with.

From the age of sixteen, half of all women in Canada have experienced at least one incident of physical or sexual violence.[12] Since abuse is so prevalent, it is a subject that bears studying.

There are many forms of abuse. These include: physical, sexual, emotional, verbal, financial, spiritual, and stalking. Often an abusive relationship suffers from more than one type of abuse. The likelihood that abuse might happen is greatly increased when a marriage suffers from frequent conflict.

Since we are living in relationships that operate spiritually on different levels, miscommunications and disagreements are common. We are vulnerable to conflict. When faith enters an argument, differences are magnified. When stress and angry emotions get added into the mix, you have the perfect recipe for an abusive situation.

As Christians, we tend to think that if we are trying to win our spouse for Christ, we must be demonstrating love always—even to the detriment of our own health and safety. It's easy to assume that kindness and politeness will placate every quarrel, but that doesn't work in an abusive marriage. Often love is confused with obedience, and forgiveness is given without consequences.

---

[12] See http://www.canadianwomen.org/facts-about-violence

We read this verse and may mistakenly believe that this applies in all circumstances:

> *To the rest, I say this (I, not the Lord): If any brother has a wife who is not a believer and she is willing to live with him, he must not divorce her. And if a woman has a husband who is not a believer and he is willing to live with her, she must not divorce him.*
> — 1 Corinthians 7:12–13 NIV

Friend, there is nothing in the Bible that tells us to put ourselves or our children in harm's way. Living with an unbeliever does not include living with violence or disrespect of any kind. If you are questioning your situation, you need to evaluate whether you are suffering from persecution or abuse.

> *No temptation has overtaken you except what is common to mankind. And God is faithful; he will not let you be tempted beyond what you can bear. But when you are tempted, he will also provide a way out so that you can endure it.*
> — 1 Corinthians 10:13 NIV

This verse promises us that God will provide a way of escape during times of trial. God always has a bigger plan. It is us, our motivations, and our interference that gets in the way of God doing His greatest work. We need to trust the leading of the Holy Spirit.

Abuse was common in the community where I lived during the 1970's. I watched in horror, as one of my newly-married best friends, a Christian, started coming to work wearing sunglasses, and having bruises on her face and arms. Despite the risk to her life, she stayed living in this marriage, chained in slavery to her husband and his needs. Where had this man learned this behavior? From his parents and his older brother. The children of this marriage also watched and learned, potentially perpetuating a generational cycle of violence.

Back then, there were few laws to protect women, so the police rarely interfered. There was no public education on domestic violence. The public had no information on how to identify a problem or how to help. Fortunately for western society, legal protection is now more readily available. But this is not the case everywhere. In some societies and cultures, domestic violence is still accepted.

Domestic violence is a generational cycle that doesn't end without intervention. It often doesn't raise its ugly head until after the wedding ceremony. Unless you are well-educated on this issue, you won't know what to look for before you get married. Often, the abusers are publicly charming and liked by their peers. They can be pillars of society. But that nice guy turns out to be a bully at home when someone says the wrong thing at the wrong time. Sadly, red flags, such as bruises, long sleeves, or turtlenecks that are commonly recognized in social or educational settings, are too often ignored in the church.

At home, violent arguments are quickly ended or covered up with flowers or expensive gifts. The abuser expects his wife to be overjoyed with these exaggerated apologies and believes that she will brag to her friends about her husband's generosity. The overt apologies and the calm between the storms, together with financial dependence, are some common factors that keep women in abusive relationships. Women that live in isolated areas or are introverted, have few friends, or avoid social gatherings are prime candidates for a spouse with an abusive disposition.

I worked as a professional social worker for fifteen years. During that time, I witnessed many types of abuse. I've also personally experienced horrific physical, sexual, and emotional violence. Recovering from those traumas has required years of intensive therapy and inner healing. I've also experienced mild verbal/emotional persecution related to my faith. But my experiences pale in comparison to what many Christians suffer in other parts of the world.

When you are living in an unequally yoked marriage, *and* you are very dedicated to your faith, you are going to come up against resistance, obstruction, and persecution. That is a guarantee. Abuse, however, is never acceptable. Sometimes, being able to tell the difference between abuse and persecution is a fine line.

Recognizing Abuse

How can you tell the difference? If the conflict stirs up intense fear, anxiety, or physical danger—it's likely abuse. If the attack is specifically directed at your faith, it may be persecution. However, it might also be an easy way to fling verbal assaults your way. Ask yourself—is he attacking you, or is he attacking your faith? You will need to rely on the voice of God to understand how to define what is happening. Remember, God's perfect love casts out fear (1 John 4:18).

Please get advice from a professional if you are unsure of what is happening to you. My opinion is based on my own experiences, and observation of and conversations with affected people. Please don't be a martyr and put yourself in harm's way.

If your life or the lives of your children are in danger, you need to get out immediately. Emotional and sexual abuse can be just as devastating. Never tolerate violent disrespect of your body or your mind. Also, never tolerate violence of any sort toward your children.

We all bear scars of our childhood from things that people said or did to us. Some people suffer their entire life because of one single incident that made them feel worthless. Always protect your children and be open to their interpretation of what they are experiencing. Some children cannot tell in words what they are feeling, so they may act violently or demonstrate other dramatic behaviors. Be perceptive. A sudden change in personality in your child almost always signals that there is something wrong. Find out what the problem is and act quickly. Get help before things escalate!

Sexual Abuse in Marriage

I knew a lovely Christian couple that married when they were both very young. Both had been raised in Godly families that attended the same church. Joe was naive when he was introduced to pornography at work. Sex was new and exciting. He enjoyed learning about novel and creative ways to enjoy his young bride. Eventually the pornography became an obsession, and it didn't take very long for the sex to become abusive. The obsession stole their intimacy, destroyed communication and robbed the family of valuable time.

On numerous occasions, Jane cried out for help to church leaders and people she respected. But no one believed her. In fact, many turned around and blamed her for not being a very good wife! Despite an upbringing that taught her that divorce was wrong, there came a point when she knew that Joe had crossed the line, and she needed to protect herself and her children. Eventually, Jane made the difficult decision to end the marriage.

What an incredibly sad story! What I find the most appalling about her story is the fact that no one in her church believed her or supported her. Friends, let us never disbelieve someone when they are crying out for help!

Unfortunately, sexual abuse in a marriage—especially a young marriage—is almost impossible to see. Open displays of sexual affection are commonplace in our culture, and sexual perversions are laughed at. Pornography has become the accepted cultural sin in society. There are more and more reports coming out about church leaders who have been caught in this satanic web.[13]

---

[13] See www.charismanews.com/culture/54853-pastors-get-honest-about-porn-the-struggle-is-real

Pornography not only tears relationships apart, it also destroys those who participate in it. It is subtler than alcohol, and more destructive than drug addiction. There are now scientific research studies of the brain that show that pornography changes the structure of the brain in the addict.[14]

The sex industry is a ruse for human slavery. Why would anyone want to support slavery? Please educate yourself about the sex-trafficking industry. Check out websites, such as A21.org[15] and polarisproject.org[16] to further educate yourself.

Emotional Abuse, Manipulation and Fear

Gaslighting is a form of abuse in which a victim is manipulated into doubting their own memory, perception, and sanity.[17] This type of abuse is common in emotional or verbally abusive relationships.

When frequent misinterpretations happen, you might begin to think you are losing your mind. This is more likely a sign of poor communication skills (that can be corrected with professional help), or a sign of interference by the enemy. The enemy looks for ways to create conflict, and if he can twist something someone says to create stress in a relationship, he will do that. He loves to play mind games.

We live in an unseen spiritual world. The enemy desires to steal, kill and destroy (John 10:10). That means he will do and say anything to cause chaos in relationships and families.

I often test communication misses by first inviting the Lord into the situation. Then I use the mental imagery of the cross, place that image between myself and my husband, and then visualize an

---

[14] "Brain Activity in Sex Addiction mirrors that of Drug Addiction." ScienceDaily. https://www.sciencedaily.com/releases/2014/07/140711153327.htm
[15] Visit www.a21.org
[16] See https://polarisproject.org
[17] See https://en.m.wikipedia.org/wiki/Gaslighting

open communication pathway. If the disagreement stops in response, then I know the miscommunication is coming from the enemy. If not, then it's one of us. We need to stop miscommunication before it gets out of control. Miscommunication can lead to hostility. Hostility can lead to abuse. Abuse causes fear. The enemy loves to create fear in relationships. Fear is not from God.

> *There is no fear in love; but perfect love casts out fear, because fear involves torment. But he who fears has not been made perfect in love.*
> — 1 John 4:18 NKJV

However, not all fear is real. Fear dominated my life for years. A break-in at our house triggered nightmares and old memories of an abusive situation. I was terrified that these things would happen again. I had difficulty falling asleep, and was unable to sleep soundly. The doctors prescribed a variety of antidepressant and anxiety medications, but that only kept me in a constant state of numbness. Psychological assistance was ineffective. I also asked for support from a few Christian people and pastors. They offered to pray with me, but could not offer me any other advice.

Eventually, I became agoraphobic (I couldn't leave the house). Then, when everything was falling apart in our home and chaos was reigning supreme, I seriously contemplated suicide. I was hospitalized and diagnosed with PTSD. The special programs at the hospital and daily structure provided some great education and many creative therapeutic tools to control my symptoms. The staff were kind, helpful, and very encouraging. Unfortunately, their nightly checks at midnight only triggered my night terrors. Nothing helped to take away my fear.

After my worst episode, I spent four years reading the Bible, praying, listening to audio tapes, and searching the Internet for online support. I knew if I just pressed more into Jesus, eventually my fears would go away.

One day, when I was out walking and talking to the Lord (which is one of my favorite times to talk to Him), a thought suddenly came to me. "This fear is irrational. It has absolutely nothing to do with my life today. In fact, I don't really think this fear belongs to me. I bet it's an evil spirit intent on destroying me." And with that knowledge, I said, "Fear, in the name of Jesus, I command you to leave and never come back."

Immediately, I felt something lift off my shoulders. The knot in my stomach and the fear in my mind were both instantly gone. I was completely free! It was that simple.

I needed to reach that point when I recognized that my thoughts are not always *my* thoughts. It also meant learning how to hear the voice of Jesus. That took time and practice. The "School of the Spirit" course with Dr. Mark Virkler encouraged major growth in my spiritual life.[18]

People who have suffered serious abuse may experience distorted thinking and understanding. These distortions can be caused by structural changes in the brain. This is like the brain damage seen in an addict's brain. Pathways in the brain become entrenched, causing difficulties in comprehending the difference between the past and the present. This is the reason some military vets end up homeless. They are still living that old war in their minds and can't cope with the real world. Their perception of reality is completely distorted.

As I said earlier, *not all fear is real.* But the enemy will keep you focused on that fear to stop you from living the life God has destined for you.

If you want to understand more about how the brain changes because of trauma, please check out some of the videos and online

---

[18] School of the Spirit can be found at
https://www.cluschoolofthespirit.com/shop/diploma-in-applied-spirituality/
?affiliates=84

teachings by Dr. Caroline Leaf at drleaf.com or Dr. Daniel Amen at amenclinics.com

Always Seek Help

One final note about the subject of abuse. If you or your children are in physical danger—leave, and do so quickly. Get help. Love should not hurt.

If you feel that your marriage is abusive, but you are not sure whether you should leave, seek guidance from a Christian counselor. Fast and pray over this serious decision.

I've met many Christians married to violent, alcoholic or drug-addicted persons, who really felt that the Lord didn't want them to leave their marriage. Some of these spouses eventually got sober, ended the violence, and the marriage improved over time. Others eventually came to know the Lord. Some of these individuals needed to leave for a season until their spouse agreed to quit drinking or using drugs. Then they returned, and rebuilt their marriages through a lot of hard work.

Being married to an addicted spouse is a difficult life and sets a very bad example of married life to your children. However, please listen to the leading of the Holy Spirit before deciding to leave the relationship.

If you are married to someone with an addiction problem, or have someone in your family that struggles with addiction, check out the support available through the *Al-Anon* organization.[19] They have helped many individuals and families develop boundaries and coping skills to survive in some very difficult situations. This support is offered at no charge, and there is a chapter in every town or community. Some churches also have Christian support

---

[19] See "Al-Anon Family Groups" at www.al-anon.org.

groups or programs, such as *Celebrate Recovery*,[20] that can provide help for coping with many life issues. Check with your local church for their recommended resources.

Leaving a spouse is a painful decision, even more so for those who have been enduring an abusive relationship for a long time. Accepting the inevitable is very difficult. It is easy to become codependent on the abusive partner. Perhaps you can't imagine living alone, especially without the financial and physical support that you have been receiving from your spouse. Perhaps you are afraid that he/she will continue to terrorize you after you leave.

First...let me assure you that removing yourself from that abusive relationship may be tough at first, but you will be much happier when you discover how strong and independent you really are. Second...there are ways to prevent your spouse from hurting you. There are emergency shelters and mental health groups that will gladly help you to find safety. Never fear—God is here. The angels will always show up exactly when you need them.

It's worth mentioning also, that we must guard our own actions so that we are not accused of emotional or spiritual abuse when we are sharing our faith with our loved ones. Our loved ones are already under conviction by the Holy Spirit, and we don't want to get in His way! Jesus was all about building relationships—not tearing them down. He set up clear boundaries of what He considered acceptable and unacceptable. He battled the enemy, He took frequent rest breaks away from the demands of His job and away from people, and He spent lots of quiet time with His Heavenly Father. When He was energized, He jumped back into His job. At all times, Jesus needs to be our example.

---

[20] See "Celebrate Recovery" at www.celebraterecovery.ca

If you're abused because of Christ, count yourself fortunate. It's the Spirit of God and His glory in you that brought you to the notice of others. If they're on you because you broke the law or disturbed the peace, that's a different matter. But if it's because you're a Christian, don't give it a second thought. Be proud of the distinguished status reflected in that name!
— 1 Peter 4:14–16 MSG

Blessed are the peacemakers, for they shall be called sons of God. Blessed are those who are persecuted for righteousness' sake, for theirs is the kingdom of heaven. Blessed are you when they revile and persecute you, and say all kinds of evil against you falsely for My sake. Rejoice and be exceedingly glad, for great is your reward in heaven, for so they persecuted the prophets who were before you.
— Matthew 5:9–12 NKJV

For more information about abuse, please see the Appendix located in the back of this book, and review the United Nations definitions of violence against women. Further resources are available at canadianwomen.org/facts-about-violence

SECTION TWO

———◦———

Your Spiritual Support System

In Section One, we reviewed the basics of our faith and sorted out the confusion between justification, sanctification, and progressive sanctification. We defined the why and what of the unequally yoked marriage, and we touched on some of the social and personal struggles that we face. We ended the section with the sobering reality of domestic abuse in our society, and how to differentiate between abuse and persecution.

In Section Two, we examine your spiritual support system and find answers to the following questions:

- Why do we often feel alone in the church?
- Does church leadership make decisions about our spiritual fitness based on our home life?
- How do we ask for help from others inside the church?
- Are there other ways to get the spiritual support that we so desperately need?
- What are the pros and cons of social media and modern technology, and the importance of staying connected with other believers?
- What is mentorship, how can it help you, and how can you help others?

CHAPTER EIGHT

The Church Social Scene

Let the word of Christ dwell in you richly in all wisdom,
teaching and admonishing one another in psalms and
hymns and spiritual songs, singing with grace in your
hearts to the Lord.
— Colossians 3:16 NKJV

Church attendance is often seen as a family affair. Our spiritually unequal family is not a regular part of that scene. Although the pastor preaches about the importance of connection and reaching out—"single, but married" individuals may feel limited to do so. Some feel uncomfortable simply attending service, believing they don't fit in.

A new church can be intimidating. It's lonely sitting unaccompanied in that church pew. We feel conspicuous. We may see ourselves as modern day lepers of proper church society. Scanning the sanctuary, we see single people that are clustered into young-and-dating groupings, or blocks of the elderly and widowed. Divorced single parents sit with their children, or with other divorced single parents.

Since we don't want to be alone, we look around for others like us—hiding in a corner or in the back row—away from the crowd. But Christian partners of unequally yoked marriages don't jump up and down shouting, "I'm married to a non-believer!" Instead, clothed in false shame, we discreetly arrive late, sit in an unassuming row and participate unobtrusively. At the end of the service, we slip out the back door to avoid detection. For the most part, we struggle in this journey alone and unaided.

Finding the right fit with a congregation and socializing with other Christians can be overwhelming. It takes time to find a level of comfort, become familiar with other congregants, and learn the Christian lifestyle. Although a friendly face greets us when we walk in the door for the first time and invites us to fill in a newcomer's card, we hesitate to do so.

We suffer a contradictory dilemma. We want to participate and feel like we belong, but we don't want to have that newcomer sticker tattooed to our forehead. That identity will result in questions, such as: "Where are you from? Are you new in the community? Do you have family here? Are you married? Does your spouse work weekends?" or that dreaded invitation, "Please come to our newcomers' potluck!"

These queries may be genuine offers of Christian connection, but with our marital situation being what it is, those innocent remarks tend to make us uncomfortable. We don't want to explain the spiritual status of our marriage. Sadly—experience has taught many of us—when we start to give details, the reaction we usually get is a sympathetic but blank face, and the response of "Oh! I'm sorry." Few believers know how to reply, nor do they know how to encourage us.

We are left with this dilemma of what to do, what to say and how to act. This internal conflict leaves us feeling like a pariah in the church community.

Feeling like we don't fit in leaves us ashamed and embarrassed. Although we don't want to talk about these negative feelings with everyone, we do want to share this pain with people who truly understand. Our desire is not for sympathy, but rather for spiritual connection—relationships that can feed us socially and spiritually, and encourage us in our struggle. We want growth to happen, and we need support in our day-to-day struggles.

Despite this need, we tend to find excuses *not* to socialize with other Christians, nor others who are in our very position! Why is that? Is it because we don't want to put pressure on our unsaved spouses by having too much religion in the house? Do we feel guilty or responsible for the tension in our households? Are we trying to protect ourselves from further potential conflict?

If that's not it...*why are we not bonding?* We need to be supportive of each other. What's the best way to do that?

Early in my Christian journey, I met a vibrant older woman who had been living with an unsaved spouse for more than fifty years. Despite being surrounded by negativity in her personal life, she had learned to practice an attitude of gratitude. She encouraged herself and others around her by volunteering, both in the church library and in the secular community. Her charitable activities strengthened her joy. Her joyful attitude spread into her home. Regardless of how grumpy her husband was, she would smile and remind herself that God would meet her every need.

I don't know if her husband was eventually saved or not. Still, inspiration like this is both motivating and encouraging. Gratitude in difficult circumstances keeps our mind set on heavenly things.

Being cheerful and grateful is difficult when we can't find like-minded people to share our common challenges. There is an emotional limit to our distress. We need understanding friends. Our search within the church reveals that we don't fit into the married couples home church group, nor the singles group, neither do we fit into the mature unmarried, widowed or divorced groups. It's rare to find someone in these circles that can identify with our challenges. We may feel misunderstood, abandoned or rejected.

In Christian social settings, we may also feel excluded. We know that if we want to make Christian friends in the community, we need to attend some of these social events. Friendship is imperative in encouraging our walk with the Lord. However, if we attend alone, it raises questions that we don't want to answer. If we drag our spouses along, we're worried they might be uncomfortable. It seems to be a no-win scenario.

Sadly, it seems that there are few couples wanting to be friends with a spiritually-divided couple. Either I will be the cause of a perceived social division, or my spouse will be. In both cases, awkwardness prevails.

Our struggles may be difficult for others to understand. It's not unlike the experience following a death in the family. When someone dies, people (who mean well) come to you and say, "We're so sorry for your loss", or "I know exactly what you are going through. I once lost someone special too."

The truth is, they don't know what you—uniquely—are going through. Not really. Yes, people can sympathize and empathize, but each person's experience is going to be slightly different. I can only share my experience with you, and you can share your experience with me. Then we can sit down together and say, "OK, this part you get. This part you understand."

We may think that our Christian brother or sister doesn't understand our situation, simply because their everyday life appears so grounded in their faith. But you won't know their story until you take the time to listen to them. At that point, you also need to step up to the plate and share your narrative. In sharing we learn, grow, and help each other.

Too often we miss opportunities for growth, simply by avoiding potentially painful conversations and events. Perhaps you avoid the church's "getting to know you" events by arriving at the meeting late and leaving early. You rationalize that you can still participate in the worship service and listen to a great message. You can learn the Word and attend Bible Study or home group without actively participating.

But wallflowers live in diminished sunlight. The light of the Holy Spirit provides the spiritual vitamins and nutrients that we need to grow. This energy is activated when planted in the soil of Christian interaction. Interaction describes relations between two or more people. Growth happens very slowly in isolation.

Growth also requires introspection. To grow personally and spiritually—we need to examine, analyze and evaluate ourselves— to discover those areas where we are missing the vital nutrients for growth. Through intentional introspection, we make better decisions and grow in spiritual maturity.

Introspection done with the feedback of others allows us to better see our own blind spots, and make those changes that we need to make. If we refuse to interact with other Christians, or if we refuse to challenge ourselves, our spiritual growth will be stunted. We will remain spiritual babies, feeding only on the milk and not progressing to the meat.

> *In fact, though by this time you ought to be teachers, you need someone to teach you the elementary truths of God's word all over again. You need milk, not solid food!*
> — Hebrews 5:12 NIV

Learning and growing requires doing. Growing in Christian faith requires more than a Sunday sermon. It flourishes when connection happens.

Do you stay home from church services or social events because your spouse won't go? Do you fear potentially embarrassing questions from curious believers? I know this can be scary, but I want to encourage you. If you don't attend church, you are not only missing out on Christian growth and potential friendships, you are also missing out on contributing your wealth of information and special gifts to a community that needs you. Take the risk and go. If you are shy, it's OK to start with arriving late and leaving early. Then gradually start greeting one person at a time. Eventually you will find a new church home and a few new friends.

If you don't have a home church, visit a few to see which one is a fit for you. It may take some time to find the right one. Don't let this discourage you. There really is something for everyone. Over the years, I've attended dozens of different types of churches with varying worship styles and values. I've grown to appreciate diversity in the various Christian denominations.

Our focus should not be on which denomination is better or worse than another. Instead, our focus should be on spiritual growth. Every person is at a different stage in their Christian development, and if we are sincere, we will crave growth in our relationship with the Lord. Part of growing can include attending churches that teach different aspects of the faith.

I don't believe in church-hopping just because you don't like what a certain church teaches. However, I do believe that the Lord moves us to different areas of the Body of Christ—so that we can learn different things at different times in our lives, or to be a blessing to the people in the congregation in which you are planted.

Seating yourself with a group of believers that can encourage you in your Christian walk will also be a support in your daily struggles. If you can't get that support in the church you currently attend, then perhaps it's not the right fit for you right now. Just remember that it's not only about what you receive, but also about what you can give. Take your time and seek the Lord's guidance. He will lead you to the right community at the right time.

It may help to know that many churches struggle with finding effective ways to outreach the unchurched. Getting people in the door requires an evangelistic approach that is both time-consuming and strategic. It also requires volunteers with good people skills and possibly good media skills. These resources are often lacking, and consequently the potential available in the unchurched population remains untapped while the social fabric of the church goes stale.

If we remember that churches are comprised of Christian volunteers who are simply doing the best that they can, then perhaps we can be more forgiving when we don't receive the immediate reception and acceptance that we are looking for. When we look for a caring community that can help us overcome our feelings of loneliness and isolation, we also need to receive that family with love and acceptance, understanding that they are in fact, imperfect...just like us.

In the following chapters, I discuss some strategies that will help us to bridge that gap between church and home.

CHAPTER NINE

Church Involvement

Evangelicalism is a movement in the Protestant church shaped by differing but clear emphasis on four beliefs: the centrality of the Bible, the centrality of the atoning death of Christ, the centrality of the need for personal conversion, and the centrality of an active mission to convert others and to do good works in society.
— Scot McKnight[21]

Being a missionary in your home is a daunting endeavor. Spiritually, we fight on the front lines in an invisible war zone. The bullets fly—even in the mess hall. So how does a warrior keep continually fed, with shield up, and sword sharp?

Reading the Bible daily is the first step. A second step is keeping ourselves encouraged through fellowship with our peers. A local church congregation provides opportunities to grow in our spiritual walk, and allows us to make new friends. That is our easiest, accessible relief station and emergency room.

We can learn a lot from our Christian peers—observing and interacting with other Christians gives us a deeper knowledge of the Scriptures. When we intermingle through multiple arenas (i.e., church, workplace, and social venues), we learn how to live day by day and how to fight many challenges.

---

[21] Scot McKnight, Is Evangelicalism Ending? 26 December 2012.
http://www.patheos.com/blogs/jesuscreed/2012/12/26/is-evangelicalism-ending/

Although our mission calling may be primarily at home, the great commission demands that we "go into all the world and preach the Gospel" (Matthew 28:18–20). Part of preaching the Gospel includes living a life that attracts others to us. How can we be effective witnesses for Christ if we don't know how to witness in our immediate surroundings?

Interaction with others in our Christian circles provides an ongoing education that—in addition to biblical knowledge— teaches us to accept both criticism and encouragement. This is our practice for the war zone. Practicing hones the skills that we need to become better warriors.

Christianity demands involvement and participation. The more you grow in faith, the more you must give both to your church and secular communities. As Jesus said:

> *From everyone who has been given much, much will be demanded; and from the one who has been entrusted with much, much more will be asked.*
> — Luke 12:48b NIV

As we grow in knowledge and wisdom, our faith grows. As we share our faith with others, we too grow in faith. The same is true of our spiritual gifts, which can be more clearly defined as those natural talents or skill sets given to us by our Creator. The more we use our gifts, the more our skills are developed, and the more our wisdom and knowledge grow.

When I first began writing, I knew very little about the art and science of writing itself, and I really wasn't sure how much I knew about the content matter. The more I studied, practiced my writing skills, and expanded my knowledge—my skills and knowledge grew. Now my knowledge has grown to the point that I can share something with you. I consider it to be an incredible privilege that God has allowed me the opportunity to take on this challenge.

But this book would not have happened if I had not stepped out in faith and signed up for self-publishing school. I could have signed up for the course and just listened to everyone talk about their weekly achievements. I would have grown in knowledge, but my *skills* would never have grown. For my skills to grow, I needed to practice writing. Picking up a pen and writing things down was the next part of this growth process.

There are stages to learning and there are stages to growing. Every time you learn something new, you need to practice it until you are ready for the next stage. Your God-given skills are waiting to be developed and used.

Part of church involvement is either contributing your existing skill set to the church body, or developing new skills to encourage and help others. If you've conquered your fears of the social scene by attending home group, making friends, and attending the occasional potluck—you may feel ready to volunteer in another capacity.

When it comes to being given a leadership position or any dedicated volunteer position in the Evangelical church, in my experience, there is a glass ceiling for those with unsaved spouses. It doesn't matter what our background, secular job, or experience might be. We may be allowed to help in the coffee shop, library, or bookstore, maybe even in the church nursery—but it's unlikely that we will be offered a leadership role in which someone might be directed to come to us for advice.

One might have all kinds of degrees, even Christian ones, but too often our gifts and talents seem to be overlooked. In my experience, if your spouse isn't saved and attending church with you, it may be assumed that you lack spiritual maturity, or that you don't have the emotional and moral support at home that you need to undertake a leadership role at church. We often need to prove ourselves before we will be seen differently.

All churches have their methods of selecting leaders, which they believe are correctly interpreted from Scripture. The most commonly used Bible passage is this one:

> *In the same way, deacons are to be worthy of respect, sincere, not indulging in much wine, and not pursuing dishonest gain. They must keep hold of the deep truths of the faith with a clear conscience. They must first be tested; and then if there is nothing against them, let them serve as deacons.*
> — 1 Timothy 3:8–10 NIV

Although each expression of the Body of Christ interprets the qualifications from Scripture differently, we must demonstrate our humility and willingness to learn before we can serve in a position of influence.

If you have been a Christian for many years and have never been able to volunteer, but now are—then it's up to you to tell your church leaders. Otherwise, a lot of assumptions can happen from both sides. The leadership will continue to think that you are not ready, or not willing to become involved, and you might think that you are simply not wanted. Having a frank conversation with your leadership helps them to understand your spiritual readiness.

The church that you attend has guidelines on how, where, and in what capacity a newcomer can volunteer. Those guidelines will vary from congregation to congregation, and from denomination to denomination. You can either accept the guidelines that are put before you or you can make the choice to attend another congregation that may have more opportunities reflective to your skill set.

It is imperative to remain humble and grateful for whatever options are presented. Like any job, our attitude will determine our altitude. The more we do, the more we will be asked to do. If someone offers you the opportunity to make coffee on Sunday morning, and you turn it down because it's "not your thing," be prepared that you might not get other offers in other departments. Churches need volunteers in all departments, but those volunteers are monitored and tested before they are given more challenging tasks.

If your church attendance is spotty because of your marital situation, it will interfere in your capacity to volunteer. Explain your dilemma to your pastor or home group leader. There may be other things that you can assist with on an occasional basis or in an off-site capacity.

If that is not a possibility for you, consider volunteering in your local community in a secular organization. God needs His people everywhere. The Bible is full of commandments that we help the less fortunate. The Apostles wrote of situations when the first Christians helped others in their societies—not only in their own church group. James writes:

> What good is it, my brothers and sisters, if someone claims to have faith but has no deeds? Can such faith save them? Suppose a brother or a sister is without clothes and daily food. If one of you says to them, "Go in peace; keep warm and well fed," but does nothing about their physical needs, what good is it? In the same way, faith by itself, if it is not accompanied by action, is dead. But someone will say, "You have faith; I have deeds." Show me your faith without deeds, and I will show you my faith by my deeds.
> — James 2:14–18 NIV

Faith is active. Our testimony is visible to others by the way we conduct our lives. We demonstrate the love and mercy of God in our interactions with others and in using our skills in whatever situation we find ourselves. What that looks like varies from person-to-person.

Not everyone is fortunate enough to live in a resource-rich Christian community, or have the freedom to participate in one. If you are not able to go to church or connect with Christian friends, you need to find other ways to keep yourself encouraged. Internet technology might be the answer that you need.

CHAPTER TEN

---◆═══◆═══◆---

Technology

And let us consider how we may spur one another on toward love and good deeds, not giving up meeting together, as some are in the habit of doing, but encouraging one another—and all the more as you see the Day approaching.
— Hebrews 10:24–25 NIV

The Christian in the unequally yoked marriage needs continual encouragement and inspiration. Some of us are restricted from attending a local church or a home group, either because of our home situation, or from physical or economic limitations. If this describes your situation—this chapter is for you.

Modern technology gives us many options to access vital Christian support from around the world. Your local church may be live-streaming their regular worship service. If not, they likely have weekly messages available in audio or video on their website.

Social Media Platforms

The internet is an amazing tool. Social media groups exist for persons of every faith, denomination, and interest group. If you are not connected to Facebook, Twitter or another social media platform, consider this as a reason to join. (If this seems daunting to you, ask a friend or family member to help you.)

When you have successfully registered on one or more of these social media platforms, search for prayer groups, Christian groups, or specific churches. Ask for recommendations from trusted Christian friends or pastors.

Social media sites contain both public and private groups or lists. Private groups may be referred to as secret or closed groups. Public sites/forums/groups are open to anyone, and do not have any privacy protection. Be careful about disclosing any personal information on public sites. Secret or closed groups provide somewhat more privacy, as they are restricted to members only. They require a personal invitation and approval by the group monitor before full access is granted. This privacy promises that anything that you post there is protected from prying eyes. This allows you to share information without worrying about the curiosity of family or neighbors, or being the target of someone's negative comments. Always check a site or group's privacy settings before posting any comments.

Private groups provide the opportunity to meet new people and stay informed regarding events in the group's community. A private group from your local church allows you and other congregants to get to know one another. Sometimes these groups act as an online support group, where you can request prayer or post for help for specific needs.

Online or virtual churches draw believers together to worship, provide mutual support, and disseminate helpful information. This type of church is especially good if you live in a remote area, or are restricted from attending church. Some online churches have house church options, where congregants can connect with others in their town or neighborhood. The virtual church allows for anonymity, while the house church provides the support you need within a secluded setting.

Check out xpministries.com/shilohfellowship as one example of an online church that utilizes a home-based satellite approach. Search the internet to find a church that fits with your needs and doctrinal beliefs.

Connecting with People Online

Online friendships can be both spiritually enriching and personally exciting. The world becomes a much smaller place when you can talk instantly with friends around the globe. Social media allows you to stay in touch with people that you've only met a few times.

When I travel, or attend conferences, I often meet interesting people that I'd like to get to know better. Sharing contact information has allowed me to make new friends and learn about other cultures. Hearing people's stories and sharing our lives together online, encourages me to stretch myself personally, spiritually and socially.

A virtual church may not replace the face-to-face interaction required to stretch and grow your faith, but it can often give you the connections you need to begin making Christian friends in your community.

Online friends don't always translate into offline friendships. The shift from online to a physical friendship entails a certain level of intimacy and some dedicated time. It also crosses the privacy barrier. For these reasons, some people prefer keeping online friendships online.

It's a good idea to get to know that virtual friend well, before sharing personal information or meeting at the local coffee shop. Sadly, this world is full of people whose physical and cyber personas don't match up. Be wise in this area. Pray about your online friendships before taking any real-world steps.

Options for Limited Internet

All friendships need regular contact to flourish. Online friendships need a regular internet connection. This may be tricky if you live in an area with limited internet support.

I lived in a remote rural area for eighteen years. My internet support was extremely limited and very expensive. I had an internet day once a week, when I took my laptop to the town library (where there was free and fast internet). There I downloaded Bible Studies, watched Christian videos, listened to Christian podcasts, caught up on social media and global news, and interacted with friends around the world.

Just a word of caution if this type of internet access is your only option. All public internet connections come with security concerns, and libraries are no different. All computers store history. That includes your browsing history online, and information that you type into forms on websites. Library administrators should be continually clearing history from public computers, but that doesn't always happen. That means personal information is easily discoverable by anyone who knows how to look for it. If this is your only option, be sure to logout of all websites properly and clear the browser history after each session. If you don't know how to do this, ask the library's staff to show you.

Online Biblical Studies

Your spiritual knowledge can blossom through online access. In addition to church services, other avenues of learning include devotional studies, Christian videos and Bible School classes. Some seminaries or Bible Schools provide full credit courses, permitting you to earn a degree online from your home. Many of these schools or programs have "connect groups," allowing you to meet other Christians in your program of study. Check with your church and other Christian contacts for recommended listings. I highly recommend Christian Leadership University.[22]

While enjoying those videos, take notes and compare what you learn online to what the Holy Spirit shows you in your daily Bible readings. This will help to clarify what you learn, and ensure that what you are learning is consistent to what the Lord is showing you.

Studying the Word through various sources helps to implant it in our hearts. This encourages us, keeps us focused on the right path, and aids in deflecting the attacks of the enemy.

> *Your word I have hidden in my heart, That I might not sin against You.*
> — Psalm 119:11 NKJV

Apps for your Smartphone

The Christian community has been quick to create apps for our smartphones. These apps are very versatile in hostile environments, as they can be quickly added or removed as needed. One of my favorites is the *Daily Audio Bible* app, which features a daily Bible reading followed by a short commentary. You can read along or just listen. I love this pastor's insight and historical knowledge as he takes us through the entire Bible in one year.

This app is connected to a global prayer and support group that is available via both website and telephone. As prayer requests are made, the community is encouraged to support and pray for each other. Online support is provided through a free membership. This is an encouraging and supportive resource, but be aware that prayer requests are broadcast throughout the world and can be heard by all members of the site. Daily Audio Bible also hosts retreat weekends and trips to Israel.[23]

---

[22] Visit www.cluschoolofthespirit.com?affiliates=84
[23] Visit www.dailyaudiobible.com

Many electronic Bibles are free and easily available for download directly to your computer, smartphone, e-reader, or other portable electronic device. Currently, the most popular versions are YouVersion, Bible.com, and Olive Tree. I like the Bible Gateway site for research and quickly looking up verses in different versions and translations.[24]

The internet is a powerful tool that can enrich your spiritual and personal life. You don't have to struggle through your Christian journey alone. Now you have instant access to online support and Christian educational resources. If you can't attend your local church, you can still listen to or watch regular worship services and stay in touch with the ministerial staff and other congregants.

Online interaction gives us the opportunity to stay connected with old friends and discover new ones. Spiritual and social connections help us maintain ties to our Christian communities, and strengthen our faith. Please consider these valuable avenues to encourage your faith, bolster your hope, and share your concerns with others.

---

[24] Visit www.biblegateway.com

CHAPTER ELEVEN

Home Groups

Therefore, confess your sins to each other and pray for each other so that you may be healed. The prayer of a righteous person is powerful and effective.
— James 5:16 NIV

The internet provides a great option for strengthening your spiritual growth and making new friendships, when local church attendance is difficult. However, connecting with and getting involved in a local church still provides the best opportunity to meet like-minded Christian brothers and sisters.

The weekly church service provides education and an opportunity to worship, but it is rarely interactive. You can meet people on a superficial level, but you must go beyond this venue to develop a Christian network. Meaningful connections require effort and time. Most churches have easily accessible options available. One of these is a community of believers that may be called "home group," "connect groups," or "prayer meetings."

These groups are simply a small, intimate coterie of believers that meet during the week in congregants' local homes or sometimes in the church building's facilities. They may require a formal sign-up process, or they can happen in an informal drop-in style. The focus may be Bible study, book focused or community prayer. Some may include a social aspect, such as seasonal parties or community dinners. Many are open to people that don't or can't attend their local church.

These groups aid in encouraging mutual support and in developing Christian friendships. If you want to deepen your understanding of the Christian faith, and want to discover how to put what you've learned into practice—a home group is an excellent way of doing that. Additionally, if you need or want to be held up in prayer, this body of believers can provide that support.

Getting to know people in an intimate setting, such as a home group, can be intimidating. Are you worried about being pressured to reveal too much about yourself? Are you concerned that you won't have anything in common with others in the group?

While it's quite possible that you won't meet anyone in these groups who also has an unsaved or uncommitted spouse—fellowship with other believers is essential to your spiritual growth. Growing in your faith requires taking a few risks that includes sharing with others. There is no rule that says you must commit to something forever. Try it for a short time and see if this fits for you.

Most churches have more than one group, and often more than one type of group, so you may have several choices to pick from. Take your time to visit each one until you find your comfort fit. Some groups focus on Bible Study, and do very little mutual sharing or praying for one another. Others focus extensively on prayer and mutual support. Both types are beneficial to new converts and old believers. Your needs may vary from season to season, or you may feel that you require multiple levels of teaching or support. Attending more than one venue is perfectly acceptable.

The Home Conflict

A word of caution here. Although it's exciting to spend several nights a week joining with other believers to study the Word or pray about mutual concerns, this should not be used as an excuse to escape your home life. The amount of time you spend away from home will impact your family and affect your witness to them.

Growing in your knowledge of the Lord and learning new ways to implement your Christian faith in your everyday life may be exciting for you, but the time that you are away from home may feel like rejection to your spouse and family. Any shift of your regular routine will impact the lifestyle of your family unit. Your spouse and family need your reassurance and continual affection, as well as attention to the practical and mundane matters that occupy every household.

This doesn't mean that you don't go, just because someone is trying to put you on a guilt trip. It means that you need to find a way to coordinate your time and activities to offset any stress that may be created. Think of this...like a thermostat. Your body is comfortable at a certain temperature. When the temperature of the room changes, whether too hot or too cold, you become uncomfortable. Your marriage and your family have a routine that has operated the same way for a long time, possibly many years. Suddenly, you decide to implement a change into the routine of your life. Like a temperature change, the family's routine is forced to adjust to a new climate—that being your new church lifestyle.

Any change in a marriage or family causes a feeling of discomfort, which we typically call "stress." It doesn't matter how well you got along with each other before the change, a disruption in anyone's routine requires adjustment to a new normal. During this time, feelings of discomfort will happen and negative coping methods may be employed by everyone, including you. Feelings of rejection, alienation, and invalidation are common during this process. Clear communication is the key.

Sharing

Our own feelings of rejection, which may come from the dismissal of our Christian beliefs by our loved ones, often leave us starving for meaningful connection with other believers. The intimate setting of a home group and the offer of prayer support, can seem like a ready invitation to "over-share" one's personal problems.

This was one of the biggest mistakes I made early on in my Christian growth. Since we live in a Christian wilderness in our homes, there is a tendency for us to dump our problems in the center of the room, and hope someone else will pick up our pieces and tell us what to do with them. Although most participants will be caring and willing to listen, over-sharing can be overwhelming to anyone listening, let alone for those Christians who have little or no understanding of what you are going through. As a result, you can easily scare away the very people that you need in your life. This can cause further feelings of alienation and rejection, and leave you discouraged.

A prayer group or home group is not a therapy group. If you need Christian counseling, see your pastors and ask them to direct you to someone in the community that they trust.

In some groups, participation rules and boundaries for cross-talk are clearly explained. More often, they are unspoken and take time to learn. Watch for cues on the internal organization of the group's process. Listen to how others share, and pay attention to how much time is allotted for the sharing of prayer requests. Answer initial questions, simply and politely. When you feel comfortable, respectfully and humbly let people know about your situation.

Do request prayer for your home life, your marriage, and your spouse. Don't disclose any information that would breach your confidentiality with your spouse or family. Keep your requests clear and simple. Once you have developed friendships that have gone beyond the walls of the prayer group, you can begin to share more of your life, while learning from your new friends about their lives.

Remember, other people will have prayer requests that they need to talk about—so be respectful of the time that the group has together. While the group is praying for your family, you should also be praying for theirs. And remember to share testimonies too. These groups want to celebrate the little and big successes in your

Christian life. Success stories are the best way to cheer other people on in their daily walk. It also encourages them to pray more for you!

One of the positive things about being married to an unsaved spouse is that we grow into prayer warriors. This is a gift that we are given. If your church is fortunate enough to have a dedicated intercessory prayer group, ask if you can join. If they don't, ask if you can start a group. Every church needs people who know how to pray!

If you are permitted to start a group, invite your church community to submit their prayer requests to the team, and encourage weekly or more frequent meetings of the members to pray together. When you start to see how God answers your prayers for other people, you will be encouraged and better able to trust that your prayers are also being heard.

> *And pray in the Spirit on all occasions with all kinds of prayers and requests. With this in mind, be alert and always keep on praying for all the Lord's people.*
> — Ephesians 6:18 NIV

Deepening Your Friendships

As you become more comfortable praying and interacting with your new Christian friends, the Holy Spirit may nudge you to interact with one special person. You may meet a new believer who needs a lot of encouragement. Or you may be drawn to learn from someone who is very easy to talk to and seems very knowledgeable about multiple areas of faith. These special friendships can take your faith to an entirely new level.

Mentoring is the art of changing lives and encouraging spiritual growth through an interactive and supportive process. The next chapter delves into this encouraging dynamic.

CHAPTER TWELVE

◆━━━━◆━━━━◆

Mentorship

Then Philip ran up to the chariot and heard the man reading Isaiah the prophet. "Do you understand what you are reading?" Philip asked, "How can I," he said, "unless someone explains it to me?" So, he invited Philip to come up and sit with him.
— Acts 8:30–31 NIV

Mentoring is a very special type of kinship involving the spiritual growth of yourself and another person. There's an old saying, "You light one flame, that person lights another flame and so on, until every light in the world has been lit." Our light is sharing our faith with others and having them share their light with us. We grow from and with each other.

Passing on the flame of spiritual understanding to others can be scary at first. It requires intentionality. Like any new friendship...meeting others, getting to know them, and finding common interests is time consuming. Good friendships usually happen slowly, but the best ones last a lifetime.

While most Christian connections may seem emotionally supportive in that they keep you walking the path, not all are helpful in targeting specific areas of needed growth. You need many levels of support to help you to develop into a mature, stable, and well-grounded person of faith.

A new plant doesn't only need water—it also requires good soil, fertilizer and sunlight, and possibly some strong stakes in the ground to protect it from the winds that threaten to destroy it. So too, we desire to grow in our Christian walk. Growing involves sharing. This is almost intuitive to us. As a plant grows and matures, it produces seeds. Those seeds drop into the ground and new plants emerge from the nourished soil. As we share our faith, we are dropping seeds into soil and hope they will grow. We do this both intentionally and unintentionally.

Sharing our faith causes an explosion of growth within us, resulting in increased faith. The root system of a plant wraps its thread-like fingers around rocks, grasping for stability to strengthen its base, while branching out to search for richer soil and more nourishment. So too, sharing our faith is the root system that broadens us and encourages us to look for new opportunities to grow deeper and stronger. As we cling to our rock (Jesus), and connect with others, we become better able to stand upright in the storms of life. Sharing makes us stronger.

Mentorship provides us with an awesome opportunity to strengthen the roots of our souls. In your ongoing search for Christian friendships inside the church community, you may meet someone who also struggles with being married to an unsaved or uncommitted spouse. He or she might have a lot more or a lot less experience than you do on this journey.

Although all serious Christians should love to talk about their faith, and are usually more than happy to pray with someone who asks—mentorship is slightly different from normal Christian friendship. The goal is to learn from someone who is more spiritually mature than you are, or to teach someone who is less mature in the faith. In mentoring friendships, you will share prayer concerns and pray for each other's family situations and trials of life, but you will also share practical advice, identify areas of needed growth, and share materials that assist each other in growing in the faith. Mentorships are special relationships that empower your walk with the Lord.

Spiritual Parenting

One generation commends your works to another; they tell of your mighty acts.
— Psalm 145:4 NIV

You've probably heard the term, "spiritual mother," or "spiritual father" before. Most often you will hear these terms spoken from the pulpit as a term of endearment for someone who has taken that person under their wing and nurtured them in the faith. It's not just pastors or evangelists that need these encouraging people in their lives—we all do. Spiritual mothers and/or fathers are mature Christians who we respect, can learn from, and share our struggles with. They know our intimate pain, and they can cry with us and pray with us. These are people that we can call—day or night—for prayer or emotional support. These type of "parents" are difficult to find, but what a joy when God brings them into our lives!

A few years into my journey of faith, I was struggling and in need of care when God brought Victoria and George into my life. I connected with Victoria over a Christian ladies' luncheon in our community. Although their home was in Texas, they purchased a summer home in the northern Canadian community where I lived. I followed the Holy Spirit's promptings to befriend Victoria. That's when my spiritual life really took off.

Victoria taught me things that I could never have learned in a church service. She encouraged me and pointed out my spiritual strengths. She carefully admonished me when she had concerns. Both stood by, prayerfully, when I went through my deepest, darkest struggles. Today, even though we can't physically get together as often as I would like to, I know I can still call either one of them anytime—day or night—and receive prayer and spiritual direction. I'm sure they still pray for me...as I do for them.

If you don't have a spiritual parent in your life, ask the Holy Spirit to guide you to someone who can mentor you. Pray diligently...until you meet that one you are sure about. Spend time with that person. Listen, learn, and just get to know them. Make sure that this is the person God has put in your path to be your confidant, your Christian advisor, and your cheerleader. Test their spiritual qualities by asking questions, as well as asking for support in different areas. If they are the right fit for you, you will feel that sense of joy and connection in your soul. I often feel like my spirit does a "happy dance," when I meet the right people that God wants in my life!

Mentoring Others

> *Even when I am old and gray, do not forsake me, my God, till I declare your power to the next generation, your mighty acts to all who are to come.*
> — Psalm 71:18 NIV

Just as it is important to have a mentor to encourage you in your life, it is also important that you encourage others. Although you may already be doing this as part of a home group, a one-on-one relationship with someone who is struggling or new in their faith can be invaluable to their spiritual growth, and encouraging to you at the same time.

When you feel ready to take on the challenge of mentoring others, pray for the Lord to draw you to the right individual. You may be pulled to encourage a teen who is a new Christian, or you may be led to a peer who also struggles with an unsaved spouse. Start with an offer of friendship. If the friendship is meant to grow into a mentorship, it will naturally move in that direction. You can encourage a relationship to move that way through the offer of books, internet and video resources, and discussions on common

Christian topics. If a person isn't interested in a more focused friendship that mentorship is designed to be, they will likely indicate that.

The difficulty of mentoring others while living in an unequally yoked marriage, is the additional time constraint that this will bring into your home life. Keep in mind that your home life is still your primary mission field. Any new commitments that take you away from your spouse and family have the potential of causing strife at home. When you are mentoring others, you need to find regular time to get together and discuss concerns that your mentee raises. Be sure that you consider this time stressor before you make a commitment.

How much time this new friendship requires partly depends on the comfort level of the relationship, the ease of getting together, and the maturity level of your mentee. You need time to both follow up and research answers to the questions your protégé brings forward, and to search for new study material.

Finding physical space to meet can also be an issue. A home environment generally provides more privacy, but that may not be possible or practical. If your spouse permits you to entertain Christians in your home, then the battle for time and space are easier. If that is not possible, then you must carve out time to meet elsewhere during the week.

Regardless of where or how you connect, this must be taken as a serious commitment in your journey of faith. Part of growing in your Christian life is sharing what you are learning or have learned with others. This is more difficult to do when you can't be open with your faith in your own home. Complicating your life with a mentorship requires a big commitment that includes setting boundaries not only around your personal schedule and your family life, but also within the mentoring friendship itself.

Boundaries in Mentoring Relationships

Walk with the wise and become wise, for a companion of fools suffers harm.
— Proverbs 13:20 NIV

We all need to apply wisdom in our friendships. When it comes to mentorships, you need to be vigilant in establishing boundaries early in the relationship. Your "disciple" is looking up to you as an example of Godly behavior. What you say and how you say it can have profound and long-lasting effects on others.

If you tend to complain about your spouse, family or home situation...it would be a good idea to clean up that part of your own thought-life...before you take on helping someone with theirs. If you frequently struggle with anger, resentment, jealousy, or other sins of attitude, then perhaps you are the one who needs the mentor. I recommend holding back on mentoring others until you feel you can set a positive, loving and encouraging example to others.

Wholesome and encouraging conversation should always be in the forefront of any interaction. It is never helpful for either of you to complain about your spouses or demean or belittle another's character. Gossip should never be a cover for prayer requests. In your difficult family life, there may be plenty of fodder for venting, and you might desire to do so frequently. There is a time and place to do that, and it can be done with prayerful intent. Keeping negative circumstances bottled up inside is not healthy. Everyone needs to share with someone who understands. Unresolved problems find new solutions when you share difficult circumstances with a trusted friend. But in the end, you need to give it all over to God, and encourage others to do the same.

When people start feeling comfortable in a friendship, it's easy for conversation to flow into many areas. Certain topics, strong feelings and simmering emotions can shift relationships. When it comes to male–female interaction, opposite sex mentorships are generally not advised, unless there is a significant age difference. (Significant enough that there would never be a chance of misinterpretation by those involved or by outsiders who see the two of you together.) Most pastors agree that it's not wise to start a male–female friendship if you are married. This opens a door to temptation in the relationship or it can aggravate conflict in the home. Don't complicate your life in this way.

There are certain times when input from an opposite sex friend is helpful in resolving a difficult problem. In general, men and women have different mental mindsets. They look at things differently, approach problem solving uniquely, and usually enjoy differing things. An opposite sex friend can provide a new way of looking at things that you never thought of before, but this is no excuse to start a mentoring relationship with the opposite sex.

If you are in a younger–older, parent–child type of mentorship, you can discover a whole new way of relating and problem-solving. Young people are especially helpful to an older generation in teaching them about technology, and keeping them abreast of current societal trends. Seniors love to share stories from their own lives, and help young people work through their career and family struggles.

In every relationship, sensitive topics—such as sex—should be addressed with great caution. Remember that you are to set an example to others. It is not wise to share about intimate issues with a member of the opposite sex. If your understudy discloses *their* intimate struggles, it's appropriate for you to provide biblical support to help them find the answers that they are looking for. Encourage them in their growth by providing quality Christian resources.

It's perfectly acceptable for you to talk to your spiritual parent about your personal issues, or have your younger mentee tell you about their issues—but don't share details of your intimate personal life with those you are mentoring and don't expect your mentor to discuss their intimate details with you. This can skew a relationship in the wrong direction and destroy a good friendship. Keep the hierarchy of parent–child going in the right direction. Either you are the parent or you are the child, but you can't be both. If age differences are minimal, you can still be friends. Some relationships start out as friends and end up as mentorships, others do the opposite. Shifts happen, but if the goal is to enrich both of your lives spiritually, then keep a watchful eye on your boundaries.

Mentorships are unique intentional relationships—focused on spiritual growth in an atmosphere of friendship. Clear, positive boundaries encourage respect, provide a direction for growth, and aid in setting wise examples. Although we all need mentors in our life, becoming mentors to others may be subject to the restrictions in our home.

SECTION THREE

Life at Home

In Section Two, we looked at our spiritual support systems. I covered the subject of loneliness in church, interfacing with church leadership, getting help from others, and finding a support group. I addressed the pros and cons of social media and modern technology, and the importance of staying connected with other believers. Then we looked at mentorship, what it is, how it can help you, and how you can help others.

In Section Three, we are going to put it all together. Here's where our faith "hits the pavement."

- Does everything we know and understand about our faith, and everything that we are doing for our spiritual life, relate practically to our life at home?
- How do we get through those day-to-day struggles?
- How do we survive when we mix faith, cultural differences, social inequality, injustice, and disparate ideologies into a marriage and/or family that is full of strife?
- How can we improve our relationships through the practice of forgiveness and better communication?
- How do we handle those difficult subjects of sex, money and parenting?

- How do we manage compromising situations and establish effective boundaries around activities, friendships, and home life?
- How and when do we need to access professional support?
- How do we keep ourselves spiritually strong in the midst of battle?

CHAPTER THIRTEEN

The Marriage Relationship—
Surviving the Storms

*Love is patient and kind; love does not envy or boast; it is
not arrogant or rude. It does not insist on its own way; it is
not irritable or resentful; it does not rejoice at wrongdoing,
but rejoices with the truth. Love bears all things, believes
all things, hopes all things, endures all things.*
— 1 Corinthians 13:4–7 ESV

L iving as a Christian in a church building is as simple as
showing up. Participating in Bible studies and growing your
faith in various ways takes more time and intentionality.
Understanding our faith is an imperative in deepening our
knowledge of it. But this is all worth nothing if we can't put it into
practice in our homes.

Our spouse and our family watch our life, listen to the words we
speak and observe the actions and attitudes behind those words.
You might think that no one notices—but talk to anyone who has
lived this life and come out the other side, and you will learn that
there is a magnifying glass being held up to your life and conduct.

Every married person wants their marriage to survive the storms
of life. Each couple looks forward to a lifetime of dreams,
conquering new territories, and growing old together. No one
starts out with a plan for failure, even those who might callously
say, "Well if it doesn't work out, at least I tried."

True love believes in success and is determined to survive. This is the reason that weddings are such a royal affair. Our "royal wedding" is, we hope, a once-in-a-lifetime event that includes throwing the most lavish party of our lives. This celebration signifies to the world that we have found the love of our life and we feel fulfilled.

After the ceremony is over, we live in a pink cloud of bliss for a few months, or, if we are fortunate, a year or two. Although we know that inevitably there will be conflict between us, we expect that as a married couple we will struggle through those conflicts together. Even difficulties that involve only one of us become a shared burden. Marriage implies unity.

Coming home after a long, difficult day and having someone there waiting to listen to us vent about our darkest frustrations, or join with us to celebrate our thrilling triumphs is comforting and fulfilling. The daily sharing of our most intimate selves with someone we trust, implies an end to our own personal loneliness. This perceived full acceptance by another human being means we can truly be ourselves around them. Our deepest desires for happiness, love, acceptance and stability have finally come true. We feel grounded, our life feels complete.

When a rock falls onto our marital path, we gingerly step over it. If it's just one little stone, we deal with it and move on with our lives. But in every marriage, sooner or later—rockslides happen. These episodes produce confusion, and inevitably, some conflict. Since they are almost always temporary, we forgive and (usually) forget. After the crisis ends, we breathe a sigh of relief that we got through it unscathed.

The dilemma of faith differences throws a boulder onto that path that was likely not anticipated. If you knew about the faith differences in your respective backgrounds when you married, then you may have expected that eventually there would be some rocks in your path. At the time, they seemed surmountable. But if you fell in love with Jesus after you were married, your life now looks very different. You may feel like you've just encountered a landslide upon the path of your relationship. You have no clues as to whether you should climb over, crawl under, or walk around the mountain. Your solution may be to pull your partner along, but if they bray like Balaam's donkey, you will find yourself at a stalemate. That dream of a perfect marriage seems like it is about to be dashed, possibly even trashed. How do you keep it together?

Problem-solving can pit spouse against spouse. Even though we know all conflicts should have a unified resolution, they often don't. All too frequently, a dispute gets "resolved" with one person winning and the other losing.

When Christ comes into one person's life *after* the problem-solving thermostat has been set, the unsaved partner now has a new dilemma. The temperature has changed. They are no longer fighting against only their spouse—they are now fighting against a person, and an invisible being. Suddenly there are three in this marriage, and their saved mate is now asking for time to consult with this foreign, invisible entity. How incredibly frustrating! How does one fight against something or someone they cannot see?

Added to this problem-solving dilemma is the shift caused by the saved spouse spending more time with their God than with their spouse and family. The dagger of jealousy now presents itself as a sword that slices through the veil of unity—exposing anger, resentment, and insecurity. That mask of togetherness threatens to dissolve into two distinct personalities with nothing in common. A third party in the marriage is perceived as a threat to its stability.

In a true Christian marriage, God *is* in the center of the marriage, and this bond of three is desired as a sign of strength. In the unequally yoked marriage, we can pursue this model in love, even if our spouse does not yet believe.

*A person standing alone can be attacked and defeated, but
two can stand back-to-back and conquer. Three are even
better, for a triple-braided cord is not easily broken.*
— Ecclesiastes 4:12 NLT

Biblical problem-solving involves teamwork rooted in love, that
includes seeking God's opinion. Wisdom advises us to take time to
think things through and consider the consequences of a decision.
This doesn't mean that all problems are resolved without conflict.
I've never met a Christian couple that don't argue. Marriages
between Christians have plenty of days when partners live on
different spiritual levels, just as we do.

The ideal relationship holds to a biblical hierarchy of God first,
marriage second, family third (see Deuteronomy 5; Ephesians 5;
Ephesians 6). When a conflict cannot be mutually resolved, some
in the church may teach that the final vote goes to the husband. In
most healthy marriages, there is give and take. Sometimes the final
vote goes to the wife. The desired resolution of any conflict is
unity.

Unity requires agreement and peace. Praying before major
decisions are made...brings clarification to achieve them. When
God is consulted, solutions to problems manifest in ways that we
never thought possible.

This problem-solving method works well in marriages where
serving God is of primary importance to both spouses, but it's
harder in an unequally yoked marriage. If the unsaved spouse is
totally focused on serving self, how do you argue that you need
spiritual advice before you can proceed?

You can still pray about the issue and ask the Lord and your
Christian advisors for advice. If your spouse is intent on their own
solution, then it is doubtful they will be open to your need for
spiritual guidance. Sometimes you simply need to ask for more
time to think things through, or indicate that you don't feel good
about a decision. This is an easy non-religious way to take the time

you need. All problem-solving needs to be done in a loving and non-threatening way. The biblical view really is about respecting and honoring your spouse.

> *However, each one of you also must love his wife as he loves himself, and the wife must respect her husband.*
> — Ephesians 5:33 NIV

Unfortunately, the constant push–pull between your desire to honor God and your spouse, can result in God's will not being done effectively. Bad decisions are made—even though you've received spiritual input and have tried to argue for your viewpoint. But take heart! All is not lost! The fact that you respect and honor your spouse, despite bad decision-making or poor problem-solving—is part of your testimony. Love is the most important part of your testimony, so swallow your pride and let love be your highest aim.

> *Wives, in the same way submit yourselves to your own husbands so that, if any of them do not believe the word, they may be won over without words by the behavior of their wives, when they see the purity and reverence of your lives.*
> — 1 Peter 3:1–2 NIV

In my conversations with those who have been won over to Christ by their believing spouses, I repeatedly hear the comment, "It wasn't what he/she said, it was what he/she didn't say." The Christian spouse was respectful to the non-Christian spouse, especially around the topic of spiritual beliefs. As these verses in 1 Peter state, it is our actions and attitude that will win our loved ones for the Lord.

While we are not justified by God through our works, we are being judged by the non-Christian world by our works, which includes our conduct and attitude. Sadly, there are many non-Christians that seem to live more righteously than we do. Those who live with us see every blunder that we make. In some marriages or families, one mistake can call forth a bevy of verbal persecution against our faith. It is important for us to remember that we are human, and subject to human frailty just as all others.

The major difference between us is that we have the Spirit of God not only living in us, but also directing our lives (1 Corinthians 2:16). God is our compass, not our dictator. Jesus is our Lord and Savior, the author and finisher of our faith (Hebrews 12:2). Our perfection is in Him, not in us (2 Corinthians 5:21). We worship the triune God and give Him the glory not only because He is the Creator of all things (including us), but also because He has made a way for us to be accepted by Him through His blood sacrifice. We are the grateful prodigal sons and daughters of the King returning home (1 John 3:1–3). We now wear the robe of righteousness that covers our scarred past.

Our scarred past is not our present reality. God gave us free will; He allowed us to roam and dip into the devil's pool because He wanted us to make a very clear decision to whose family we want to belong. We took time (perhaps a great deal of time) to make that decision. God was patient with us while He waited for us. We need to afford our spouse and our family members the same patience that God afforded to us. If we are criticized by our loved ones for missing the mark (or if we see the error of our ways before they do), we can reply, "Please forgive me. God is not finished with me yet."

Don't be too hard on yourself. Remember—no relationship is perfect. All couples have conflict. It is so easy to judge someone else and miss the wayward part of our own soul. Examination of our souls is the prerequisite for change. Self-examination may be painful, but change cannot happen without it. If we want change, it must start with us. If we give God the permission to change us, the changes in our soul will be reflected in our actions and our attitudes. Our attitudes determine our altitude. We can learn to fly high and avoid the storms of life by changing our attitude.

Your spouse sees how you handle conflict and discouragement. Right now, you may be in a pressure cooker of stress. You may feel depressed. The thermostat in your house may have been adjusted one too many times and now the temperature has become uncomfortable. Take heart! The positive aspect of stress is that it reveals our underlying attitudes and our coping strategies. It is here where our light can shine. Don't give in to frustration. Remember that Jesus is our model, and the Holy Spirit is our reflector and our deflector.

When conflict surrounds you, amp up your spiritual life. Take time to meditate on the Word, take the space that you need to breathe in the breath of life, quiet yourself down to listen to His voice, and take time to reflect on your part in the situation. Take the first step by recognizing *where* you are wrong, and admit your mistakes.

Notice the choice of words here. *Where*, not when. If we understand *where* we are in error, we will truly understand the change that is needed. If we only admit *when* we are wrong, we often haven't internalized the truth of that mistake. This can lead us into a prideful attitude, where we stand in judgment over the other person.

Although every conflict takes two...it only takes one to shift the atmosphere. Be that one. Do not allow the pressure of perfection to overshadow your joy. Allow your spouse to see the joy that is in your soul—not the despair of your heart. Let them see the joy that only Christ can bring.

Overcoming the storms in our marriage is easier when we look at the problems through different lenses. Our different cultures, childhoods, and past traumas—all influence how we view and react to the problems that we encounter. Let's look at the dynamic of culture next.

CHAPTER FOURTEEN

Cultural Differences

...a true Jew is one whose heart is right with God. And true circumcision is not merely obeying the letter of the law; rather, it is a change of heart produced by the Spirit. And a person with a changed heart seeks praise from God, not from people.
— Romans 2:29 NLT

The educational journey of our lives began with a value system. Our parents trained us in the way that they thought was right. They influenced our thinking with their ideals, their values, and their cultural and ethnic heritage. We learned our most important lessons about marriage and family life from watching and listening to them.

All of that was adapted as we listened and learned from our own modern culture—our scholastic and religious training, the music of our generation, the media we listened to, and the ideals of our peers. We collected all these pieces of information and it influenced who we are, how we think, and what we cherish. Our own experiences with life further shifted our interpretation of that imprinted information. Long before we entered a romantic relationship, we had expectations and values about what it would mean. Shortly after we were married, the baggage of our life, delivered as a wedding present, was unpacked.

The baggage we bring to our marriage either matches or clashes with the baggage that our spouse brings. Some of us bring more baggage than others. Some of it may be very damaged and in desperate need of repair. Parts of it may be twisted and warped. Regardless of the shape that it is in when we begin our lives together, it all forms our value system and our own personal cultural construct. Our cultural value system influences our conduct, behavior, our communication, and our interpretation of the actions and attitudes of others. Considering this, it should not come as a surprise that when two people with different life experiences try to put their baggage together, there are bound to be some mismatches.

Faith by itself can cause significant misinterpretations. If your spouse has no prior experience with Christianity, and believes it is interchangeable with any other religion—they will have little concrete understanding of the Christian language or Christian cultural experiences that you bring into your marriage. If they have no religious background of any kind—the concepts of sin, salvation, and eternal life will be completely foreign to them. You may encounter a lot of resistance to learning and understanding. These situations take a great deal of patience, understanding, education, and of course, much prayer. How you explain things to your spouse and how they interpret what you are saying is another important step in encouraging their spiritual growth.

Faith and religion are not interchangeable terms. Faith, according to the Bible, is confidence in that which is unseen (Hebrews 11:1). Religion is a set of prescribed rules or doctrines about the interpretation or practice of that faith. Those doctrines become belief systems within a religion. All religions have variations within their belief systems, and Christianity is no different. Often culture itself can be embedded in doctrinal differences and vice-versa.

For an easy example, think of Judaism. When you think of Judaism you may think of the religion—but you may also think politically, as in the country of Israel, or you may think of food. Who doesn't love blintzes or matzo ball soup? Do you think the religion of Judaism has affected the politics of Israel or the food?

Or has the politics or food changed any of the religious perspectives?

Now when I mentioned blintzes and matzo ball soup, did you think that encompasses all Jewish dinner tables? Would it surprise you to know that those dishes are primarily on the tables of only a certain group of Jews, primarily those originally from northern Europe? Jewish food culture covers the entire world, because Jews live all over the planet. If you lived in South America or Africa, you may have a different perspective of Jewish food or the Jewish faith. Just like food differences, Jews have differing opinions about the country of Israel; just like Christianity, there are denominational differences within the religion. The compounding of religion and culture is a common occurrence in most religions, as well as in secular society.

Culture encompasses so many things. It can be hard to tease out which part of our belief system is connected to our ethnic or racial heritage, and our family's interpretation of that ethnicity. Our political exposure or beliefs can also affect our religious views. An American evangelical may have very different political beliefs from that of a Canadian evangelical, even though they attend churches of the same Christian denomination. Our political exposure, our method of government, and our educational system all influence how we see and deal with life. Hence, Christianity is reinterpreted through layers of varying cultural lenses.

A marriage brings together two people who are often of differing backgrounds. Even without ethnic, cultural or political differences, there are enough landmines to wade through to keep us guessing how someone is interpreting a situation. Perhaps our marriages might be easier if we had only doctrinal differences to sort through. But it's not that easy. Our perspectives are slanted in so many ways. Christians come from every walk of life and reflect the cultural diversity of the world. Those diverse cultural lenses can become enmeshed with political views, sociological views and yes, even food!

In my first marriage, my husband and I were from the same ethnic group and Christian denomination. Our marriage had less cultural and religious conflict, but we had different early life experiences. Ethnicity and culture dominated our interpretation of our faith to such a degree that when we were removed from that protective environment, our faith quickly fell away. Neither of us really understood what we believed or why.

When I met my second husband, I was far away from the Lord, and wrapped in anger and pain. Not only was my husband from a different cultural background, he also had a very limited knowledge of Christianity. His "worldly" lifestyle was normal to him, but unusual to me. Although I introduced him to some aspects of my cultural background and former Christian lifestyle, I was the one who was more readily willing to absorb and adapt to his secular lifestyle.

In returning to the Christian faith, I didn't blindly accept everything I heard at church. I listened, I evaluated, and I wrestled. I was determined that if I was going to return to Jesus, I needed to know what part of my former belief system belonged to my early cultural and ethnic roots, and what part belonged to the Christian faith.

My confusion between "cultural Christianity" and "practicing Christianity" was further exacerbated when I explored the various denominational belief systems. Although many of the belief systems sounded the same on paper—once immersed in the church culture and its surrounding social environment—I quickly learned that every denomination has slightly different interpretations of how Christianity is understood, and how it is to be practiced, both within the church body and in a social setting. It was many years before I truly understood what I believed and why.

During my years of spiritual struggles, my unsaved husband watched and listened to my ups and downs and constantly-changing ideologies. Since he had no personal experience with

Christianity, he had no idea how to help me. Raised in an irreligious background, he lacked the cultural foundation needed to understand the basic concepts of spirituality. His religious construct relied on three principles of life: being a good person, having integrity, and being a financial success. Essentially, that was and is his cultural construct of spirituality.

Trying to explain my faith to my husband is confusing for him. He doesn't have any Christian language to rely on for interpretation. He has never read the Bible. Almost everything he knows about Christianity comes from Hollywood. He has no social experience within a Christian community. He has no way to categorize my commitment to Christ in a cultural construct. *To him, it is a foreign language and a foreign culture.* He has difficulty understanding that which is seemingly irrelevant to his lifestyle. After many frustrating years of trying to explain my faith and my beliefs, I realized that where I am failing is not recognizing where he is stuck.

Getting trapped in our own cultural mindset is not new. One of the conflicts in the early church was a cultural clash between the Jewish and Greek cultures. Many of the early Judeo-Christian believers continued to practice many of the Jewish laws and customs. Some teachers of the faith were trying to impose those laws and customs on the new gentile Greco-Roman believers (see Acts 15).

One of those customs was circumcision. Paul explains that although circumcision had been used in the past as a sign of God's covenant with man, that symbol was not required after Christ's death and resurrection. Instead, Paul states that God is looking for circumcision of the heart, not of the body. Circumcision of the heart involves a change that casts off the old ways and mindsets, and exposes a new heart, one willing to serve God.

Today's cultural conflicts seldom involve circumcision, but is still apparent in other ways. Sexism (or sexual disparity) is still very common in many cultures and is often translated accordingly into our homes, as well as in church and workplace environments. Racial issues continue to cause conflict in many communities. Political diversity is common in many families. One person's rigid political stance can create communication barriers and intra and inter-familial conflict.[25]

These examples are all potential barriers that can cause misinterpretation of our faith within our homes. People can be "pro-Christian," or "anti-Christian," solely because of their understanding of what the term means. The word 'Christian' is often connected with cultural and societal tags that are unrelated to our true faith. What the unbeliever presumes when they hear you say that one word, can start or stop your conversation. Maybe that's why some Christians are beginning to use the term "Christ-follower," or describing themselves as "a follower of Jesus Christ." Perhaps this is a valid move to distance ourselves from the misunderstood Christian label and an approach to open the communication doorway of our faith.

Ethnic heritage, societal culture, and religious upbringing significantly impact comprehension of faith differences. This is our "macro" environment. We both absorb the culture that we are immersed in, create our own micro-culture, and pass on our cultural interpretations to others. Understanding how someone views Christianity in the wider cultural context is important to know before you can begin discussion on it. If we want to share our faith effectively with others, we need to learn how their cultural lenses will color the way they understand the Christian message.

> *"After this I looked, and there before me was a great multitude that no one could count, from every nation, tribe, people and language, standing before the throne and before the Lamb."*
> — *Revelation 7:9a NIV*

---

[25] See this page re multiculturalism: www.cultureclashes.org/book/8-conflicts/

CHAPTER FIFTEEN

Communication

Don't shoot off your mouth, or speak before you think.
Don't be too quick to tell God what you think He wants to
hear. God's in charge, not you—the less you speak, the
better.
— Ecclesiastes 5:2 MSG

Living with a spouse who doesn't understand your faith means
that there is already a breakdown in understanding
surrounding your Christian culture and language. Poor
communication styles will only widen that gap and open the door
for more misinterpretation. If you want to share your faith, and
keep your marriage healthy and conflict to a minimum—you must
intentionally work to improve this area. Clarifying communication
in a positive way helps to keep your testimony clear, since you are
setting the example for pure and honest speech.

Communication studies show that as little as 7% of
communication is verbal.[26] A quick internet search shows divorce
lawyers claiming that 56% of divorces happen because couples
argue too much.[27] These shocking statistics demonstrate how
important communication is, and why we need to pay more
attention to this subject. The abundance of self-help books,
television shows, blogs, and social media sites confirm that
communication is the most common conflict zone in marriages.

---

[26] Messages: The Communication Skills Book, Matthew McKay, PhD, Martha Davis,
PhD, Patrick Fanning, New Harbinger Publications, 2009
[27] See http://www.wf-lawyers.com/divorce-statistics-and-facts

We all know that the words we speak can have either positive or negative impact on the receiver of those words. But what we say is often less important than how we say it, or ensuring that the other person understands what we mean. We may think we know what the other person is saying, but do we take the time to really listen to each other? It's so easy to nod appreciatively during a conversation (which gives them the impression that we understand), while carrying on cooking dinner or answering that message on our phone. At one time or other, we have all been guilty of this lack of consideration to those we love the most.

Good communication contains several important elements. Since this isn't a book on communication, I'm only going to mention a few of these that I feel are critical. There are plenty of good communication books that you can reference if you want to study this in more detail.[28]

Timing and Setting

When you live in a busy household, communication gets taken for granted. With never ending to-do lists, it's easy for everyone to be preoccupied with what needs to be done today or tomorrow. Everything seems urgent. We start every day waking up with a to-do list in our head and go to bed with a checklist. Sometimes we can go days or weeks without having a quality conversation. When something dramatic happens to one person—time suddenly stands still, if only for a moment. As soon as everyone has a chance to catch their breath and reorganize, the flurry of activity resumes.

Consequently, important conversations, whether they are about family issues or faith, require intentionally setting aside time to discuss those matters. Blocking off a time in your mutual calendars and finding space away from the rat race will help to ensure that your specific points will be addressed and understood.

---

[28] I recommend *Messages: The Communication Skills Workbook* by Matthew McKay, PhD

A quiet, private environment is ideal, but not always possible. Background noise, such as a television or radio blaring, or children screaming—makes for a stressful, unproductive talk. Remove yourself from noisy environments, and turn off any electronics (including your phone) that might be an intrusion in your conversation.

When my second husband and I were first married (before cell phones existed), our blended family of six included two with special needs. The children's ages ranged from toddler to teenagers. We had our hands full. To add to our stress load, my husband's work schedule as an airline pilot was erratic, with lengthy times away from home and an upside-down sleep schedule. My work schedule frequently conflicted with his. Our lives were crazy and disorganized. Trying to find a good time to connect required deliberate planning by both of us. Honestly, I don't know how we got through it.

My husband's way of finding time to talk was to take me to a coffee shop. Unfortunately, one hour often turned into several hours, which left me feeling stressed. It meant the kids and my to-do list were being neglected. I also didn't like discussing personal issues in a public space where we might be overheard. This lack of privacy caused me to freeze up inside. Feeling conspicuous and trapped, I often just nodded and smiled rather than be honest about how I really felt. I much preferred either going out for a stroll in nature where I felt relaxed, or sitting at the kitchen table. I had difficulty putting my finger on the real problem, which was my inability to discuss this very issue with him. My reluctance to be open caused him to feel frustrated. He felt that I wasn't listening to him. Many problems never got resolved. This caused negative feelings to build, until eventually, a heated argument would ensue.

We carried on with this dysfunctional pattern until my kids left home a few years later. After that, a quiet house created a less urgent and more practical lifestyle. Looking back, I can see where I was wrong in not making my needs understood. Sadly, at the time

I was too focused on my job and my kids, and I couldn't see where the real problem lay.

My husband's idea of finding time and space to talk was right. My preference for what that looked like was different. Even though we both wanted to resolve the problem at hand, our poor communication prevented that from happening. We needed a functional atmosphere in which we could both freely express our feelings.

Focus and Attention

A serious discussion needs a well-planned meeting with a clear agenda. Choosing the right atmosphere, in which both people are comfortable, is the first step. Picking the right time and a neutral setting helps both of you to stop the rat race in your heads and listen to each other. If you want to be a good communicator, you must learn to be a good listener. You can't have a conversation with someone if you can't get their attention.

Restaurants are interesting places to watch how couples interact with each other. Some couples pull out their smartphones and start texting almost the second they are seated at the table. Or, their conversation is interrupted with a lengthy phone call. The phone conversation takes precedence, leaving the partner sitting across the table completely ignored until the food arrives. What message is this sending? To me, this shouts that your partner is not as important as the person on the telephone. Turn that gadget off! If you are in a restaurant with your spouse, the only call you should be accept is one from the babysitter or in a family emergency. I often think, "How in the world did we ever manage to survive without cell phones?"

If you want the other person to feel understood and validated, you need to shut down all potential distractions. Whether it's cell phones, kids, or background noise, you must ensure that your spouse knows that they are the most important person in the conversation. If your spouse isn't a good listener, express your need for their full attention. If it's you, admit your weakness and start working on this!

As simple as it sounds, not fixing this issue results in one or both persons feeling unimportant and invalidated. This in turn, leads to further breakdowns in communication and a feeling of dissatisfaction in the relationship. This negative, spiraling staircase leads only downward.

A good listener displays positive body language, makes good eye contact, and engages you in a conversation in which you feel understood and validated. Making yourself receptive and open doesn't guarantee a successful conversation if your spouse isn't interested in having this talk. However, by simply watching their body language, you can very easily ascertain when they're ready to listen. Good communication involves your entire body.

Non-Verbal Communication

According to the book *Messages: The Communication Skills Book* by Matthew McKay, PhD, Martha Davis, PhD, Patrick Fanning, 55% of our communication is non-verbal. Communication isn't just talking. It includes the way you phrase your sentences, your tone of voice, your body language, and your eye contact. Physical touch is also non-verbal communication that is too often underestimated. A pat on the hand, a warm hug or a slap on the back all display emotions without words.

We are born knowing how to project our emotions into our voices, and we learn quickly how to understand that in others. Just watch the interaction between a new mother and her baby. The baby cries, the mom knows exactly what the problem is. Whether it's the need for a diaper change, food, physical stimulation, or fatigue— Mom has it figured out just from the way her baby cries. Mom didn't know this information before the baby was born, but she learned very quickly after a few diaper changes. In turn, the baby also learned very quickly how to project his discomfort into his/her own voice so that Mom would recognize that certain sound or tone. We understand emotions long before we understand the words to describe them.

This is our earliest method of learning—non-verbally. As the sister of a deaf brother and deaf sister-in-law, and the parent of two intellectually-challenged adults, I can confirm from personal experience that non-verbal language is often more communicative than words. Before either of us learned any sign language, my brother and I communicated with facial expressions and body language. As you can imagine, our early years were very dramatic.

Later in life, I applied many of these learned skills to my parenting. Children with intellectual challenges often have difficulty with verbal communication and the parents must know how to communicate and interpret communication without words.

Have you ever entered a room and just sensed that something was wrong? You could feel the tension in the air and couldn't wait to get out of that room. I'm sure you've also had the experience when someone is talking to you, but their body language or tone of voice doesn't match their words. Something is amiss, but you can't put your finger on it. Words can often be incongruent with body language. Experts in non-verbal communication can detect immediately when a person is lying. The details spoken through facial expressions, posture, eye contact, body positioning, tone of voice and inflections speak volumes. Have you ever watched a customs officer at the border? One of their many skills is interpreting body language.

Non-verbal cues provide a context for negative and positive emotions in what someone is saying, and how they are feeling about what they are saying. It's the sound in the words, the inflection in the voice, and the facial expressions—that are given to those words that give them meaning.

Your tone of voice can be heard over the telephone. Just listen to how telemarketers sound when they call you. You can hear the smile in their voice right over the telephone. They want to sell you something, so they smile, sound cheerful, and ask encouraging questions to get you to respond with "yes." This is a good skill to practice if you wish to improve your receptivity in your conversation with others. You can practice by talking to yourself in front of the bathroom mirror! Eventually, it will start to feel natural.

There are cultural differences in body language that may be applicable to your personal situation. For example, in North American and European societies, the lack of good eye contact is often seen as a sign of disrespect and may feel devaluing to the receiver. In other cultures, the avoidance of eye contact is a sign of respect.

It's completely normal for someone to look above you or temporarily focus elsewhere when they are thinking deeply about a subject or searching for a response. But that generally lasts for a few seconds, while the thought process is engaged. Deliberate refusal to engage in eye contact usually indicates a serious problem in the relationship. Encourage sitting down and casually talking about everyday things to see if you can pinpoint what is really going on. If that doesn't work, you may want to use a more direct approach. Anger, resentment, spiritual churning, or a guilty conscience, is often demonstrated by your spouse pulling away and not wanting to have an intimate conversation.

If you want to make sure that your words aren't refuted before you speak them, pay close attention to your own non-verbal communication, and watch for receptivity from the other person. Positive communication works two ways. The best indicators include what is often referred to as "open body language." Typically, your arms are relaxed at your side or on your lap, with hands soft and unclenched, facing the other person, and maintaining good eye contact.

Negative body language includes clenched fists, crossed arms, tight facial muscles, a refusal to respond to a smile, or returning eye contact with a glaring look. These can indicate either stress, anger, or an unwillingness to listen. When someone is standing with their arms crossed, fists clenched, lips pursed and glaring at you at the same time—well, who wants to have a conversation with someone who obviously has their mind made up already? In that case—walk away and wait for them to cool off, or just drop it. In the big scheme of things, most issues aren't worth fighting about anyway. Forgiveness goes a long way in resolving disputes.

In the middle of conflict, make sure you are heard and that your viewpoint is understood. Be firm, calm, unhurried, and just loud enough to be heard clearly. Emotions—such as anxiety, nervousness, anger and even fatigue—can change the tone of your voice and the volume of your speech.

It is better to identify your emotion up-front...so the receiver doesn't misinterpret the conversation before you've had a chance to say anything. If you are sensing a scary emotion coming from the other person, ask if your perception is correct. Often people can be upset about an unconnected issue. However, because it remains unprocessed— it will come through their interactions and with everything else that they are saying or doing. Invalidated emotions can often trigger unwanted arguments.

Active Listening and Validation

Everyone should be quick to listen, slow to speak and slow to become angry.
— James 1:19 NIV

Both visual and auditory cues are essential parts of successful communication. Listening effectively helps to make the other person feel validated and understood. There are many courses and videos online to help you improve your communication style, and ensure that what you say and how you say it is received appropriately by your audience.

"Active Listening" is a therapeutic term that refers to clear communication that makes the other person feel heard and understood. It includes those audio and visual cues that we just talked about, as well as providing verbal feedback, such as paraphrasing, asking clarifying questions, reflecting on what they are saying, and allowing them to speak without being interrupted. Responding positively without judgment keeps conflict to a minimum.

This doesn't mean that you must agree with everything someone says. You can learn to "agree to disagree," without allowing bad feelings to surface. A positive conversational style brings honor and respect into the conversation. One way of doing this is to ask encouraging and clarifying questions.

A clarifying question, such as "I'm not sure I understand. Would you mind explaining that further?" helps both parties know that they are on the same page and ensures that each one feels heard and understood.

Questions that encourage a person to speak, demonstrates interest in the other person, and lets them know that what they are saying is important. Open-ended questions are those that do not require a "yes" or "no" answer, but rather invite the responder to share information. Starting a question with "how" or "what," invites feedback and helps a person focus on the question's content.

If your spouse comes home from work and only answers your questions with a "yes" or "no" answer, check the way in which you are asking your questions. Asking, "Did you have a good day?" invites a different response than, "Tell me about your day." Re-wording your questions can stimulate a conversation. Great conversations begin with well-placed questions. Bear in mind that when you invite conversation to begin—you also need to, physically and emotionally, be positioned to engage. If you don't respond appropriately, your loved one feels shut down, which in turn causes negative reactions.

When asking questions, making comments, or giving feedback, be aware that certain words or phrases can be interpreted differently by others, from what you intended. These mix-ups can cause some very unwanted reactions. Miscommunication happens when things are taken out of context. This can turn into hurt feelings, bad decisions, and arguments. Doors get slammed, and a whole fridge full of ice gets dumped between the two of you.

Every relationship, regardless of how good it is, will have communication issues at some point or another. Ideally, it is best to learn to communicate effectively early on in your marriage, rather than later, when patterns are set in stone. It's very difficult to change a pattern of relating after years of miscommunication.

Understanding Personality Differences

> *Let your conversation be always full of grace, seasoned with*
> *salt, so that you may know how to answer everyone.*
> — Colossians 4:6 NIV

Miscommunication can also happen when you are paying attention only to your own needs or priorities, and are insensitive to your spouse's needs and personality style. Asking if it's a good time to have a conversation—goes a long way in making sure you will be heard when they are ready to listen. Knowing each other's personality type and conflict management style helps to ensure success in communication.

Is your spouse an introvert? Most introverts tend to be very guarded about disclosing personal information, and will feel bullied if you ask them too many questions too quickly. They need time to feel comfortable with the conversation and to formulate their own thoughts and feedback. Perhaps your spouse needs a wind-down time after work before they are ready to start a conversation. An extra thirty minutes of patience might mean the difference between a romantic dinner conversation and a wall of ice.

Perhaps it's just the opposite. Maybe you are the one who needs the extra time to process information. Be open enough to share that. If you feel pressured into committing to something that you are not ready to agree to—step out of your comfort zone and say so. Hold your ground. Just because you are trying to set a Christian example in your communication does not mean that you are a doormat. Be clear in your needs and in your communication.

Oversharing can be just as frustrating as those who keep everything to themselves. If you are at home all day with the kids, you might be dying for an adult to talk to. The minute your spouse walks in the door, you dump every detail of your day in their lap. Unfortunately, they are still processing their day and are not ready to listen to you. You might get a grunt, a smile, a nod, or you might get an unwelcome angry response. Change your strategy—give them some time to unwind.

Conversely, maybe your spouse is one of those people who come home from work and want to dump their entire day onto your lap. They might love to overshare or get very detailed in their storytelling. If your agenda (or dinner, or the kids' activities) is interfering with their sharing, they might feel rejected. This can create a negative atmosphere, and potentially escalate into an unwanted argument. If you know this about their personality, communicate that you want to hear more, but it's not a good time. In situations like this, it's best to get agreement on a regularly-scheduled time—when you can give each other your full, undivided attention.

Communicating effectively with difficult personality types can be challenging. Sometimes it's hard to know whether it's personalities, job stress, communication styles, cultural issues, or faith differences that are interfering in effective communication. Some people have poor boundaries, poor impulse control, or simply lack effective listening skills. If you don't know what is causing your communication impasse, I advise getting professional help.

Recognizing Different Conflict Management Styles

You can choose the right time and the right place to have a conversation, and make sure your body language isn't sending any negative signals. You can watch for the right opening time by simply watching your spouse's body language. You can schedule a routine conversation hour. You can give them 100% of your attention. This can all help to mediate potential blow-ups, but if your conflict management styles are entirely different, you may still find yourself on a collision course with disaster. Here's where knowing each other's family background and communication style is helpful.

We model what we see when we are growing up. Our parents' marriage and our family of origin were the only models that we had. It's what we assumed was normal. Unfortunately, what's normal for you probably looked very different in your spouse's family. Whether you grew up in a traditional two-parent home, or a diverse multi-generational household, each of you experienced and learned different conflict management styles.

For example, if you came from a home in which your parents screamed, yelled and slammed doors—that is exactly what you will think normal looks like. If your spouse came from a home that never fought openly, but lived in silence and internalized conflict— that will be what looks and feels normal to them. Neither of these patterns of communication are healthy.

If unhealthy conflict management styles are contributing to unresolved issues in your marriage, you must fix this. Before you can fix it, you need to know what is wrong. Fault-finding and blaming is not helpful. You are in a relationship and communication is a two-way street. Both of you must be willing to work and improve this. Letting things slide will only contribute to a deteriorating, dysfunctional relationship.

Understanding each other's conflict management style requires a planned discussion as to what is considered acceptable and what is not, and why. How does your current conflict management style make you feel? Do you feel heard and understood, or rejected and unimportant?

If you can articulate this and get a consensus of what makes each other comfortable or uncomfortable during a conflict, you can often stop an argument in its tracks. Having an agreement ahead of time, as to how conflict is to be managed in the future, can go a long way to prevent escalating emotions. A mental checklist or a written "Plan of Action to Resolve Conflict," may help. It's generally known that writing things down gets better success than just keeping mental notes.

Understanding your partner's communication style will help you to minimize conflict, and will aid in knowing when and how to start important conversations. Continual strife will diminish any effectiveness in sharing your faith. Having an honest discussion about faith differences requires a relationship that demonstrates positive communication skills. If your communication is a constant challenge, it may be time to get professional help.

A good relationship has positive and clear communication. Sometimes our past gets in the way of expressing our needs. If you find yourself struggling with negative thought patterns that impact on your relationship, perhaps some deeper reflection may be helpful.

CHAPTER SIXTEEN

Attitudes and Forgiveness

You're familiar with the command to the ancients, 'Do not murder.' I'm telling you that anyone who is so much as angry with a brother or sister is guilty of murder. Carelessly call a brother 'idiot!' and you just might find yourself hauled into court. Thoughtlessly yell 'stupid!' at a sister and you are on the brink of hellfire. The simple moral fact is that words kill.
— Matthew 5:21–22 MSG

Two of the biggest barriers to good communication are negative attitudes and unforgiveness. Tucked into the corners of our blind spots are old resentments, often previously forgotten until an argument happens. In the heat of anger, "remember when" comes out of our mouth landing on our loved ones like boiling water on an open wound.

Are you guilty of this? Are you carrying a resentment against something or someone? Are you bitter toward your spouse for something they did or said? Or are they carrying a resentment against you, perhaps? Do you know how to say, "I'm sorry," from the depths of your heart, forgive completely and move on? Too often, hurt feelings get buried under a pile of other hurt feelings. Like dirty laundry, the feelings build until they spill over into everything that you think, do, or say. Negativity breeds negativity. The only way to get rid of dirty laundry is to wash it or completely replace it. We can do the same with negative attitudes. We can wash them with repentance and positivity, and change our mindset. Unfortunately, changing a mindset is a little harder than changing a shirt.

We've discussed several ways to view your marriage and your belief system through different lenses. Much of that work is pointless if you or your spouse are holding grudges against each other.

Holding a grudge is unforgiveness. It's a resentment that says, "Wait until it's your turn; I'll get you back." Resentments are a way of measuring the pain of your past with the perception of your present or future. It's holding onto that old pain in your relationship, and using it as a wedge between the two of you, instead of lovingly serving the person standing before you.

An offensive attitude becomes more negative with each offense. This build-up of old hurts destroys your ability to see the beauty around you. Eventually, the person sleeping beside you isn't the amazing person you once married. Instead, they are a constant reminder of the pain in your relationship, which you believe they have caused. The pain you feel is projected onto them, and over time, they become unattractive and unappealing to you.

When you can no longer focus on the beauty that someone brings into the world—your focus isn't on today, it's on the past. If you can't focus on today, it's difficult to focus on your future and set realistic dreams that spell happiness. If you want to be happy in the now and in the future, you need to let go of the past. Your ability to live successfully in this unequally yoked marriage includes learning to "Let go and let God." Forgiveness is part of our Christian testimony. Jesus said:

> *For if you forgive other people when they sin against you, your heavenly Father will also forgive you. But if you do not forgive others their sins, your Father will not forgive your sins.*
> — Matthew 6:14–16 NIV

If we want to be forgiven, then we in turn, must forgive others. That means we must find a way to let go of the past and press on toward the marvelous future that God has in store for us.

The story of Lot's wife in Genesis 19:26 shows us that when we look backward, we are frozen in time. When we look backward, we can't look toward the land of milk and honey. You can't go forward, toward happiness and success, when you are looking backward on destruction and chaos. Going forward requires forgiveness of the past.

Letting Go

Forgiveness isn't forgetting the memory that caused the pain. It's accepting that it happened and being able to acknowledge the truth of what happened, while releasing the pain that continues to hold you tied to that memory.

Maybe this experience taught you that the person who hurt you suffers from an unresolved old wound or also struggles with forgiveness. Understanding the humanity behind the pain that was caused is often very helpful in learning to let it go.

Pain causes awareness of our emotions and decisions. When we are hurt—we feel, we think, we ruminate, and we process. This encourages us to grow. Whether we grow into a more mature and mentally-stronger person because of it, or an insecure and negative person, is up to us. We can take the lessons and apply them to our lives in whatever way we want. God wants the best for our lives—He wants us to mature healthily. We can't grow when we allow ourselves to be caught up in the net of discouragement and despair that came because we were hurt. If we get too wrapped up in how we are feeling, we get stuck like Lot's wife—looking over our shoulder. And then we wonder why our lives are such a mess.

Often our lives are in a mess simply because of our selfishness. Selfishness interferes in our everyday relationships, because we take more than we give. When the recipient pushes back because they feel ignored or neglected, verbal knives get thrown, and suddenly a wounded person is standing there. There isn't always a calculated reason why a person hurts someone else. Usually it is completely unintentional. People will react out of their own frustration, personal limitations, or their own pain.

Hurt feelings frequently develop over simple misunderstandings. How many times have you heard stories of families splintered because of misunderstandings? This can happen when we are so wrapped up in our own daily lives and our own issues that we have no idea how we are coming across to someone else. Selfishness can be defined as a lack of sensitivity to others and a lack of awareness of our own behavior.

If we can become more sensitive to how our behavior might be interpreted by someone else, then we can learn to become more compassionate when our loved one misses the mark of perfection. Increasing the compassionate side of ourselves is one of the hallmarks of learning to forgive. A compassionate person is a forgiving person.

Forgiveness is rarely easy, especially when you have been deeply hurt. But if you truly love someone, and you want the relationship to continue, you *must* forgive. Everyone is human and we all make mistakes. We have all hurt someone and we have all experienced the pain of being hurt by someone we love. If we want to heal from the past, we need to learn to forgive. Sometimes, that might require forgiving someone else, but it almost always involves forgiving ourselves as well.

Forgiving Old Hurts Helps Us to Focus on Our Present and Future

Why do we need to forgive ourselves? What if the entire situation was someone else's fault?

I was in a serious car accident in 1990. It happened a week into the contentious separation from my first husband, so the timing couldn't have been worse. I sustained lifelong injuries which included brain trauma. That affected my decision-making abilities and my emotional stability. My personality changed. I became confused easily and had difficulty working full-time. My former ability to multi-task was gone. Verbal exploration of abstract thoughts was exhausting. I had trouble following the simplest of conversations.

The thing that kept bugging me was that I didn't cause the accident. I was stopped, preparing to turn left onto an alley. A truck driver—who was in a terrible hurry because of a late delivery—failed to notice my brake-lights and my turn signal. He drove straight into the back of my car, crushing it like an accordion and pushing me into the oncoming lane of traffic. I was fortunate to survive. The accident wasn't my fault, yet I still blamed myself.

I was insured under a silly no-fault law that was in place for only a couple of years. That meant getting compensation for my injuries through civil litigation was impossible. Medically and financially I was stuck suffering with my injuries for the rest of my life. I was frightened of the future and angry at the situation.

Even though there was nothing I could do about my legal or financial situation, I was still angry at the legal system. My unabated anger included the truck driver who caused the accident, and my ex for leaving me at such a vulnerable time and not pitching in to help. My stressed financial situation and the never-ending legal battle with my ex fueled my resentments. For years, I ruminated on thoughts, such as "If only I had done this...if only I had done that," and "How could that truck driver not see me?" and "How could my ex be so insensitive and not stick around and help?" I thought I must be a stupid person, for surely a smart person could have avoided all that. I was trapped in a cycle of revolving negative thought patterns that went nowhere. I brought all that anger into my new marriage.

Secular therapy helped me to function again. They pointed out that my negative mindset was keeping me stuck and possibly contributing to my pain levels. Because the trauma was multi-faceted (accident, brain injury, physical injuries, and contentious divorce), I couldn't just "let it go." I needed to understand and analyze the many contributing components. During this time, I was told that forgiveness wasn't required...instead, I was encouraged to emotionally process my anger and my grief.

During these lost years, I became an embittered, resentful person who lashed out at everyone. I was mad at the world and I was determined to make everyone pay for my suffering. This contributed to a negative attitude that impacted my relationships with others. I shook my fist at God, refusing to listen to Him or look at what He was trying to show me. I became a victim instead of a victor. Holding onto unforgiveness not only blocked my physical healing, it also disconnected me from God and others.

From a secular point of view, there were plenty of good reasons to be angry. From a spiritual perspective, those reasons translated into onion layers that needed to be peeled back before forgiveness could enter. The layers of pain and resentment included the truck driver, the insurance system, the legal system, my ex, the medical system, myself, and God.

Why did I need to forgive myself when this accident wasn't my fault?

First, I needed to repent for holding anger and resentment toward the situation and everyone either directly or indirectly associated with the accident. Holding on to unforgiveness was like pulling the scab off a festering wound. There was no way I was going to heal if I didn't put the right "ointment" on the wound. Forgiveness was that "ointment."

Secondly, through unforgiveness, I was holding myself hostage. I resented myself for being in the wrong place at the wrong time. As silly as it sounds, I had to forgive myself for believing that lie. The truth was I couldn't go back in time and undo that situation. I could only move forward.

Thirdly, I resented my body and my brain for no longer functioning at my previous optimum performance. Hating myself was putting up destructive walls in my life and keeping me chained to the past. If I wanted to move forward in my life, I had to put down the gun that was keeping me from receiving my healing.

When I began to realize how unforgiveness was damaging my relationships with God and others, I could start moving into forgiveness. Healing was a lengthy process that required moving through forgiveness one layer at a time. Slowly, a heavy weight lifted from my soul, giving me a clearer perspective of my life. My relationship with the Lord improved. Instead of living in regret, I looked up and saw the Savior's love. Eventually I grasped how He had been there in that accident with me, and not only saved me from death, but also sent compassionate people into my life both that day and in the months following. I realized that even though I wasn't pursuing Him at that time, He was still in the background guiding my circumstances.

That accident helped me to understand the trauma that car accidents cause and the difficulty people have in recovering from them. Coincidently, at that time, I was working as a social worker in the field of personal injury. Even while I was still walking in unforgiveness, the accident gave me an awareness and compassionate understanding into my clients' lives that few other professionals had. If the accident had never happened, I wouldn't have that insight. It was the diamond inside the darkness that helped me to move toward forgiveness.

There is always something good that comes out of anything bad. God can teach us how to look at things through a different lens if only we let Him.

Forgiving Childhood Hurts Helps Us to Put the Past in the Past

Isolated incidents that involve strangers are often easier to forgive, especially when it was obviously accidental. When the situation is more intimate, as in childhood sexual abuse, it becomes more challenging. How do you forgive someone who deliberately committed a criminal act (perhaps multiple times) against you? Those are wounds that can destroy a life forever.

Sexual crimes send their victims into a head-spinning world, in which they can no longer figure out who is safe and who isn't. They lose the ability of knowing where to place personal boundaries in order to protect themselves. They have difficulty identifying safe environments. Consequently, victims of sexual abuse are incredibly vulnerable to further abuse and often put themselves in harm's way, sometimes intentionally because they think they belong there. Sometimes they fall into addiction and self-sabotaging behavior. Often, they struggle with finding healthy relationships.

Being the victim was a destructive pattern that I fell into. Childhood abuse taught me that I was not permitted to say "no." Time and time again, I found myself in the wrong place at the wrong time with the wrong people. Vulnerability set a trap, causing me to blame myself every time another evil situation crossed my path. In searching for love and answers I kept turning into blind corners and slamming into destructive walls.

The word 'repentance' means, "to feel such sorrow for sin or fault as to be disposed to change one's life for the better."[29] To change from being a victim to a survivor was a process that took many years. I needed to learn to think like a survivor, something that I was unfamiliar with. This required learning about healthy

---

[29] Source: www.dictionary.com/browse/repent

boundaries, what they are, and how to place them appropriately in my life. Learning to say "no" was part of this process.

For many years, I had seen myself as a trash heap...unworthy of respect and love. In many ways, I was a co-conspirator in my own destruction. But I needed to be saved from that self-sabotaging behavior. I needed to learn to see myself as a valuable person, worthy of God's love and grace. The conflict that I felt in comprehending this point was that if I was worthy of God's love and grace, then so were the perpetrators. For the longest time, this was inconceivable to me.

Jesus said that if we don't forgive other people when they sin against us, then God will not forgive our sins (Matthew 6:14–16). If I wanted a clear pathway of communication between myself and God, I needed to remove the block of unforgiveness standing between us. That required repenting to God—for my unforgiveness, hatred, resentment and anger that was dominating my life and interfering in the relationships in my life. I needed to repent for my self-sabotaging behavior and thinking like a victim. This process included giving up on pursuing vengeance and agreeing that justice belonged to God.

Vengeance and justice are not the same thing. Vengeance is a spiritual attitude. Justice is a legal process. Repenting for pursuing vengeance means changing our attitude and heart. Repentance leads us into forgiveness. Forgiveness leads to healing. This doesn't mean that all your pain instantly vanishes. It does mean that you can now, if you are willing, allow the Lord to give you a new perspective. You now have Him to lean on, to help you recover from your wounds. The Master Healer wants to heal you, but you must do your part to let that happen. We do not have to be helpless victims. God wants us to be overcomers.

Many people protest the idea of forgiveness, especially in the case of child abuse. After all, how could a loving God allow such a thing to happen to a defenseless child?

It's a good thing that God understands anger. There are plenty of stories in the Old Testament about what happened when God got angry. However, we need to understand His anger isn't toward the sinner, it's directed at sin itself. God is a compassionate and loving God who hurts when we hurt. He doesn't cause evil. He hates it (Isaiah 61:8, Psalm 5:4, Proverbs 8:13). The choice between good and evil rests with us. When bad things happen, He promises that justice will happen in His time and in His way (Romans 12:19, Deuteronomy 32:35).

In my case, I overcame my anger toward my Heavenly Father when I truly understood that God gave us all the freedom to choose. All the men that abused me had a choice, and they chose badly. As a child, I didn't have a choice, so therefore I wasn't responsible for that sin. I was responsible for the sins of self-hatred, self-condemnation and rebellion against God, and the hatred toward my abusers. I was responsible for the sin of unforgiveness. God helped me see that my abusers were damaged people who needed Jesus.

When I repented for my anger, my resentment, and my unforgiveness—I could forgive myself. When I forgave myself, I could take that first cut, that first deep wound, and hold it up to God and say, "Please heal this. I don't want to carry this pain anymore." When that pain healed, I still felt sad that the damage happened, but there was no anger and there was no desire to "get even." Instead, I felt compassion.

Feelings of resentment fade after forgiveness takes place, not before. Our load is now lighter, and we can face the future with hope and a smile in our hearts.

Revenge Belongs to God but Laws Protect People

As trauma victims, we tend to nurse our wounds over and over, expecting justice to happen, thinking that will take away the pain. We think justice will bring closure. Often there is neither justice, nor closure. Our reaction is to drown ourselves in a stew of brokenness. The result is that healing doesn't happen.

When we sit in brokenness, we sit in blame. When we blame others for the sins committed against us, we are declaring that we are God and we have control over others. Blame stops us from looking at ourselves. It keeps us focused on the offender and the offense. Forgiveness starts by looking in the mirror. We must first "take the stick out of our own eye" (Matthew 7:5).

God says revenge and justice belong to Him. Our attempts to interfere frustrate the Father's plans. Our job is to listen to His voice for our lives and walk in His ways. He says:

> *Dear friends, never take revenge. Leave that to the righteous anger of God. For the Scriptures say, "I will take revenge; I will pay them back," says the Lord. Instead, "If your enemies are hungry, feed them. If they are thirsty, give them something to drink. In doing this, you will heap burning coals of shame on their heads." Don't let evil conquer you, but conquer evil by doing good.*
> — Romans 12:19–21 NLT

God says it is His job to avenge:

> *I will take revenge; I will pay them back. In due time their feet will slip. Their day of disaster will arrive, and their destiny will overtake them'.*
> — Deuteronomy 32:35 NLT

Leaving things up to God doesn't negate the consequence of damage that has been done to us. Criminal acts require legal intervention to protect the public and to call the criminal to accountability. The Bible agrees that laws are required to protect the public. The Laws of Moses were instituted for governmental use to protect the innocent and punish the guilty in a way that was effective in that society at the time.

It may be hard to contact the authorities when we think we are supposed to be all-loving and all-forgiving. This is a common struggle for domestic violence survivors. For many years, there were few laws to protect individuals within families from one another. Men were legally permitted to beat their wives and children. Sexual abuse within families was ignored. Sadly, people who hurt people rarely stop after injuring only one. They will continue to hurt others, so it is our job to do our part to protect others.

> *Learn to do good. Seek justice. Help the oppressed. Defend the cause of orphans. Fight for the rights of widows.*
> — Isaiah 1:17 NLT

There are many verses in the Bible that speak about the importance of helping people who are easily hurt and taken advantage of. We are not only to help them, but also to defend them. That means if someone hurts us in a criminal way, we shouldn't feel guilty about getting the legal system involved. We have the obligation to protect others from being hurt. We also have the right to have our body respected and kept safe from those who would do it harm. Since our body is the temple of the Holy Spirit, it is our job to enforce boundaries to keep ourselves safe. We are not doormats!

I want to clarify that the legal system is *not* a substitute for forgiveness. If you have ever gone to court to try to get justice for a wrongdoing, you will understand this. You still must do the work of repentance and forgiveness.

Offense is a spirit that clings to any negative feelings. It festers and grows with each new wound. It doesn't matter who or what hurt you. Hurts from your childhood will cling to hurts from your marriage and become one huge, tangled ball of pain. If you don't start somewhere, you'll never get it untangled, and eventually your marriage will fall apart. Without working through this you will become a person with negative attitudes that repels others. Repentance and forgiveness free you from the spirit of offense.

You might think that forgiving someone whom you will never see again might not be that difficult. After all, there is something to the saying, "Out of sight, out of mind." But our soul doesn't forget the pain from old wounds until we release it to God. Getting saved opens the pathway to healing, but we still must walk that path and do the work. If we don't release it, that pain infects our mindsets, and our present and future relationships.

Boundaries Protect the Heart

Protecting others and ourselves through the court system is one way of dealing with injustice. But we also need to protect ourselves from being repeatedly hurt by the same people or type of situations. It is here where boundaries become important. This is what is meant by guarding our heart.

> *Above all else, guard your heart, for everything you do flows from it.*
> — Proverbs 4:23 NIV

God knows that our heart is tender. This is a good thing. A tender heart is compassionate and loving...always able to see the good in people...always willing to help. It needs to be protected from becoming calloused and hardened. Boundaries are not defensive walls that don't let anyone in, but rather, strategic checks and balances to ensure that whatever or whomever comes into your safe place is in fact, safe. This process requires having discernment and the wisdom to put limits on repeat offenders.

Most children are taught the development of boundaries as they grow up. Without safe personal boundaries they become rebellious, callous and disrespectful, often violating the safe zone of others. A person with good boundaries sees such a person as an unsafe person—someone to stay away from. A person with poor boundaries can cause incredible pain to others.

Maybe you were a person who had poor boundaries before you came to know the Lord. You continually got hurt because you didn't know what the problem was. So, you built a defensive wall and kept everyone out. You now realize you don't need a wall, you just need safe boundaries. Through repentance and forgiveness, you are now making the required changes in your life. Please understand—this process is never easy and it is never instantaneous. Be diligent in continuing with this important work and get help from a Christian inner-healing program if you are stuck.

Forgiving the Unforgiving Spouse

What if you are living with someone who has a caustic attitude and calloused spirit? Do they have difficulty receiving or giving love? Do they keep a running tab of everyone and everything that has hurt them? Perhaps your spouse struggles with deep hurts that project venom at everyone they meet. There doesn't seem to be a single rose in their negative mindset. Perhaps they cope by taking addictive substances, or have crude friends that feed their angry personality. You have tried to make them happy, but everything you do is the wrong thing. You have prayed and prayed, but nothing seems to change.

What do you do when someone you love hurts you over and over? Do we really have to forgive "seventy times seven?"

> *Then Peter came to Him and said, "Lord, how often shall my brother sin against me, and I forgive him? Up to seven times?" Jesus said to him, "I do not say to you, up to seven times, but up to seventy times seven.*
> — Matthew 18:21–22 NKJV

If forgiveness is about releasing our pain and our hurt, then it also includes the person who did the hurting. If you choose to continue to live in a painful marriage with a difficult person, then you need to keep forgiving each offense as it happens. If your spouse won't do the work to heal their own hurts, you can strengthen your own boundaries to protect your heart.

You can start this process by gently explaining that you are setting limits for inappropriate behavior, and they will be enforced with consequences. The consequences need to be clear and meaningful. You need to be prepared to follow through with consequences, otherwise they lose their impact.

If you can't do that, then ask the Lord what your next step should be. Sometimes all we can do is forgive ourselves for allowing hurt to enter our heart, and then release the person who hurting us. As we hold our broken heart to the Lord and ask Him to heal it—we still wait for a breakthrough for our spouse.

In marriage, saying "I forgive you," can sometimes be difficult when the other party is the offender. We are so tempted to nurse our hurts and play the victim. Marriages suffer when one person holds a resentment, even if the other person has done the work of forgiveness. Relationships cannot move forward if there is no forgiveness from both sides. Deep wounds require deep healing. Without healing, there can be no restoration or true happiness. Resentment blocks happiness. Without happiness, love cannot blossom and grow. Happiness is a motivating factor to step out of that negative mindset. If we can keep our desire for happiness at the forefront, we can release the pain and forgive our partner with every ounce of strength, compassion and grace that God gives us.

We Must Take the Initiative When we are Wrong

What happens when we are the offending party? We can apologize, but what if they don't want to accept our apology? Sometimes, our spouse is the one holding a grudge against us. We may find ourselves in an ice-cold room for days. So, what do we do when someone has something against us, and they are not willing to forgive us?

Therefore, if you are offering your gift at the altar and there remember that your brother or sister has something against you, leave your gift there in front of the altar. First go and be reconciled to them; then come and offer your gift.
— Matthew 5:23–24 NIV

Jesus is saying that if you are aware that someone is holding something against you, and you do nothing to make that relationship right, then your offering to the Lord is basically of no value. When you know what the problem is and you don't try to fix it, then you are just as guilty as the person who is holding the offense against you. Our repentance will not be genuine if we are deliberately holding darkness in our soul. Our prayers will bounce off the ceiling and go nowhere.

As Christians, we are to shine our light and be an example to those around us. Genuine love needs to be pouring from every pore in our body. Not just to our church family, but also to our own family...even when they are exasperating. We can't worship God with an open heart by pretending that everything is perfect in our lives, when there is hostility at home. Sometimes to reconcile an argument, you need to compromise. Jesus said:

Settle matters quickly with your adversary who is taking you to court. Do it while you are still together on the way, or your adversary may hand you over to the judge, and the judge may hand you over to the officer, and you may be thrown into prison.
— Matthew 5:25 NIV

Compromise, whether in a legal situation or at home, is often necessary to bring peace into the situation. Settling matters quickly helps to prevent the matter from escalating. In marriage, it doesn't take much for an emotional outburst to escalate into a full-blown fight. Taking the initiative through compromise, can stop a downward spiraling situation from getting out of control. Admitting that you also were wrong helps the forgiveness happen faster. When mutual forgiveness happens, you have peace. With peace, comes happiness.

We must be vigilant not to fall into the trap of unforgiveness and bitterness. Remember that there is an enemy who wants to destroy our marriages and steal our joy.

> *Be sober, be vigilant; because your adversary the devil walks about like a roaring lion, seeking whom he may devour.*
> — 1 Peter 5:8 NKJV

If we want our marriage to be happy and healthy we must follow these biblical steps:

- When we are wrong, we must be humble and repent quickly.
- When they are wrong, we must approach the situation with a heart full of love and forgiveness. Accept repentant behavior with humility and thankfulness.

The Apostle Paul tells us that once we have agreed to forgive, we must show that our forgiveness is genuine, and we must work to restore the relationship with love. This is our mandate in Christ.

> *If anyone has caused grief, he has not so much grieved me as he has grieved all of you to some extent—not to put it too severely. The punishment inflicted on him by the majority is sufficient. Now instead, you ought to forgive and comfort him, so that he will not be overwhelmed by excessive sorrow. I urge you, therefore, to reaffirm your love for him. Another reason I wrote you was to see if you would stand the test and be obedient in everything. Anyone you forgive, I also forgive. And what I have forgiven—if there was anything to forgive— I have forgiven in the sight of Christ for your sake, in order that Satan might not outwit us. For we are not unaware of his schemes.*
> — 2 Corinthians 2:5–11 NIV

We should never hold old sins over someone's head. If we do that, we are proving that we have not genuinely forgiven them. This type of behavior is destructive to any relationship, and keeps the offender in a place of "excessive sorrow," where they feel that they can do nothing right to repair the wrong that was done. This attitude keeps people in bondage and keeps them from fully experiencing the light of Christ. When you say that you have forgiven them, mean it from the depths of your body, soul and spirit.

God showed us what true forgiveness looks like. He created humankind so that He could have a relationship with us. But He gave us choices because He wanted our love to be genuine, not mandatory. We were not created to be puppets on a string.

When Adam and Eve destroyed their perfect relationship with God through prideful rebellious attitudes, God met their sin with a consequence, but He didn't stop loving them or us. He still wanted a relationship with us. He came to earth in human form, in the person of Jesus, to show us what true love looks like. He showed us and taught us how to love one another.

God's perfect plan of relationship is pictured in the cross. The vertical bar of the cross demonstrates the relationship between us and God. The horizontal bar demonstrates the relationship between us and our fellow human beings. Together, they form a cross that is representative of sacrificial love...perfect love. This is what true forgiveness looks like.

> *Therefore, as God's chosen people, holy and dearly loved, clothe yourselves with compassion, kindness, humility, gentleness and patience. Bear with each other and forgive one another if any of you has a grievance against someone. Forgive as the Lord forgave you. And over all these virtues put on love, which binds them all together in perfect unity.*
> — Colossians 3:12–14 NIV

Forgiveness and good communication are essential to a good relationship. But finding common ground to get through the tough times can be complicated. The doorway of professional help may provide the answers we need.

CHAPTER SEVENTEEN

Counseling and Choosing a Therapist

Don't have anything to do with foolish and stupid arguments, because you know they produce quarrels. And the Lord's servant must not be quarrelsome but must be kind to everyone, able to teach, not resentful. Opponents must be gently instructed, in the hope that God will grant them repentance leading them to a knowledge of the truth, and that they will come to their senses and escape from the trap of the devil, who has taken them captive to do his will.
— 2 Timothy 2:23–26 NIV

Poor communication and unforgiving attitudes contribute to negative atmospheres and stressful relationships. If slamming doors, screaming, frequent tears, or the wall of ice are a common occurrence in your home, you might be thinking of throwing in the towel. You might be questioning whether or not you are still in love.

Take a minute right now and think back to your wedding day, and remind yourself about how you were feeling on that beautiful day. There was something very mysterious and attractive about your relationship with your spouse at one time. Visualize that, and then bring those feelings into the present. Does that change how you feel?

This is hard to do in the middle of an argument. Conflict tends to disrupt the rational part of our thought process, allowing our emotions to take over. This in turn creates a lonely feeling and a perception that each person is on the opposite side of a glass wall.

You can see angry body language, but words are barely heard. The cognitive ability to process those words is disrupted by your distress. To get your point across, it's easy to amplify the volume and use blaming or derogatory words.

At one time or another, we have all been guilty of getting sucked into this negative spiral of poor communication. The Bible has plenty to say about this topic. If we study the Bible and invite the Lord's presence into our circumstances, His grace can transform us into better communicators. When we learn to become better communicators, we can encourage our loved ones down the same path.

At the end of the day, our efforts in this area only work if both people are willing to work on their issues, and are equally open to seeing their own blind spots. Blind spots are called that because we can't see them. When you look in the mirror, can you see the back of your head? No. You need another mirror that reflects into the one you are looking at.

Our life is the same. We need someone else to point out our problem areas. That requires an open attitude to criticism and a willingness to change. However, if either person is continually offended by the other's criticism, or if one person is continually critical—then it's time to get outside help. Frequent negative chatter in the home and the feeling of being demeaned or invalidated can destroy love quickly. There may be deeper problems here that are interfering in your relationship. Unfortunately, if you wait until your marriage is at a crisis point before seeking help, you may have waited too long.

Marriage counseling is an important way to iron out small differences before they become big problems. Many people see marriage counseling as the last straw before the lawyers get involved. This is wrong thinking, and is one reason why marriage counseling gets a bad rap. Since it is the last place people go before the lawyers draw up the divorce papers, people fear it almost as much as they fear the legal process.

There's something unnerving about talking about your personal marital issues with a third party who doesn't know you. You get this gut wrenching feeling that you are going to be judged or admonished. It's almost like being called to the principal's office when you were in grade school. It can feel humiliating. You really don't think you've done anything wrong, but what if you did? And how do you fix it?

Admitting that you need help is always the first step. Having the "I think we need help," conversation with your spouse is almost as stressful as having that first appointment with the therapist. All kinds of fearful thoughts accompany this conversation. Are you in the wrong...or are they? Will you be pressured into giving up your faith? Will they be pressured into giving in to you? The one you committed to spend the rest of your life with is someone you've dreamt dreams with, built a home with, and perhaps had children with. Is it all going to come tumbling down?

It might be helpful to know that every marriage goes through tough times. Marriage counseling does not mean that it's over. It's a safe place to talk about difficult issues that you can't seem to talk about at home. It's also a place to safely share your differences and concerns, and find new strategies to old problems. If you are frequently arguing about the same issues, or if every molehill turns into a mountain, you need a new strategy that is non-threatening to both of you.

It's easy for any couple to get stuck in a rut with dysfunctional communication patterns. It's getting out of that place that can be tough. A good therapist will assess your communication skills, discover the roadblocks that are impeding good communication, and help you to uncover a new smoother path to walk upon.

That smoother path is not designed by the therapist. It's designed by the two of you. Your therapist is simply a conduit to a new doorway that neither of you have opened yet. It's not their job to judge you or control your lifestyle. Their job is to point out where each of you are falling, and try to help you find mutually-agreeable ways to help each other stand up together. They provide a non-judgmental third perspective on the presented problem, and help to discover the root causes underlying the friction that you are experiencing. Sometimes this can be uncovered in just a few sessions. In more difficult cases, it may take several months. But the good news is that most marriages can be saved if the couple want it to be saved and both are willing to make the necessary changes.

Finding a Therapist

Once you've decided that it's worth the risk to make that phone call, the next logical questions are: Where do we go? How do we know that this therapist will be right for us?

If your pastor has been certified in Christian counseling, this is a good (and most economical) place to start. They might offer counseling, or recommend that you go elsewhere instead. Since you have a relationship with the church, your spouse may feel intimidated and pressured into a situation where you already know the counselor. It's fine to consult with this pastor for yourself—but when it comes to marriage counseling, it's usually recommended to get a neutral therapist. Your pastor can refer you to someone that you can interview to determine if they are a fit for your situation.

Most therapists are quite open to an initial interview. You need to feel comfortable with them, and they also want to make sure that they are skilled enough to deal with your specific needs. Before you book that first appointment, it's important to ask about their qualifications.

You will want someone who is accredited specifically in marriage counseling. If there are easily identifiable problems (e.g., addictions, anger, money management, etc.), it's important that the counselor is also accredited in that field. It doesn't matter if they are a psychologist, social worker, or a pastor. Ask about their qualifications, and years of experience in marriage counseling, family counseling, addictions, or any other additional certifications that you think you might require. Ask if they have a Christian faith-based approach to counseling. They will be more than happy to tell you.

It is possible that your spouse may not be open to seeing a Christian therapist. If that's a concern, try to find someone who is open and willing to assist with faith-based differences. It's important to keep in mind that all therapists, by nature, are compassionate individuals. Some are more skilled in one area than another. If they are not comfortable in counseling faith-related issues, they may refer you to someone who is qualified in that area. After all, they want to make sure that you are happy with their services. No one wants to be the contributing source of a family breakdown or a marital split. All therapists want to be known as someone who can help heal people, relationships, and families.

When the day comes and the appointment arrives, put on your best smile and let your spouse know that no matter what happens at the meeting, you love them. Reassure them that you really do want to work this out, you just need a better way of doing it. Let them know you are just as apprehensive about the end results as they are, but with God's help you will both come through this with healthier mindsets and a stronger marriage.

Prior to each session, pray for God's guidance in the words that you speak, and ask for courage for both of you. Pray that you will each have the wisdom to accept constructive feedback from the therapist. Also pray for the therapist...that he or she will have the spiritual discernment to understand and interpret the issues that you are struggling with.

The famous Serenity Prayer is helpful at times like this:

> *God grant me the serenity to accept the things I cannot change; the courage to change the things I can; and the wisdom to know the difference.*
> — Reinhold Niebuhr, 1892–1971

Faith differences are one thing we can't change. The Holy Spirit is the one who instigates change. Our job is to listen to His voice and obey His leading.

CHAPTER EIGHTEEN

——◆——

The Conversation
About Church

*For the message of the cross is foolishness to those who are
perishing, but to us who are being saved it is the power of
God.*
— 1 Corinthians 1:18 NKJV

Compromise and forgiveness in our day-to-day interactions are
essential for good relationships. We need to seed our marriage
with the salt of grace and water it with the truth and light of
Christ's love. This can be a challenging call to action. It's easy to
get frustrated and discouraged. You might be thinking, "If only I
could get them to come to church, they would see what they are
missing!"

"If only..."

It's easy to live in that space in your head that focuses on the
fantasy of a perfect future. Living in the future doesn't help you
deal with today. Today the reality is that they're neither interested,
nor ready. Tomorrow might be different, but only God knows.

Dealing with today does not mean one stops praying or gives up on
hope for things to change. Life is always changing and the future is
unpredictable. You can plan a path that is more hopeful and more

encouraging, but there is no guarantee that your plan will play out as you want it to.

Ask yourself, "Who am I planning for?" If it's for you and you alone, that's being goal-oriented. If you are attempting to manipulate another's path, then you are setting the stage for potential conflict. Backlash can happen and suddenly you fall into the trap of your own manipulation.

You want your spouse to go to church with you, but they aren't interested. So, you plan and scheme on a way to achieve your goal. You talk yourself into a method that seems reasonable to you, and before you know it, you have crafted the perfect manipulation. Of course, this is all in your mind. You haven't presented the scenario to them yet.

The sin of manipulation often appears attractive after you've spent months or years begging, nagging or badgering. What you've accomplished up to this point, is building a wall of resentment and a platform for further conflict. To appease you, they might grudgingly accept your invitation to that special event at church, but they won't acknowledge an appreciation of the content at the end of the event. Essentially you are receiving a push back against your manipulation. Is that really what you want?

Accept their "No thanks," with understanding. They are not ready to make that leap with you. If, and when they want to join you, they will show signs of interest. Pushing your own agenda can conflict with the work the Holy Spirit is already doing. We can't be the Holy Spirit in someone else's life. We don't know all things. We need to be patient and trust Him. If we frustrate the Holy Spirit by getting in His way and trying to "help," we usually end up making the situation worse.

One night, when I thought I was being completely innocent in attempting to convince my husband to attend a Christian concert with me, I heard the Lord say this:

UNEQUALLY YOKED

The heart is deceitful above all things, and desperately wicked; Who can know it?
— Jeremiah 17:9 NKJV

Who, me? I didn't listen and continued to push for my own agenda. As it turned out, there was a person attending the concert toward whom my husband had a resentment. My husband couldn't enjoy the evening, because his attention was distracted from the concert to the person who he felt had wronged him. What should have been a beautiful evening turned out to be a disaster. When the Lord sends a strongly-worded message, it's important to listen. I learned my lesson the hard way. Manipulation, no matter how well-intentioned, is dishonest, and therefore, sinful. Backlash happens when we try to take personal control of someone else's spiritual path.

I realize that you are anxious for the right opportunities, the right people, and the right experiences to expose your spouse to the Father's love. Church attendance helps to ignite that desire within the soul to crave the good things available to us from the Heavenly Kingdom. But walking into a church building to attend a regular church service can be intimidating to a newcomer or unbeliever.

The door to this conversation can open when you least expect it. Our society affords us plenty of opportunities to walk into a venue that includes a church service. It's almost impossible to avoid. After all, weddings, funerals and other special occasions are frequently held inside church buildings and hosted by Christian leaders.

Then there are those seasonal expressions of Christianity— Christmas and Easter. Sadly, Easter has become more connected with the beginning of Spring than the resurrection story, but resurrection plays can still be found in many communities. Christmas holds a more overt expression of Christianity than any other time of year with music reflective of the birth of Christ, decorative manger scenes, and an abundance of activities that take place inside church buildings.

In some families, it's traditional to attend Christmas and Easter services, regardless of whether you are a practicing Christian or not. Churches anticipate a higher attendance on these occasions and frequently aim the service and the message toward those who rarely attend. This might be the easiest time, with the least conflict, for you to invite your spouse to attend church.

Personally, seasonal expressions of Christianity help me to reflect on my childhood days—a time when everyone in the community attended church during special occasions. In my marriage, I've impressed upon my husband that family church attendance during these times helps to make the seasons more festive for me. I'm honest with him that I need him to attend with me...for me. I am clear and honest with my intentions. He comes because he thinks it will make me happy. After the service, I don't push the subject matter, and I don't grill him on what he learned. I'm excited if he wants to talk about it later, but most times he doesn't. I've learned to be patient and let the Holy Spirit do His work.

Family members will often do things for one another, such as attending church, because of Mom or Dad's pleading. That doesn't mean that they will enjoy it. They may just go because you have insisted. In this case, let them know how appreciative you are by thanking them and adding a warm hug. You might want to demonstrate your appreciation by doing something for them in return. A nice lunch at a favorite restaurant usually goes over well.

These special occasions can be the start to an open door for further conversation. You can casually ask, "What did you think about the service?" to open the door. They may or may not walk through that door, and if they don't, then don't push it. Let the Holy Spirit do His job. But if they do, be prepared for questions, and don't answer with a dissertation. Questions need to be answered simply and specifically. Allow time for information to be absorbed.

When your loved one starts to ask questions about your church, your Christian friends or more specifically, about your faith—listen closely. The kindling of interest usually starts with questions. How you answer might peak their curiosity. Their questions may be a sincere quest for learning, or just curiosity to understand a specific point. Reflect on your answer before you speak.

If your spouse indicates that they want to attend church with you more frequently—carefully consider whether or not your church would be appropriate for someone who is searching.

Some churches are geared toward searchers and new believers. Others are very theological, and more suited to deep thinkers and those well-educated in the faith. Unless they are highly educated, most aspiring believers would be bored, intimidated, or overwhelmed at this latter type of church. Keep in mind that newcomers, although curious, will be confused easily when too much information is presented too quickly. First impressions can either kill future interest, or encourage it. Since we want to encourage further attendance, it is important to make sure that interest isn't stifled by the style of service or an intimidating atmosphere.

People who have never attended church or only attended on formal occasions have preconceived ideas of what a church service looks like. Hollywood has done a great job of showing us three different styles: the traditional and liturgical (such as the Catholic churches), the average Protestant church, and the "deep Southern Gospel" style. These are true reflections of some churches, but there are many variations of those themes.

Your church may not look anything like these three dominant styles. You picked your church because there was something about that group that appealed to you. Spend some time thinking about this. What was it about this church that attracted you? Was it the worship style, was it the preaching style, was it the relevance of the pastor's message as it pertained to your life, or was it the variety of programming? Does it match with your learning style? Be prepared to answer the question why you go where you go. Be open to attending elsewhere temporarily if your spouse isn't comfortable with your church's style. While you might be comfortable with a loosely-structured setting, they may require a more traditional and liturgical approach (or vice-versa).

When we recently moved into a new neighborhood, I searched for a church that could meet my needs, and with some traditional aspects that would be comfortably-suited for my husband to attend during those seasonal occasions. Initially, I chose a middle-of-the-road approach, hoping it might appeal to him. Sadly, my attempt to compromise and guess at what he might like, backfired. After keeping me company a couple of times, he declined to continue. He said he didn't like the worship music...but it could just as easily have been something else.

My husband and I clash on musical tastes—especially worship music. He describes modern worship music as irreverent. I appreciate that he voices that predilection. I enjoy a loud, joyful style, in which I can dance and sing. Although a sensitive compromise is important to encourage his participation, stifling my spiritual needs to compensate for his style preferences isn't the answer. We need to find a balance that works for both of us.

Although most times I prefer a celebration of joy, I also appreciate a quiet, stoic, liturgical service when I'm going through tough times and I need to be more reflective, or when I am going through a period of deep intercession. However, my primary need at this point in my life is learning how to be joyful in difficult circumstances. A church that celebrates my faith and encourages me to interact with others helps me to do that.

Childhood memories may have impact on where or when we attend church. Although my memories involve traditional church celebrations during Christmas and Easter, my husband did not grow up in a religious or Christian family. He doesn't share similar memories. I didn't know that about him until I asked questions about those times in his life. I was surprised by his answers. It's so easy to assume that our spouse's childhood was like ours. We need to take the time to ask the right questions.

When a person doesn't understand spirituality, neither do they know what they need to do to encourage their own spiritual growth. As we try to help them through what we think they need, we assume that we have the answers. We become frustrated, feeling like failures, because we are trying to force them to look through our eyes. In turn, they give up trying to comprehend spiritual things, because they are trying to understand through our eyes. This doesn't work. It may seem to us that they are blind, but it is God who gives the eyes to see, not us. We need to wait on the Holy Spirit to implant the hunger in our loved ones, and give us the guidance that we need. Only God knows how quickly the next step will happen. Be patient.

Lee and Leslie Strobel, in their book, *Surviving a Spiritual Mismatch in Marriage*, recommend two things:

1. Go to a church where you feel comfortable worshipping with the spiritual depth that you require at this stage of your journey.
2. Find another church where your spouse might be comfortable for those times that they may want to go with you.[30]

Finding the right church that will be comfortable for your non-believing spouse takes time. You want to be sensitive to their previous experiences with Christian churches, their learning style, their personality style (i.e., whether they are introverted or extroverted), and their theological outlook.

Fortunately, in this technological age, you can go online, research the various churches in your neighborhood, and watch or listen to live-streamed services without leaving the comfort of your home.

---

[30] Strobel, Lee, and Leslie Strobel. Surviving a Spiritual Mismatch in Marriage. Grand Rapids, MI: Zondervan, 2002.

It's wise to do your research long before you will ever need it. A peaked curiosity can expire at midnight. If your spouse is showing interest in attending with you, but you feel that your church is not appropriate for spiritual seekers or new believers, explain that to them and offer an alternative church to attend.

In thinking of alternatives, you might think that staying home and watching church on television or live-stream might be a good way to introduce them to Christianity. This may or may not work. If they are willing to watch with you, it can provide education about your Christian beliefs, while encouraging you in your faith at the same time. This approach provides a more relaxed environment for a faith-based conversation. However, be cautious about falling into a situation in which you can be accused of bombarding your home with "religious propaganda." Christian television can be a turnoff to some non-believers. If your spouse is antagonistic about the Christian faith, pray about this approach, and allow the Holy Spirit to guide you into making the right decision in this area.

Secondly, technology can be a slippery slope. It provides a temptation to stay at home and eliminate that feeling of being conspicuous in the church. It's easy to isolate yourself with a church service on television or read that Christian book you've been planning to read. Remember this—it doesn't take very long before staying home becomes a habit.

Another drawback of technology, is that it does not immerse you in the Christian environment with all the experiences that go with church attendance. Part of attending church is communal interaction. Connecting with other believers, enriches and deepens your faith. Interaction with others helps you to practically implement biblical principles into your day-to-day life. More importantly, the mighty presence of the Holy Spirit is powerfully activated when believers come together in community. Even if you don't talk to another soul while you are there, you are being strengthened and encouraged in that environment. The TV doesn't provide the same exposure.

Your community church is one of the few places where you can meet Christian friends who share common interests. If your spouse chooses to attend with you, they will meet believers and have opportunities to make friends who can lead them further in the faith. The experience of a church community will allow them to encounter Jesus through the eyes of others. Hearing about the Lord from someone other than you, both solidifies and clarifies their learning, and provides confirmation that the joy evidenced in you, is also visible in the lives of other believers.

If your spouse is not at this point yet—don't despair. Look for opportunities to open the door to an invitation. Pray for this to happen. Set aside time for a conversation about this, but don't be discouraged if they say no or come back with a nasty rebuke. If they refuse to attend church with you, continue to live in love— keep your attitude in check, practice forgiveness, and work on your communication skills.

Demonstrate joy in your life. Be Jesus with skin on. When you wake up in the morning, ask the Lord to show you how to be a beacon of light for your family today. Jesus said that our lives reflect what we believe. We can talk about our faith, but if our lives don't show the truth of what we believe, then our lives accuse us of hypocrisy.

> *He replied, "Isaiah was right when he prophesied about you hypocrites; as it is written: 'These people honor me with their lips, but their hearts are far from me. They worship me in vain; their teachings are merely human rules.'"*
> — Mark 7:6–7 NIV

Let us not give any room to hypocrisy. Our most important testimony is at home with those we love. We want to win them to the Lord with love, not fear. We want them to make the decision of coming to Christ because they are convinced that the message is true *for them.* Allowing them to come to that decision requires that we demonstrate love and grace in our communication and our actions. At all times, we must maintain a respectful attitude in presenting the Gospel message. A joyful engaging attitude helps to encourage others to peek inside our Christian world.

CHAPTER NINETEEN

———◆———

Submission, Respect and Grace

Unless the Lord builds the house, the builders labor in vain.
— Psalm 127:1 NIV

When Adam and Eve made the conscious choice to disobey God, they committed the ultimate sin of rebellion. This attitude of "I know better," and "I want to be in control," is still our basic human nature.

When we are frustrated that our prayers aren't being heard, we assume that God wants us to get involved and help solve the problem. As human beings, we tend to put ourselves on the God pedestal. After all, "I am," the ultimate problem solver. We think we know better. Sadly, time after time, we mess things up. Our perfect solution ends up as a disaster. Our dreams become illusions of grandeur, as we watch our goals dissolve into thin air. The answers that Scripture holds, seem to be meant for everyone else but us. It takes patience and trust to let God be God.

Part of growing in our faith is studying the Word. Initially we may struggle to comprehend the full meaning of a passage. As we begin to understand, we look to mount the next step of putting it into practice. However, in the unequally yoked marriage, we may question whether or not some aspects of Scripture apply to us. One of those confusing topics is the subject of submission, especially this (often misunderstood) verse:

Wives, in the same way submit yourselves to your own husbands so that, if any of them do not believe the word, they may be won over without words by the behavior of their wives, when they see the purity and reverence of your lives.
— 1 Peter 3:1–2 NIV

What does this mean?

Does submission mean giving up control? To what? To everything that my husband wants to do? Must I agree with every decision that he makes? How does this apply in the unequally yoked marriage?

In our "equal rights" society, submission sounds like a dirty word. We wrongly interpret the word 'submission' as subservience, something that is not acceptable in our modern world. After all, women work just as hard (if not harder) than men. We can do any job in the marketplace that a man can do. And men also cook, clean the house, and change diapers. Most modern marriages operate in a team approach to household management and problem-solving. So then, how exactly are we supposed to interpret this passage of Scripture?

Sadly, this famously misquoted verse has often been used to denigrate women and keep them in a subservient place. Therefore, it's important to have a look at the word 'submit' and get a clear understanding of its meaning and context in this verse. The word translated 'submit' here, is from the Greek word '*hypotassō*,' [31] which is defined as follows:

- It originated from a Greek military term, meaning "to arrange [troop divisions] in a military fashion under the command of a leader."

---

[31] Hupotasso, also spelled Hypotasso, #G5293New Strong's Exhaustive Concordance by James Strong, Published by Thomas Nelson, 2003.

- In non-military use, it was "a voluntary attitude of giving in, cooperating, assuming responsibility, and carrying a burden."[32]

These two very different interpretations carry some heavy implications. In many Evangelical circles, people interpret the text using the first definition—the military use of the term. This understanding seems to advocate for a home that uses a military chain of command, where no one can make a move without the approval of the chief commander. This can implicate a lifestyle that encourages fear. That is a horrible way to live and raises the risk for domestic violence.

Considering that Jesus encouraged equality between everyone, it's hard to believe that He would be in support of a man dominating a woman, or anything that would resemble one person controlling another. That doesn't sound like God's plan for relationships and family.

If this negative interpretation isn't consistent with the message of love coming from the Savior, then surely it wouldn't be endorsed by the Apostle Paul. Thankfully, Paul explains what he means by this when we read the rest of this verse. He says that when we submit, we are demonstrating "purity and reverence," in our lives. The King James Version translates this as "chaste conduct accompanied by fear." The English Standard Version translates this passage as "respectful and pure conduct."

The Merriam-Webster Dictionary defines 'reverence' as "honor or respect that is felt for or shown to someone or something." Synonyms of reverence include honor, homage, and deference, which all mean to respect and show esteem to another.[33]

In Ephesians 5:33, Paul clarifies this a bit more. The Amplified Bible (Classic Edition) expands this as follows:

---

[32] Source: http://www.biblestudytools.com/lexicons/greek/nas/hupotasso.html
[33] Source: http://www.merriam-webster.com/dictionary/reverence

"...let the wife see that she respects and reverences her husband [that she notices him, regards him, honors him, prefers him, venerates, and esteems him; and that she defers to him, praises him, and loves and admires him exceedingly]."
— Ephesians 5:33b AMPC

The Apostle is saying that we should have an attitude of cooperation, voluntarily carrying our spouse's burdens, and taking responsibility for our attitudes and actions, so that we are always demonstrating honor and respect in our marriage.

Respect and honor are characteristic of a Godly life. It should be evident in all our relationships, not just with our spouse (see 1 Peter 2). Paul isn't saying anything new here. His words are consistent with Christ's message. Jesus demonstrated respect and honor to everyone, while maintaining an attitude of servanthood. The example that we need to follow is Jesus.

Jesus is still known as the greatest leader that ever walked on this planet. Despite being the greatest teacher and rabbi, He carried a submissive attitude. He practiced servanthood to others. As the perfect man, He taught us how to love completely, how to show respect, honor and give dignity to every human being. As God, He showed us what relationship looks like. He taught us life isn't about our own selfish desires—it's about what we can give—and not about what we can get.

When it comes to our relationships at home, how do we reflect that submissive, servant attitude? How do we demonstrate honor and respect? How do we maintain an attitude that reflects Jesus?

Firstly...we must be conscious of our attitudes, our actions, and our words. Everything we do needs to flow in the undercurrent of love. Without love, our actions and our words mean nothing.

*If I speak in the tongues of men or of angels, but do not have
love, I am only a resounding gong or a clanging cymbal.*
— 1 Corinthians 13:1 NIV

Love shows in our motivations. We need to examine ourselves as
to why we do what we do, or say what we say. It is very easy to fall
into "control mode," or play the blame game. If we are only
grudgingly doing something because it's the "Christian thing to
do," then we have the wrong motivation. We are then making it
about ourselves and a salvation of works, trying to work our way
into Heaven and getting those diamonds in our eternal crown. This
is where our works become gongs or clanging cymbals. People can
sense fake love. If your motivations are not based on love, it will
come through in your attitude. This is especially true in marriage.

If we want to demonstrate love in all our actions, then we need to
keep our motivations pure, and demonstrate honesty and integrity.
If you don't feel very loving to your spouse because of something
that happened, then explain that to them. Don't walk around with
an attitude of rebellious pride. Pride is selfish, and causes us to
blame others for the problem. Pride prevents us from honestly
evaluating ourselves and searching for solutions.

Putting it into action is difficult. Practically speaking, we can read
the Bible and listen to a sermon on pride. Pride is incompatible
with honesty and gentleness. In the middle of an argument, when
you think you are right and the other person is wrong, being
honest and gentle is easier said than done. It hurts to bite our
tongue when we want to scream angry words. It's especially tough
when your loved one doesn't have the same standards of honesty
and integrity that you do. This is where your Christian witness can
speak volumes.

For example, what do you do when the one you love asks you to lie
for them?

Answer: You either say no or you find a way to deal with the issue
without compromising your integrity.

This also applies in our jobs. When I worked as a legal secretary after high school, my boss sometimes instructed me to tell clients that he wasn't in. More than once, he walked into the room exactly when that same client was standing at the reception desk. Embarrassed by my lie, I quickly learned to change my words. Using the phrase "He's not available," allowed me to maintain my integrity and accomplished my boss' request.

That example is perhaps simplistic. But have you ever asked your spouse to lie for you about being home when a certain phone call was expected, or called your employer to say you are sick when you are not? How are we demonstrating Christian truth and integrity when we participate in these "little white lies"?

One way of checking whether or not your conduct is respectful and your integrity is intact, is to picture your six-year-old child watching and hearing you. Would they be disappointed in your actions? Would it be something that would be OK for them to do at home, school, or in a public situation? Did your words and actions just teach that child a positive thing or something you might regret? I know we ask, "What would Jesus do?" but sadly, sometimes it's easier to be dismissive of the Lord's reaction than it is of a small child. It's easy for us to get hooked into what others might think and allow that to control our actions. Since we live on different spiritual levels—honesty and integrity can sometimes be confusing to identify. Truth can sometimes have different levels, depending on which stairway you are standing on.

If we have experienced abuse in our lives, our value system can be compromised. Since abuse tends to warp core integrity, survivors sometimes need to learn from others how to evaluate truth, determine the correct action for the situation, and learn what is acceptable behavior and what isn't.

Conversely, allowing others to have too much influence in what we do and how we think, can lead us into codependency, and make us vulnerable to further abuse. Codependency is a battle many of us face as we unknowingly enable negative behavior in others. It's tough to stand up in a crowd and disagree. Disagreeing with our family members can cause unwanted strife. It's often so much easier to just give in.

Strife is a form of warfare. A negative home breeds negative attitudes. Negative attitudes produce stress. Stress increases the hormone cortisol, that is designed to help us in times of crisis. Continually elevated levels of cortisol interfere with our ability to stay healthy. Long-term negative stress affects our breathing, our digestion, our immune system, and our sleep. It interferes with memory and learning. Negative stress is unhealthy. If we live in strife, the stress of it can literally kill us.[34]

God wants us to be healthy, and live long, and prosperous, years. He encourages us to live in love and in peace.

> *Do not repay anyone evil for evil. Be careful to do what is right in the eyes of everyone. If it is possible, as far as it depends on you, live at peace with everyone.*
> — Romans 12:17–18 NIV

Living in peace does not mean compromising our values of truth. But it may require that we set aside our pride to achieve peace. Perhaps I need to defer to my husband, even if I don't agree with him. The consequences could mean that some bad decisions get made. Take heart that bad decisions eventually prove themselves. Few bad decisions are fatal, although they might be emotionally or financially difficult. It's how we treat others and show respect in the decision-making process that is reflective of our Christian attitude.

When bad decisions are made, they require grace and mercy. Grace manifests itself in an attitude of kindness and forgiveness. It is not a synonym for acceptance. It helps to maintain your loved

---

[34] Source: https://www.psychologytoday.com/blog/the-athletes-way/201301/cortisol-why-the-stress-hormone-is-public-enemy-no-1

one's integrity, while allowing them to learn in the way that they learn best. Learning by your mistakes can be humiliating. Grace holds out a supportive hand while one or both of you suffer through the consequences of bad decision-making. You may be tempted to say, "I told you so," but that is pride rearing its ugly head. Grace and pride don't go together. Grace and integrity do.

Grace is not codependent. It doesn't enable the other person in repetitive bad decision-making. It doesn't include throwing up our hands and saying, "Do whatever you want." Sometimes showing grace involves stepping back and allowing consequences to happen, and sometimes mercy requires us to step in and rescue.

At times, rescuing can be codependent. Sometimes rescuing doesn't allow a person to learn from their mistakes. There's a big difference between rescuing a five-year-old child having a tantrum who runs into the path of an oncoming vehicle, and rescuing your spouse from the effects of alcohol by diluting the bottle of vodka with water because you don't want them to get drunk again. Protecting a child from dangers they don't understand is wise. Protecting an adult from the consequences of their actions is a form of control that interferes in relationships.

Good relationships are based on submitting to one another (see Ephesians 5:22–33). The underpinning of love shows itself through respect, honor, and always maintaining one another's integrity. It is visible in the way we speak to one another, how we speak about one another to others, and how we treat one another. It values the other person above ourselves. This is love. This is what Christ taught us. This is how He wants us to live.

> *Love is patient, love is kind. It does not envy, it does not boast, it is not proud. It does not dishonor others, it is not self-seeking, it is not easily angered, it keeps no record of wrongs. Love does not delight in evil but rejoices with the truth. It always protects, always trusts, always hopes, always perseveres.*
> — 1 Corinthians 13:4–7 NIV

CHAPTER TWENTY

Living your Faith at Home

How then shall they call on Him in whom they have not believed? And how shall they believe in Him of whom they have not heard? And how shall they hear without a preacher? And how shall they preach unless they are sent? As it is written: "How beautiful are the feet of those who preach the gospel of peace."
— Romans 10:14–15 NKJV

As we reflect on what we've learned so far, we recognize that we are far from perfect. Admitting our imperfections, asking for forgiveness, and changing our mindsets to more righteous ways of thinking are part of our daily journey. Even though we will never be perfect, we need to focus inward with humility, and accept criticisms of our attitude or actions with graciousness.

How do we show our faith in the different and often-challenging situations imposed upon us in our spiritually diverse and often divisive home life? How do we show grace, when we are being unfairly attacked? Accepting criticism from those we love hurts. Sometimes it can be completely unjustified. Understanding where this nastiness comes from can help us empathize with another's spiritual state.

People strike out at others, sometimes without obvious provocation, because of their own inner pain. It is here where we need to show mercy and understanding. Anyone who doesn't have the love of the Lord within them doesn't have that resource to grasp for added strength. They depend on their own strength. They are striving to do the best that they can with the skills and understanding that they have. They are not willing to open themselves up to the One who can provide the comfort and reassurance that says, "This too shall pass." They can't "let go and let God," because they have no idea who the real God is. Their fight for self-survival is evident every time a crisis happens.

It is during these times that our carnal nature rises in rebellion, pushes to the forefront, and wants to strike back. It's very easy to get hooked into a pattern of negatively reacting to our spouse's behavior. It's hard to be understanding when you are facing a bear. It takes a lot of discipline to keep your mouth shut and back away quietly.

> *Finally, all of you, be like-minded, be sympathetic, love one another, be compassionate and humble. Do not repay evil with evil or insult with insult. On the contrary, repay evil with blessing, because to this you were called so that you may inherit a blessing.*
> — 1 Peter 3:8–9 NIV

It is difficult to repay evil with blessing. Going into your "prayer closet," is probably the wisest thing you can do. Asking the Holy Spirit for the right words to say and how to say them can change a bear into a puppy, or at least turn down the fire of fear that's attempting to start a blaze.

Stopping ourselves from saying something that we might regret takes discipline. Our innate need to control our environment (including other people) often hooks us with our own religious pride. We want to step into the danger zone and start preaching. After all, we think we have the answer to their dilemma. Or at least, we believe that God has the answer, and we justify our lame preaching efforts with that explanation. And it is precisely that which we should not do.

Nothing turns an unbeliever off more than saying, "The Bible says..." or "God told me...." There is a time and place to have a discussion on faith, and it's not in the middle of an argument, or when someone is so absorbed in their pain that they are in no position to reach for joy or salvation. When people are in pain, they need comfort and understanding. When your loved one is angry at the world, they need space to process their feelings. Anything you say at this point has the potential for backlash.

It's important to acknowledge your loved one's pain or discomfort. People in pain want to feel that someone understands. They need comfort and reassurance that they matter in the world, and that their emotions have validity (even if those emotions seem unreasonable to us).

An angry person can get so lost in the pain of that emotion that they are oblivious to how they are coming across to others. People that are angry need to hear from others that their anger is valid, but that their demonstration of anger might not be appropriate. If we can learn to empathize with detachment—we deflect and diffuse the negative emotions of others. This is an essential skill that prevents us from getting hooked into confrontations.

Detachment is not disconnecting. It is being an observer, and not getting caught up in the drama of the situation. This is a skill that professional therapists practice with all their clients. It's why they don't take their problems home with them. (If they didn't do this, they would burn out quickly.)

In detachment, you observe the emotions and the effects that those emotions are having on the afflicted person. While you acknowledge the feelings, you remain cognizant that those emotions belong to the person who is experiencing them—not to you. It's a difficult skill to learn, especially for those who didn't grow up with a healthy modeling of conflict management at home.

When we detach, we are modeling a healthy way of dealing with stressful situations. We are also taking care of our own emotional and physical well-being. As mentioned previously, stress can kill. Detachment is a tool to keep stress outside our "safe zone."

When Jesus was verbally attacked by His accusers, or when His critics attempted to drag Him into a conflict zone, He detached. He regarded the situation for what it really was. He stayed calm, He reflected, and He often turned situations around with questions. He never fell into a trap designed to get Him to react in a negative way. Jesus is our model to teach us how to practice detachment.

Detachment does not include an attitude of smugness or superiority. It is a genuine caring for our loved one, as well as ourselves. It says, "I care, I understand—but your feelings belong to you, not to me. Just because I care does not mean I have to experience the same emotions that you do."

When our best friend's loved one dies, we don't feel their pain because it is removed from us. But we can hold their hand and observe their pain, and help them get through their dark days. Detachment carries empathy. Empathy connects with the pain in an understanding way. It doesn't include getting hooked into the pain. Detachment with empathy is active, loving and practical. This is a way of living that reflects the love of Christ.

Reflecting the love of Christ at home is our testimony. There are times when words are necessary, but our actions always speak louder than words. Often our actions will lead others into observing us. That observation can lead to questions. Questions may lead into a discussion about faith.

Can you see the pattern now? Our actions (whether they be words, attitudes, or works) are the unlocked doors that invite others to step into our world—to a different level of understanding. On this level, grace becomes experiential. It is the door to faith.

Sadly, we often stand in front of that door to judge the correct timing for someone to walk through. Our human need to control often violates another person's decision-making process. But you can't force faith.

Faith begins with an acknowledgement of a higher spiritual power outside of ourselves. A person can deny the truth all they want, but as the Apostle Paul explains:

> *"...what may be known about God is plain to them, because God has made it plain to them. For since the creation of the world God's invisible qualities—his eternal power and divine nature—have been clearly seen, being understood from what has been made, so that people are without excuse."*
> — Romans 1:19–20 NIV

This verse explains that intuitively, most people know that God exists, but many refuse to admit to seeing His hand at work in the world or in their personal lives. Before a person is willing to open the door to see how this Omniscience interacts in their lives, there must first be some conscious awareness of His existence.

That involves taking the first step—admitting that God is real and that He is interactive with every individual on the planet. However, if someone is determined not to believe, there aren't any words that you can speak that will convince them otherwise. Neither is there anything that you can *do*. Only the Holy Spirit can create a river where no water flows.

When the well-digger digs for water, sometimes that drill must go very deep, often a thousand feet or more. The naked eye cannot see the crystal river lying deep beneath the hard, rocky soil. Something or someone needs to crack the earth so that a pure refreshing spring can burst forth. Allow me to ask you this: How many deserts did you have to walk through before you found relief for your thirsty soul?

At one time or another, we all experience the difficulty of traveling through parched deserts, towering mountains, and dark valleys. Every person's journey of faith is unique to them. Some people fall into a deep pit before they realize the need to be rescued by someone other than themselves. Others walk through life oblivious to any spiritual influence, until one day they encounter a blinding flash of light.

The Apostle Paul was an enemy of Christians and considered himself to be one of the most righteous persons in Jewish society (see Philippians 3). It was only when that "blinding flash of light" met him on his journey to murder more Christians, that he finally got the message. His belief system changed instantly, but he didn't start preaching the Gospel immediately. There were things that he needed to learn, and he needed to gain the trust of the very people he had been persecuting. That took time (see Acts 9).

Are you asking, "How can our loved ones learn about our faith if we don't tell them? Isn't preaching words part of the evangelical message?"

Yes, it is. But how and when this conversation happens must depend on the Holy Spirit's guidance and not our feelings of desperation. The words we speak are not as important as the way in which we conduct our day-to-day lives. Our behavior, our communication, our love, our language, our words, our activities, even the way we dress—carries the message of the love of Christ. The Apostle Peter says that our character needs to be our testimony.

> *Your beauty should not come from outward adornment, such as elaborate hairstyles and the wearing of gold jewelry or fine clothes. Rather, it should be that of your inner self, the unfading beauty of a gentle and quiet spirit, which is of great worth in God's sight.*
> — 1 Peter 3:3–4 NIV

It is a loving, gracious attitude that is demonstrated in everything we do and say that will show the changes in ourselves. This is our testimony. When our spouse sees how we handle ourselves in difficult situations, how we offer grace and mercy to those least deserving, how we demonstrate patience in our interactions with others, and how we are generous and loving in everything we do— then, at some point, they will admit that the changes in us are evidence of the faith that we embrace. This is how we reflect Jesus in our home. The Bible promises us that acknowledgement will happen.

> *Live such good lives among the pagans that, though they accuse you of doing wrong, they may see your good deeds and glorify God on the day He visits us.*
> — 1 Peter 2:12 NIV

CHAPTER TWENTY-ONE

Intimacy—The Holy Bedroom

*Kiss me with the sweet kisses of your lips, for your love
delights me more than wine.*
— Song of Solomon 1:2 VOICE

Sharing our faith inside a spiritually-divided household is
difficult at the best of times. We need to be vigilant about our
Christian testimony—demonstrating grace, love and joy in all we
do and say. Our lifestyle should promote an attraction to a
relationship with Jesus.

Our spiritual growth is encouraged when we exercise thoughtful
and respectful communication, actions and attitudes. A forgiving,
selfless attitude, and watching our words, are essential to
encouraging a positive atmosphere in the home. In our private
time, we encourage ourselves when we spend time in prayer, read
the Bible and other faith-building literature, and connect
frequently with our spiritual support systems.

But what about the bedroom? Does your Christian life stop
between the sheets?

Do you wonder about couples who are both completely in love with
Jesus, and with each other? How different is their sex life? Is sex
just an act of procreation and pleasure, or does the Holy Spirit's
presence make a difference? If it makes a difference, is there a way
that we can bring that presence and power into the bedroom, even
though our spouse remains uncommitted to Christ?

In my introduction, I talked about the day when the Holy Spirit got my attention as I watched a couple sing in the worship team. They were a middle-aged couple that had been married well over twenty years, but by the way they looked at each other you would think they were still on their honeymoon! Their devotion for Jesus poured out in their harmonious singing. Their eyes sparkled and their faces lit up every time they glanced at one another. I could feel the mutual hunger in their eyes. I could see their adoration for each other through their frequent grazes of arms and hands. When they sat down, they sat very close, made eye contact, and smiled and laughed together.

This wasn't the first time I had observed this couple, but for whatever reason, on that day, the Holy Spirit chose to speak to me about my life and my marriage. Over the last few years I've listened to this couple speak and sing on many occasions. I know their reputation in that church to be that of a couple very devoted to the Lord. They demonstrate this through their Christian service, both within the church, and in the community-at-large. Their intimacy with the Lord and each other is genuine. Love flows from their lives. Their love is not only romantic, it is also spiritual. This type of intimacy cannot be faked.

Maybe this doesn't sound so unusual to you, but it was to me. At that moment when I realized what I was witnessing, my heart was pierced with jealousy.

My observations that day caused me to question whether I was seeing and sensing an unusually well-matched couple, or if this was a normal trait of a Spirit-filled Christian marriage. This led me to think, question, and people watch.

I put on my old, dusty, long-forgotten social work hat and started observing and making mental notes. I began to consciously watch the body language of other Christian couples, and how they interacted with each other in public. I listened to how they talked to each other, and about each other. I watched how they sat, how they touched, and how frequently they made eye contact. To assess their love for the Lord, I watched their attitudes and listened to their speech toward their family and others, and I looked for cues about their Christian service in the church or community. I admit my research was not scientific, but it did provide me with enough general information to draw some conclusions.

My conclusion from my observations revealed an appreciable difference between "cultural Christians," and those who exude Jesus in their lives. Couples who seem happiest in their marriages are those who overtly express the love of Christ to the world.

There is a glow and a passion between Spirit-filled spouses that is not as prevalent in other couples. Frequent physical contact—such as holding hands or brief hugs, or other kind touches and direct eye contact, indicate an openness to each other. Laughter flows with ease in their communication with each other. Their public conversations are salted with positive references about their spouse. These couples seem truly filled with joy. Age and time spent married only seems to enhance these qualities.

On that day as I watched the couple, I realized that the spiritual connection between couples and the Holy Spirit is an intimate triad relationship. When couples commit themselves completely to the Lord, they are rewarded with another level of intimacy in their relationship. This is a level of intimacy that the Bible promises is available to all of us, if we only ask God.

> *May your fountain, your sex life, be blessed by God; may you know true joy with the wife of your youth.*
> — Proverbs 5:18 VOICE

God wants to bless our marriages and our sex life.

Don't we all want this type of intimacy? If we don't have it, can it be because there is a barrier between the Holy Spirit and the unequally yoked marriage? After all, Jesus hasn't been fully invited into our home. It's not surprising that we might be questioning if something is missing. The bedroom might be the one area of our lives that demonstrates evidence of that missing piece.

But is this difference spiritual or simply the reality of life interfering in the bedroom?

When you are newly married and living with rose-colored glasses, your sex life is one of the highlights of your life. However, it's generally accepted that in most marriages, things change over time. Our passions slowly dampen from a roaring fire to a flickering flame. Sexual activity slackens both in time and quality and becomes more mechanical.

As we adjust to a comfortable married life with routines, we find ourselves touching and talking less. Maybe dinner takes place in front of the television screen, and evenings in front of the computer screen. When children arrive, their needs take priority and the bedroom is the last place that gets any attention. At the end of the day, we fall into bed exhausted. It's all we can do to kiss each other goodnight.

We know that our life should be *more*. Our idealized life includes a good paying job with a pleasant boss and ideal working conditions, and plenty of leisure time to be spent with family and friends. We want more intimacy with our spouse, but we don't know where to find the time and energy to fit that in. Life crashes in on reality.

Our romantic ideals of how things should be, reflect how we visualized life when we first married. When we take off our rose-colored glasses, we see life for the pressure cooker that it is. As we adapt our priorities, our hope in the romantic storybook version of life dissipates. We accept what is, and often feel unable to change things.

But if an entire book of the Bible was written about romantic love, that's a pretty good indication of the importance of sex to God! Maybe we need to study this more and see where we can improve.

In the first two chapters of Genesis, we read the story of creation. Sex was God's design—not only for procreation, but also for enhancing a relationship with our covenant spouse. In Matthew 19:4–9, Jesus explains God's plan for relationship between a man and a woman—to be "one flesh." This was God's plan from the beginning (Genesis 2:22–24).

When you read the various passages in the Bible about marriage, one other fact is obvious: God is always present as the third member in the triad of marriage, whether He is acknowledged or not. God created us for a relationship with Him and with each other. Our marriage is stronger if He is permitted to be part of it.

> *"...a threefold cord is not quickly broken."*
> — Ecclesiastes 4:12 NKJV

The intimacy of marriage is an example of the spiritual intensity that God desires to have with us. In Ephesians 5:22–30, the Apostle Paul parallels marriage to God's love for the church. We are to love as God loves. The desire for intimacy is a normal part of a spiritual connection between us and God. It seems to follow that as we desire more of God, we also desire a deeper relationship with our spouse. This deep Eros-sharing of one soul with another is possible only in marriage, and can only happen when God is in the center of it.

When the Holy Spirit comes into our life and not into our spouse's...something shifts. We may not know exactly what it is, but we know that something is different. Something is missing. We crave this love that God talks about in the Bible. That beautiful love story in the Song of Solomon shows us what intimacy with our Heavenly Father looks like. It also reminds us of when we first fell in love. It stimulates our imagination and our senses.

It's easy to question whether sex is always supposed to be a mystical, all-consuming event. We fantasize about reading the *Song of Solomon* to our lover in bed while we suck grapes out of their fingers! We might try to improve things by lighting scented candles and playing soft music in the background. As pleasant as our momentary pleasure may be, we are cognizant that things are not the way they should be.

When I began to question what the joint venture of Holy Spirit-inspired sex might be like, I sensed that I was missing some deeper connection in my own life. I asked myself, "Is it me, or does my faith interfere with my relationship in the bedroom? Maybe I just need to be filled with more of God." So, I threw myself into more learning, trying to gain a better understanding. But even though my spiritual knowledge grew, there was still something missing.

I finally realized that God designed us for relationship. We were created to love other human beings *with* the fullness of God. The spiritual barrier in our marriage can prevent that from happening.

When your partner-in-life doesn't share your passion for Jesus, you might sense a feeling of physical or emotional disconnection from your mate. Since you can't share this important part of your soul with your best friend, there is a depth to your marriage that is missing. The Holy Spirit wants to take your love deeper. For that to happen, both of you need to invite Him into the bedroom. But that isn't happening. It seems that Holy Spirit-inspired sex is an unfulfilled gap in our lives just waiting to be completed.

Have you ever discussed this with your spouse? Are they jealous of your relationship with Jesus? Does your relationship with Christ interfere in how your husband or wife sees you romantically?

Lee Strobel, in his book, *Surviving a Spiritual Mismatch in Marriage*, says that when his wife gave her life to Jesus, he was afraid that she would turn into a prude. Instead, the opposite happened. When he researched the correlation between sexual frequency, happiness, and religious identity, he discovered that Protestant women have the happiest and most sexually-fulfilling lives, and Catholic women were second. Other religions followed, and atheists had the least fulfilling sex lives.[35]

This information really surprised me, but it validated my belief that there is something incredibly romantic when God is involved in the bedroom!

Is this information too scary for our loved ones? Few people, in my experience, have the courage to talk openly about sex. It is well-known that having a successful and happy marriage includes having a good sex life. Communication about sex is important. But a dialogue about including Jesus in the bedroom might throw a curveball into your relationship that will result in a strike-out. So how do you deal with this intimate issue when you are on such different spiritual levels? After all, you don't want to come across as a prude!

If your spouse thinks that your religion means an end to sexual intimacy, prove them wrong! Just because they don't want the Holy Spirit in their life (yet) doesn't mean you can't invite your Heavenly Lover into your bedroom. Leaving Jesus in the living room is only going to be a reminder to you of what's missing. So, include Him.

Go into your prayer closet and start with prayer. Invite the Holy Spirit into your marriage. Ask Him to soften the heart of your earthly lover toward your Heavenly Lover. Ask Him to make you a receptive vessel to your spouse's affections. If you haven't tried this yet, I can guarantee that you will be pleasantly surprised at the results!

Learn to express your love creatively, and in a variety of ways. Inside the bedroom give as much as is asked for and more (within reason). Outside the bedroom touch frequently—whether it's holding hands, a peck on the cheek, or warm hugs. Give physical

---

[35] Lee Strobel and Leslie Strobel: Surviving a Spiritual Mismatch in Marriage, Zondervan, 2002.

and verbal acknowledgements of love, show them that you love their body, and that you want them to love yours. Say the words, "I love you," often. Think back to your newlywed days and try to recreate the things that you did back then.

You don't need money to do the simple things that can make a difference in someone's day, or to encourage growth in a marriage. The brain is the biggest sex organ in the body. Simple touches and a positive attitude encourage stress-reducing hormones to flow, and help to create an accepting and loving environment. When a person feels valued, and not just desired, they are naturally more sexually receptive. How a person starts and ends their day can make the difference between a great sex life and a non-existent one. If you want a good sex life, you need to keep negativity out of your life. Start your day with cheerfulness and end it with appreciation.

Stress reduction in marriage includes setting healthy boundaries. Organize your day well. Practice good time management to keep your own stress to a minimum. Stretch your communication skills by improving your listening skills. At home, show an interest in your spouse's personal and work life. Empathize with workplace stressors and difficult everyday situations. Listen intently and ask questions, but don't offer unsolicited advice. (Unwanted problem-solving can be interpreted as controlling behavior. This can be insulting or feel demeaning to others and may cause a communication wedge in your relationships.) Show respect and dignity in your conversations.

Healthy boundaries in the bedroom start with a welcoming environment. Keep this room clean and uncluttered. Prepare your bedroom for romance by getting rid of all distractions, such as the TV, the pets, and the kids' toys. A closed door to the master bedroom should have a rule of "Do not enter!" to everyone, except the two of you. Experiment with scented candles or essential oils. Soft music always makes for a romantic environment.

Pray before slipping into bed. Ask the Lord to make you a receptive vessel and to enhance your lovemaking skills. Yes, it's important to pray about your sexual encounters! After all, you never know what will inspire your earthly lover to want to get to know your Heavenly Lover.

Stress, Anger and Medical Issues

Honest communication and stress reduction is important. Never allow yourself to be pushed into sex if your body is saying no. Never go to bed angry and never have sex while you are angry. The day's stresses need to be left at the door. Forgiveness and acceptance needs to dominate in the bedroom. This is a sacred space and should be treated as such. While you seek to bring the love of Jesus into your home, your light needs to shine everywhere, especially in the most intimate place in your life.

Anger and negative stress are dangerous enemies that shut down the very chemicals in the brain that help you to relax. Frequent angry or stressful encounters before sex can cause long-term physical problems, in both men and women, that can require medical or psychological intervention. (This is especially relevant to those persons who have suffered physical or sexual abuse at any point in their life.)

For more information about the relationship between stress and sex, check out the article by Dr. Andrew Goliszek, PhD, in his blog, entitled *How the Mind Heals the Body: The Stress-Sex Connection—How to Prevent Stress from Ruining Your Sex Life.*[36]

---

[36] Psychology Today, December 22, 2014.
https://www.psychologytoday.com/blog/how-the-mind-heals-the-body/201412/the-stress-sex-connection

Beware of the Enemy's Deception

An unhappy sex life leads to dissatisfaction within the marriage. That unhappiness can lead to other destructive actions, such as affairs and pornography. A good sex life won't guarantee an affair-proof marriage, but it will help.

The enemy stands at our door waiting to steal our happiness, kill our goals, ruin our dreams, and destroy our marriages. He is incredibly deceptive. He will try to wedge his foot in by encouraging negativity in your relationship, and tempting you with promising offers of short-term alternative ways to soothe your bruised feelings. Temptations of pornography or illicit affairs surround both of you in the workplace, in your community, and in your home.

These distractions carry the goal of destruction. Affairs destroy everything in their wake...marriages, the children of those marriages, the extended families of those marriages, and eventually the very fabric of society itself. Pornography destroys intimacy by taking your focus off your spouse and putting an unrealistic image in your mind.

Pornography is incredibly deceptive. It is an addictive process that can never be fully satisfied. It starts small—gradually desensitizing you and building your appetite to want more—more in quantity and more explicit in details. Eventually, anything goes. Once the enemy is fully engaged in your bedroom, the most sacred intimate moments with your spouse are gone. Strangers are now present in your bedroom with the two of you. The porn stars have your (and your spouse's) attention. Instead of making love, sex becomes only a momentary physical act.

Today's sexually explicit society leads many to think that "spicing up your sex life" needs to involve pornography. Many Christians are going along with this deception. If you think a little porn won't hurt anyone, think carefully about the people who are portraying that activity on the screen. That person is someone's daughter…someone's son. Would you want your child performing sex acts for money? By purchasing such material, you are encouraging more sales.

It may surprise you to know that many of the people who perform in these videos are not doing so voluntarily. Pornography is modern-day slavery. Please take some time and read up on the horrifying realities of the sex-trafficking industry.[37] If you want to keep your marriage strong, keep this deception out of your bedroom, and out of your life. There are many other ways to enhance your lovemaking. Be creative, but keep your focus on your spouse, and encourage them to keep their focus on you, and you alone.

Keep your sex life active and happy. Nothing can ever fully guarantee that your loved one might not slip into an affair with someone else. You cannot control your spouse's decisions, but you can influence them for good. Take positive steps to encourage the love in your marriage to bloom and blossom over and over again.

In your personal life, keep your heart clean and keep your armor on. This will help you to be prepared for the enemy's attack. Know the Word, speak the Word, and practice the Word. If you struggle with sinful desires, confess and repent to the One who sees all. Repent quickly to keep the enemy at bay. You can overcome this. Don't let the enemy steal your marriage or your home.

If you or your spouse struggle with lust, I suggest reading the book, *Eyes of Honor*. In this excellent book, Dr. Jonathan Welton talks about how we need to understand who we are in Christ. Once we understand our identity, it's so much easier to guard and advance against the enemy.[38]

---

[37] See http://fightthenewdrug.org/the-internet-can-be-a-very-unsexy-place-we/
[38] Jonathan Welton and Graham Cooke: Eyes of Honor: Training for Purity and Righteousness, Destiny Image 2012.

For further information on the damage that pornography can cause in your life, review my earlier chapter on Differentiating Between Abuse and Persecution.

CHAPTER TWENTY-TWO

Mutual Friendships

Above all else, guard your heart, for everything you do flows from it. Keep your mouth free of perversity; keep corrupt talk far from your lips. Let your eyes look straight ahead; fix your gaze directly before you. Give careful thought to the paths for your feet and be steadfast in all your ways. Do not turn to the right or the left; keep your foot from evil.
— Proverbs 4:23–27 NIV

Marriage is a very special friendship. It implies a togetherness with a very intimate sense of belonging. It is a partnership that encompasses every aspect of our lives—legal, financial, and social. We expect the social piece to be the easiest, but sometimes it can be complicated.

In the beginning of our union we spend all our free time together. Each partner's personal friends are pushed to the background, while we concentrate on building the foundation of our joint future. Our circle of intimacy during this stage is very tight.

Gradually, as our relationship becomes more comfortable, that circle of intimacy begins to expand. Our family and friends once again have our attention, and we explore ways and means to socialize with them. During this time, we subconsciously or consciously evaluate the quality of our external friendships. One query is whether our friends will be included in only my circle, my spouse's circle, or in both?

The fluidity of life affects the ebb and flow of relationships. This is normal. It's a rare few that grow up in one neighborhood, and keep their childhood friends for their entire lives. An enviable few stay emotionally close to their own family members throughout life, but many don't. For most of us, we can count our friends on one hand. Perhaps only one or two fingers. How many friends do you have that you can call in the middle of the night? How many take your birthday seriously (not counting social media birthday notifications)?

Making lasting friendships is hard work, requiring consistent efforts of time and attention—the reality is that we often have too little of either to effectively forge new ties. Consequently, our circle of friends may remain small. It's easier to concentrate on the relationships we already have, than to make new ones. Our energy is spent on those that we value the most, and that value us in return.

As our life changes, our friendships change. New friends with common interests, ideals, and mindsets enter—replacing those who drift out. We seek allies in similar life stages to help us problem-solve our day-to-day crises. Families with children of the same age help each other with child-rearing issues. New retirees search out other new retirees.

Unfortunately, friendships can also be a source of conflict in our marriage. These bonds can easily end with one wrong word or action. Since we want deep-rooted relationships, we work to avoid conflict. We seek to establish life-long ties, even when people move away or change in other ways.

This ongoing search for like-minded companions is one reason why marriage is so important to us. Friends come and go, but the marriage friendship is a legal contract that enforces "forever together," and thereby provides us with a sense of stability and permanency. This is the one person who is invariably there for us—regardless of the situation. We count on them to keep our secrets, cherish our dreams, encourage us during difficult times, remember those special occasions, and consistently find time to make us feel special. This is the one we can go to with our tears and fears, joys and sorrows. This one person provides us with a sense of safety and security.

That is, until we get saved and they don't.

The Dilemma

At that point, a huge shift happens. A tremor causes a boulder to fall off our secure wall, breaching the boundaries. Both partners feel a threat to the safety level of this once-stable relationship. Will this tremor turn into an earthquake? How much damage will it do?

Our friendships become extremely vulnerable during this shift. Initially, the friends we shared together are still there, but people quickly learn that something has changed. Neither our spouse nor our old friends want to sit around and talk about Jesus, church issues, or religion. It's generally known that any subject, that is debatable or based on perception alone, is a potential target zone for conflict in a relationship. Politics and religion are two hot topics that can either cement or end friendships.

When you are a new Christian, it's tough not to talk about Jesus. You want to talk about Him all the time. It's hard to step out of that pink bubble that surrounds you. Our seemingly drastic personality change can trigger our non-Christian friends to drift out of our lives. They sense that we are not the same person that they used to hang out with. Perhaps we are no longer interested in the same activities previously enjoyed together. On top of that, we now have new Christian friends that we want to bring into our marriage and include in our larger coterie.

Introducing ardent Christian believers to our unbelieving friends might seem to be a great idea from our end. However, when the topic of Jesus or church arises casually between believers, your unbelieving friends feel awkward. They quickly pick up on your evangelistic fervor, so they work very hard to talk about anything but faith (unless they enjoy debating). They want to keep your friendship, but are not too crazy about your new choices in friends. They may feel rejected or pushed to the exterior walls of your life.

In this messy mix sits your spouse. They have friends too, often the same ones. They don't want to lose these friendships that have taken a long time to build. They too, are not interested in listening to you ramble on about your church or your Jesus. They find themselves in an awkward position of staying silent, or taking sides with their friends or unsaved family members against you. Conflict ensues. The blame for tearing the family apart or tearing friendships apart is placed solely on your shoulders. Their message is clear—they want you to drop this fanatical Christian religion pronto!

One answer to our dilemma may be a separated social arrangement of "your friends, my friends," with few friends that we both enjoy mutually. This arrangement can work when life is so busy that many social engagements can be pushed to the periphery. The key to making this work is mutual respect and honor. If I respect my husband in the choices he makes and the friends he chooses, then there is a greater chance that he will respect my friends and my choices as well.

Although your marriage can survive this arrangement, discomfort happens when these worlds collide.

Our unequally yoked marriage puts us in a very difficult dilemma. We want a safe, comfortable friendship circle with both Christian and non-believing friends, but we can't push aside our Christianity to make that work. In some Christian circles, having many non-Christian friends raises eyebrows about our level of spirituality. We struggle with the question, "Do we keep both feet planted on Christian ground, or, do we plant one foot in the world and the other in the Church?" In this marriage, it seems that our life requires the latter.

Keeping one foot in both camps is a balancing act that results in daily exposure to the sins of this world. Perversity and corrupt talk barks out from media entertainment, inundating our homes with a barrage of verbal and visual garbage. We want to speak out, but we don't for fear of offending our spouse, or being ostracized by our unsaved friends. Too often, we sit on the fence or give in and participate in activities, socializing in ways that are not God-honoring. Our conscience throws a wet blanket on the party and screams, "Hypocrite!"

We justify our actions by telling ourselves that relationships are more important than our participation in, or judgment of, "unholy" things or activities. After all, Jesus wined and dined with the lowest of sinners while spreading His Good News. Isn't showing love and hospitality the most important part of establishing the groundwork for sharing the Gospel? If I just shine my light, do I really need to say anything?

Salt and Light

Jesus said:

> You are the salt of the earth; but if the salt loses its flavor, how shall it be seasoned? It is then good for nothing but to be thrown out and trampled underfoot by men. You are the light of the world. A city that is set on a hill cannot be hidden. Nor do they light a lamp and put it under a basket, but on a lampstand, and it gives light to all who are in the house. Let your light so shine before men, that they may see your good works and glorify your Father in heaven.
> — Matthew 5:13–16 NKJV

If we are the salt of the earth and the light on the hill, then our job is to spread a message of hope and peace. We need to be the beacons of the lighthouses, inviting those whose lives are weighed down and surrounded by turbulent waves to a safe harbor. This safe place is Jesus, but we are often the first light, the first glimmer of hope that can direct them to that safe passage.

If this is how we want others to see us, then our example of Christ-like living must be evident. But that evidence can only be displayed through socially engaging with others. People need to see us and get to know us before they can begin to see Jesus in us. The unsaved cannot be attracted to a light that they never see.

One light that our unsaved friends see is how we live out our faith in our marriage. They may perceive our unequally yoked marriage as unbalanced and unstable. They may speculate about how two people can have a happy relationship when one person prioritizes faith and the other doesn't.

We must be cognizant that our marriage speaks for itself without words. Attitudes, tone of voice, words of endearment, physical contact, and actions of love—these all speak volumes about the state of our marriage. How I treat my spouse in the presence of others demonstrates how my faith gives me the strength to love despite differences.

One day I was at a friend's house, waiting to go out for dinner together. When the husband came downstairs after changing his clothes, my friend yelled at him about his choice in sports coat and ordered him to change. They began to argue. Their voices became louder and louder until she was screaming. The poor man hung his head, clearly embarrassed, then slipped past me to go change his coat. I was stuck in the room with nowhere to hide while they worked out their differences in front of me. It was an awful scene to witness. That situation changed my view of my friend and of their marriage.

I learned a valuable lesson that day. Be careful how you treat your spouse in front of others. People are watching.

Setting Boundaries

We all slip from time to time. We want grace from others when we do, as well we need to show grace to others when they slip. That is part of having healthy relationships with others. But when our buttons get pressed, it's easy to over-react. Sometimes we also over-apologize. Instead of holding ourselves to impossibly high expectations, we should look at our boundaries and shift them to where they are more manageable.

Doing the Christian–non-Christian dance to try to please everyone is exhausting and confusing. Regularly participating in potentially-compromising activities can open a gate for the enemy to pull you away from your faith. The questions swirl through your head. Can I participate in this activity or this conversation and still be a good witness? How can I keep everyone happy? How can I honor the Lord while having fun in a non-Christian environment?

Living a righteous life isn't easy when those around you don't. Sooner or later the spirit of offense arises. You will get blamed for the "lack of fun" in your home or social environment. Faith differences are powerful projectiles for people to throw around when things aren't going their way. They may argue that we are trying to impose our new belief system on them. It's easy to personalize this and assume the responsibility for everyone's happiness. We tend to feel guilty, because we are the ones who have instigated the change in our lives.

If our friends and family are offended because of something that we did or said—we must seek forgiveness. Most offenses are merely miscommunications that are easily rectified. We have all been both the recipient of, and the instigator of, offence. No one is immune to this.

We must remind ourselves that we are not responsible for the words that someone else speaks, or the thoughts that they think. We are all personally responsible for our own conduct, and the words that we speak. Although we all have choices in what we say and the actions we take, we must be sensitive to misperceptions caused by faith differences. In those cases, we need to put our faith in action, and give grace even though we may not receive grace in return.

Happy, healthy friendships require grace, and safe, healthy boundaries. Before you can establish boundaries, you must work out your own foundational beliefs of what is acceptable and what is not. Then you need to exercise that foundation by changing your attitudes and desires with the guidance of the Holy Spirit.

Take a serious look at your current situation and ask a few questions. How important are the changes that you are making? How will they impact others? What is the best way to implement this within your marriage and your friendships? Will setting strict boundaries in one area cause someone to refuse to listen to the Christian message?

Your marriage is the second most important relationship in your life (next to your relationship with Jesus). There will always be an impact, either positive or negative, every time boundaries are shifted.

Too often we nitpick about little things and miss the big picture. Sometimes, we are judgmental about others, because we are struggling in the very same areas. We focus on the speck in someone else's eye without taking "the log out of our own eye." This attitude destroys relationships.

Jesus taught about healthy relationships and bringing light to a dark world. Many Pharisees of the time lived religious lifestyles, filled with pride. Their self-serving attitudes not only stopped them from seeing the truth and light of Christ, but also destroyed relationships between them and others. Eventually, it was pride and rebellion that nailed Jesus to the cross—the same sins that infected the Garden of Eden. We need to keep those sins out of our life and away from our soul. Protecting our soul requires safe boundaries—not rigid walls built with pride.

When rules run our lives instead of the Holy Spirit, we develop a self-righteous attitude that includes self-justification. And it's a two-way street. Our unsaved friends are just as rigid and unwilling to make changes. They use justification to maintain their cancerous lifestyles. Rigidity is a sickness that creeps into the lives of Christians and non-believers alike. It's part of the human condition. Few people are open to looking at their lives and seeing the long-term effects of their destructive paths. They don't want to do the work that's required to become spiritually mature or to keep their relationships operating in a healthy manner.

When we try to implement too many rules too quickly, we end up alienating people, instead of attracting them to the Lord. Banning rigidity from our actions, attitudes and thought-life requires grace. Implementing grace in our lives means that we need to recognize that our loved ones are on different spiritual levels than us. Our focus must be on love and understanding. This requires grace and flexibility.

Without implementing grace and flexibility in our boundaries, we risk building walls in relationships. A wall is symbolic of a locked door. If you can't walk through an open, friendly door—you certainly won't be climbing the wall to get into that household. Only a thief climbs walls. Conversely, proper boundaries include doors that open and close effectively.

Effective boundaries require conscious management and decision-making. We must strategize for when someone or something attempts to breach them. In the middle of conflict, fear can paralyze us. Instead of doing something, we do nothing. Instead of broadening our perspectives, we narrow them. Then we think we are a bad Christian, because we can't live up to our own value system. We give up and keep our faith to ourselves and continue to live a gray world where anything goes.

Giving up means we struggle with delivering Christ's pivotal message of love in a diverse world. We need to view differences from God's perspective. God seeded a colorful garden of flowers and plants on this planet. Nature shows us how beautiful diversity is. People are just as varied as the rest of creation. Our differences are what makes us unique. God loves us for us, not because of what we do or don't do.

Jesus loved, and loves diversity. When He walked this earth, He accepted each person's uniqueness, but elevated them to a higher plane. He challenged accepted viewpoints and changed perspectives. He changed people's beliefs. He took the lowest of society and gave them dignity. Women were no longer property. The sick were no longer responsible for their illnesses. The socially unacceptable were redeemed.

Although Jesus ate and drank with socially-unacceptable sinners, He didn't participate in their sins. Jesus had boundaries. He showed grace to the spiritually different, by offering them a new way to live, while being in their environment. Even the self-righteous Pharisees received grace. This is how we are to live.

We don't need to participate in the unhealthy behaviors that others do, but to build and maintain relationships, we may have to go into some environments that make us feel uncomfortable. You can't build relationships by staying away from people.

A healthy person doesn't fill themselves up with bad food, or live in unhealthy environments. Living on different spiritual levels means we can't always choose the healthy environment that we want. We live with others who are not ready for pure living. But there are choices we can make. If television and movies are filled with foul language, sexually-degrading scenes, and violence, we don't have to watch them. We can demonstrate purity through our language, or quietly remove ourselves from offensive conversations, or change the topic. We can demonstrate a different way to live by starting a dialogue about "garbage in, garbage out."

Sometimes, that's all it takes for other people to start looking at their own lives.

Finding a Respectful Compromise

When you have decided where your boundaries need to change, explain this to your spouse. Admit that the two of you have different tolerance levels. Try to find common ground, or a realistic, mutually-acceptable compromise. If that isn't possible, be clear on your position. There may be times when you need to temporarily leave the room, or the house, or the social environment in question. Ask them for their support with your shared friends when you are entertaining or being entertained.

Sometimes setting boundaries may only require changing topics of conversation. Other times, it may require declining an invitation. Be clear that sitting on the fence to maintain those unhealthy friendships is not a spiritually-healthy option for you. At all times work to keep respect, honor, and dignity—between the two of you, and with your friends. Be clear about your boundaries without being offensive.

Finding and keeping couple friends requires dedicated prayer and wisdom. The enemy loves conflict, and he uses our opposing views to drive us apart and destroy relationships. But sometimes those same differences can also bring us together. Temptations will come, and arguments will happen. Friendships grow, change, and unfortunately, sometimes end. We can't always get it right. None of us are perfect. We will continue to grow and change until the day we die.

We need to be open and accepting of all who are attracted to the light of Christ within us. But we must keep our light on. If we are confused about what we believe, and we don't know how to stand up for righteous living—then our light will not shine, and our faith will not be taken seriously. The Bible warns about being double-minded.

*Those who depend only on their own judgment are like those
lost on the seas, carried away by any wave or picked up by
any wind. Those adrift on their own wisdom shouldn't
assume the Lord will rescue them or bring them anything.
The splinter of divided loyalty shatters your compass and
leaves you dizzy and confused.*
— James 1:6b–8 VOICE

Thankfully, our Savior knows what we need…when we need it.
Jesus was all about making relationships. He wants us to have
healthy, happy friendships and marriages. If relationships are our
priority, then we need to focus on common interests, rather than
disagreements. But we must not be codependent, or allow ungodly
behavior to dominate our activities, just so that we can keep a
friendship. We have our own spiritual health to think of.
Sometimes our job is just to plant seeds, and it is someone else's
job to water the garden. The harvest could be many years away.

Whether your friends are saved or unsaved, single or couples—
remember that everything you do and say reflects Jesus. Keep your
thought-life clean, be respectful with your words, and be careful of
what you see, hear, and do. Be a living example of Jesus in your
conduct and lifestyle.

*Any temptation you face will be nothing new. But God is
faithful, and He will not let you be tempted beyond what you
can handle. But He always provides a way of escape so that
you will be able to endure and keep moving forward.*
— 1 Corinthians 10:13 VOICE

*Love must be sincere. Hate what is evil; cling to what is
good. Be devoted to one another in love. Honor one another
above yourselves. Never be lacking in zeal, but keep your
spiritual fervor, serving the Lord. Be joyful in hope, patient
in affliction, faithful in prayer. Share with the Lord's people
who are in need. Practice hospitality.*
— Romans 12:9–13 NIV

CHAPTER TWENTY-THREE

Money and Tithing

"Bring the whole tithe into the storehouse, that there may
be food in my house. Test me in this," says the
Lord Almighty, "and see if I will not throw open the
floodgates of heaven and pour out so much blessing that
there will not be room enough to store it."
— Malachi 3:10 NIV

Money is a touchy subject in most marriages, and is known to be one of the top causes of divorce. Managing it is a skill that few master successfully. Without wisdom and foresight, it has the potential to destroy your life and your marriage. With proper planning, you can control it and have enough left over at the end of your working life to enjoy an early retirement or some lifelong travel plans.

In the unequally yoked marriage, money is often viewed through two opposing opinions. One says it is to be used for personal pleasure and a nice lifestyle. The other view says money is to be spent in God-honoring ways. How do we find a compromise that works for both?

Life has a price tag. How you live it determines how much it will cost. Enjoyment has nothing to do with money—it has everything to do with attitude. Put the two together and you have a happy and financially-successful life. At least that's the dream that we have been taught. The problem is, we often equate happiness with money, and we can't imagine life without it. Most of us have never lived in a ghetto or been so desperately poor that we didn't know where our next meal was coming from. We can't imagine poor people being happy. So, we develop a scarcity mentality, thinking that "If I keep all my money for my own needs, then I will have enough and be happy." Sharing something that we have worked hard for is scary. Sharing might mean that we won't have enough when we really need it.

As children, we are taught to share our toys and sometimes our clothes. We share our "things," but not our money. Money is ours, and ours alone. Dropping a dollar in the homeless man's jar is one thing, but making a conscious effort to regularly give away a substantial part of our hard-earned income is a whole different ballgame. In marriage, we learn how to pool our resources to pay the bills and enjoy life together. Marriage is all about sharing—our things, our children, our friends, and our money. Mutually, that is—agreeing together about where and how the money gets spent.

When we fall in love with Jesus, but our spouse doesn't—we face another dilemma. The church that we attend preaches financial responsibility toward social issues, and asks for commitments to maintain the church's commitments. Buildings need upkeep, church staff need wages, and full-time missionaries in different places around the globe can't do their job without support. It's not only time that the church wants from us, it's also money. How do we manage this sensitive topic without upsetting the apple cart at home?

Giving money away can be a contentious issue, especially if you are an average earner on a tight budget. If you are fortunate to be married to a kind and generous mate, who understands your compassionate need to help those less fortunate and give to your local church, then count your blessings. For the rest of us, the topic of "giving money to the church," requires a delicate conversation that invites confrontation. How can we be respectful and honoring, and invite respect and honor from the other side, when our viewpoints are polarized?

Many non-Christians see churches and pastors as greedy opportunists. They sometimes accuse them of taking advantage of the vulnerable who are already struggling to make ends meet. They notice poor people who can barely afford to feed themselves giving their last dollars to the church. They conclude that the church is manipulating its congregation.

What they don't see is the attitude of charity that is taught in the church…that encourages a more unified society. They don't see us feeding the poor, giving justice to the oppressed, and helping the helpless. They don't appreciate the teaching of spirituality—as an essential service—that inspires a kinder, gentler, and more peaceful society. They don't see this, because they don't want to look inside the church or listen to the message that is preached.

Our ability to deliver the message of the need for charitable giving means we, as Christians, need to understand the why and how of giving, and be ready to explain it to our marriage partner and anyone else who asks. So just in case you're not sure about this, let me give you a quick recap of what is heard from most pulpits.

The call to donate both time and money is based on Scripture, but there are differences in interpretive beliefs between congregations. Some churches believe strongly in tithing a fixed portion of one's income. Other churches feel that this is an Old Testament principle and people should give charitably from their hearts.

Biblically, the first record of tithing is when Abraham gave Melchizedek, the high priest, a tenth of the spoils of recent conquest (Genesis 14:18–20; Hebrews 7:2–10). This was long before the days of Moses, when the law was given. Regardless of whether you believe that giving 10% of your income is still required, or whether you believe that it is part of the old covenant and no longer relevant today, charitable giving is still a part of our foundation of faith. Paul said:

"Remember this: Whoever sows sparingly will also reap sparingly, and whoever sows generously will also reap generously. Each of you should give what you have decided in your heart to give, not reluctantly or under compulsion, for God loves a cheerful giver."
— 2 Corinthians 9:6–7 NIV

How much you give is less important than the attitude that you have when giving. Anything that you give should be given with an attitude of love, and a desire to support the spread of the Gospel, and to help the less fortunate—not because you are expected to give. The amount given should support your scriptural understanding and the compassion that the Holy Spirit imparts to you.

But how do you deal with this when you and your spouse don't agree? Respectful conversations take into consideration each other's viewpoints.

To do what is right and just is more acceptable to the Lord than sacrifice.
— Proverbs 21:3 NIV

God sees our heart. If our giving is going to create havoc at home, then keeping peace and witnessing through our attitude is more valuable than any financial contribution that is here today and gone tomorrow. We have an overwhelming mission at home that has the potential to bear valuable fruit for the Kingdom. Our relationships at home and our everyday connections need to be our focus.

If you have been feeling guilty about being unable to tithe or you think your small donations are inadequate, put an end to this feeling. The stress in your marriage isn't worth it. Keep praying about this. Are there ways you can financially contribute that will not interfere in the family budget? If you can't contribute financially, perhaps you can give your time or other resources.

What are some creative things that you can do to help raise money for the church?

In my community, many of the local churches have fundraisers, such as bake sales, community garage sales, and community dinners. The money raised often goes to specific mission projects. These types of events need volunteers. There are never enough volunteers to help. Consider contributing your time for these events.

Depending on how you pool and manage your resources at home, you may be able to tithe from your own income. If you don't work outside the home but you don't have to account for every dollar you spend, are you able to you contribute from your grocery fund or personal spending account without causing conflict in your marriage? If you are worried about running out of food at the end of the month remember this: Jesus made the two fish and five loaves of bread stretch to feed five thousand people (Matthew 14:17–21), so He can easily make your groceries last through the month.

A planned meeting to talk about donations is helpful and can include the details of where, when, and how much. You might want to request an optional amount for unforeseen needs that come up during the year. In some marriages, your income level and your country's tax laws regarding donations will impact your spouse's views on donating to various causes.

If I feel the need to make a large donation to a certain project, I sit down with my husband and discuss it. One year, there was a young girl who needed eye surgery, and there was a public plea from a Christian charity to help. I felt burdened to meet this need. After sharing the story, my husband agreed, and I was so excited that we could help together. The young girl regained her sight and is now studying at school with manageable vision. She has an optimistic future. I'm praying that this inspires her to bless others too. Minimizing the suffering of another life is an awesome privilege.

Contributing to the local church has not been as easy. My husband doesn't understand the financial need to spread the Gospel, or the responsibility to contribute to the general operation of the church building and the pastors' salaries. Thankfully, almost all churches have mission projects that also need financial support. This is usually an easier topic to discuss. I explain that donating to a local church for mission projects is much more cost effective (with considerably smaller overhead expenses) compared to global charitable organizations. In my case, helping the less fortunate around the world is often received with a more positive attitude than contributing to the church's general operational expense budget.

The following information might be helpful in your discussion with your spouse.

Churches and Christian-based organizations are generally more effective in meeting local community needs than large humanitarian organizations that publicly canvass for contributions. This is partly due to lower overheads and a reliance on volunteer labor.[39] Churches are already funded by other donations for general operational expenses. This allows them to give financial contributions directly to the missionaries working in the field. (You can verify this by reviewing your local church's financial statements.)

Missionaries often speak about how food purchased by money donated to the United Nations gets caught up in political red tape, or in the hands of rebel groups. Too frequently, food, money and medicines don't make it to the people that most desperately need it. The food sits on the ground and is eaten by rats while people starve.[40]Church aid groups have a reputation for getting around rebel groups and red tape. Due to small operations, money and

---

[39] For an example compare the Christian organization mcccanada.ca to cancer.ca
[40] Clifford D. May, Special to the New York Times, 17 May 1985
http://www.nytimes.com/1985/05/17/world/in-ethiopia-food-rots-on-the-docks.html?mcubz=3

supplies are often inconspicuously carried into the needed areas. The power of the Holy Spirit does amazing things in areas where the UN and other organizations can't or won't operate. The effectiveness of a Christian organization or a church's ability to reach the most desperate need, makes for a very compelling argument for where to donate your money.

Researching financial statements online can help you to make wiser decisions. Online charity watchdog sites can help you to research some charities' spending practices.[41] This doesn't mean that one organization is better than the other. However, transparency about where your money goes should be a key factor before you donate.

The subject of money can be difficult in any marriage, let alone in an unequally yoked marriage. If your spouse says no, honor that. There's no rule that you can't ask again the next time a need arises. They might change their mind. Your desire to give should not cause undue pressure in your marriage. There's enough pressure in your life already, so don't let this topic create hostile divisions between the two of you. Flip this topic the other way—wouldn't you want them to tell you if they're planning on spending thousands of dollars on something that interests only them?

As much as your local church needs your money, they also need your help. Don't feel guilty that you can't give as much as you would like. Just remember—it's God that you are serving—not your church, and certainly not your pastor. You don't have to prove your spiritual worthiness to your church or your pastor through financial contributions. God sees your heart.

I pray this gives you some peace of mind. As I mentioned earlier, there are other ways to help your local church. If you want to have a happy, healthy marriage, respect your spouse's feelings and be honest with them—especially about money. Honesty is always the best policy.

---

[41] An example of a charity watchdog site is www.charityintelligence.ca

CHAPTER TWENTY-FOUR

Co-Parenting

Jesus said, "Let the little children come to me, and do not hinder them, for the kingdom of heaven belongs to such as these."
— Matthew 19:14 NIV

All good parents have one common goal—to raise morally-healthy children. Although the definition of "morally healthy" may seem logical at first (i.e., not lying, cheating, stealing, etc.), parents differ in their understanding of morality and in the methods of teaching the specifics to their children.

For example, is a lie always wrong, or are there times when it's morally right to lie? Life isn't always black and white; often there are shades of gray. During the teen years, the struggle to identify right and wrong in the arena of sexual expression can create some very tense family moments. The nuances of differing levels of morality are a potential conflict zone between most parents.

Christian parents have a second goal—to raise spiritually-healthy children, who love God. This goal comes with the same decision-making conflicts of the morally-healthy goal. How each parent prioritizes Christian values in the home determines how this lifestyle will impact the children long-term.

In the unequally yoked marriage, we struggle with combining both goals while keeping peace in our marriage. Our marriage partner isn't focused on imparting Christian values to your children. They may not even know or care about those standards. This creates the possibility of an additional battleground. How can you convince your spouse that spiritually healthy is just as important as morally healthy? Can you design a mutually-agreeable parenting protocol?

Parenting is one big learning curve. Through trial and error, we make decisions today, that might not be practical tomorrow. Children change as they grow, and needs and rules must flex accordingly. Consistency is easy with only one child, but when the family grows to two or more little ones, you quickly discover that each child has a different personality.

This throws in another dilemma. Different rules for different personalities, combined with two different parenting approaches. As things change and children grow—we struggle through the confusion of the myriad of information coming at us, examining our inconsistencies, and hoping that we don't end up creating a disaster.

Our struggle may not be as much with our spouse, as it is our kids. Their sharp minds and quick wit leave us agape, and often embarrassed, while we struggle with genuine answers to their many questions or keen observations. When our minds go blank, we cough up something that we hope they will buy. But they can see through our hypocrisy, and often accuse us of inconsistency in our words and behavior. Their innate, competitive nature comes to the surface, as they discover the fine art of manipulation. Their goals switch between searching for truth and getting their own way. When Mom and Dad don't agree, they learn how to play one parent against the other, in order to meet their selfish agendas.

All human beings look for the easier, softer way to do life—whether it's earning money or attending church. It's just our human nature. We hate discipline. We are born stubborn and rebellious, and want our own way. Setting goals is work. Work is stressful. Setting long-term goals requires the ability to look at the bigger picture and aligning your objectives to meet your goals. Children are not able to do that, simply because they don't have the experience in life that we have. It's our responsibility to guide them and teach them the importance of healthy goal-setting.

The Groundwork

Our knowledge about how to raise children, how to treat our marriage partner, and how to communicate with others, comes from watching our parents. What we observe as children, we integrate into our value system. Those values form the basis of our actions and reactions. We assume that the relationships we see in our childhood home are normal, even though they may not be. Relationships may be good one day, and bad the next. This makes learning confusing, and can lead a child to believe that confusion is normal. Unfortunately, children cannot differentiate between good and bad relationships without guidance.

If we learn dysfunctional relationship patterns as children—we carry these patterns into our future marriages, our communication, and our parenting. To those of us who grew up with dysfunctional childhoods, we don't realize that we ourselves, are wounded people. When we form relationships and they go badly, we often have difficulty recognizing our own flawed behavior patterns. It's tough to look in the mirror and admit that we have imperfections. We are blind to our own blind spots!

We can't undo something that we don't understand. We need someone to show us where we need to change. Few people have the capability to be introspective to the extent that they can recognize their own dysfunctional paradigms and change them. Even when our negative patterns are pointed out to us, we buck the truth about ourselves. Instead, we tend to blame our failures on other people or circumstances, and refuse to make the changes needed to have happy and healthy lives.

Emotionally healthy families produce happy, well-balanced children. If we want our children to become successful adults, we need to give them the proper tools and provide the most positive environment for them to grow up in. This means modeling a happy marriage, in a home filled with love and good communication.

A happy, healthy home is not conflict-free. Conflict is normal and healthy. It's how that conflict is handled that's important. Positive conflict recognizes differences of opinion, and communicates respect and honor. Negative conflict shuts the door on resolution, and produces dysfunctional communication. If one person is not permitted to give their opinion, or think that they have not been heard, they will feel shut down. People have difficulty trusting someone who continually violates their feelings and refuses to listen to what they say. Trust is a conditional element in a relationship. When it breaks down, the relationship is damaged. Trust is very difficult to rebuild.

Maintaining an atmosphere of trust in our unequally yoked marriage means prioritizing respect for opposing beliefs. By doing this, we convey to our children that, although as parents we have differing opinions, we respect the choices that each parent makes. Sometimes those choices will produce conflict. That doesn't mean either person is better or worse than the other—we simply have different ways of looking at the world. When we work through our polarized viewpoints with healthy communication, children see healthy conflict management.

Christian Education

The home is the first place that children learn social norms and values. The second most influential environment is the educational system. However, these environments are also affected by mainstream media—including television and online entertainment. Each of these learning environments interplay, and either enhance or negate values learned through the other.

We live in a society that implies that there are no moral absolutes, provided we don't hurt anyone else. We can be what we want, and do what we want. Despite this, those who disagree with the mainstream media and liberal moral viewpoints, are considered the outsiders, and the cause of all that is wrong in the world. This hypocritical view confuses morality with human rights, and discounts the effect one's selfish lifestyle has on others.

In schools twenty years ago, it was unheard of to have metal detectors or grief counsellors on speed dial. Today, suicides, mass shootings on school grounds, and acts of terrorism have normalized high security. Media content is hypersexualized and the threat of child sexual abuse is very real. Children are no longer protected from violence. They are immersed in it. This is the world our children see as normal. How can one feel safe when fear is omnipresent?

A world without God is a world where fear enters, and threatens to control us and divide our families. When God is the center of our lives, the home is a place of safety. Fear is pushed away as love is embraced. On a personal level, we don't need to worry about losing control over our lives when we give up control to the King of Kings.

In the unequally yoked marriage, we have the daily dilemma of figuring out how to encourage others to give up control to this God that we trust. We want our loved ones to have the freedom from fear that only comes through a personal relationship with Jesus. If our spouse isn't ready for this, we still want our children to hear the Gospel message and have an opportunity to make this decision for themselves.

When children understand that there is a Power that they can tap into that is greater than themselves, they become confident and secure. Having Jesus in their lives helps them to overcome daily obstacles, and teaches them to focus on long-term goals. A spiritual foundation enhances positive moral decision-making. It is internal protection against the decay in morality that inundates our modern world.

Sadly, our modern world rejects Christianity—declaring our beliefs to be outdated, judgmental, restrictive, and in many cases, offensive. In the unequally yoked marriage, your spouse may be one of the nay-sayers of Christianity in your children's lives. How do you teach your children these truths when your spouse doesn't see this as important?

> *These commandments that I give you today are to be on your hearts. Impress them on your children. Talk about them when you sit at home and when you walk along the road, when you lie down and when you get up.*
> — Deuteronomy 6:6–7 NIV

As adults, we understand that developing good habits requires consistency. The intentional act of church participation encourages the development of a spiritual mindset. The easiest and best time to start this mental shift is when children are very young. Regular church attendance by the entire family helps to develop a committed lifestyle that infuses the home with good values. It is much more than a weekend activity.

Church activities for children provide discipleship, wholesome entertainment, and new friends. Most young children love the rich learning environment of Sunday School, or "Kids' Church," where they learn about Jesus through entertaining Bible stories, music, and games. Older children and teens can participate in church-sponsored recreational activities throughout the week.

It's generally known that teenagers are prone to dropping out of church. The subject of God may not be "cool" in their school, where peer pressure dominates. Growing in the things of God becomes boring unless it is accompanied by plenty of entertainment. Teens want to make their own decisions and form their own opinions. When pressured to attend, they quickly look for an excuse not to go.

Children mimic the adults around them. When the two most important adults in their lives are operating on different spiritual levels, children will want to copy the adult that seems to be having the most fun. If your spouse doesn't attend church with you, they want to know why they need to go. If Dad says it's not important to him or he has more important things to do (like cutting the grass or changing the oil on the car), they begin to question why they can't opt-out like Dad does.

This pivotal point will affect the child's spiritual future. It is important that parents prepare for this discussion time with consistent, well thought-out, and wise answers. The challenge comes when your spouse minimizes the value of Christian training. If you try to explain the importance of spiritual growth, and your spouse discounts your viewpoint or undermines your faith—the strife with your children will only intensify. You may feel that everything that you've done until now is all for naught. This is a battle that you don't want to lose.

Is there another strategy that might be effective?

Have you noticed that some parents who don't attend church, will send their young children to Sunday School anyway? Biblical teaching, such as the Ten Commandments and the "Golden Rule," are generally understood by most parents as important moral foundations in life. Sending children to Sunday School helps ensure that they will learn these truths and integrate them into their lives.

If the lessons learned at home are compatible with those taught at church, a consistent message is delivered. A consistent message increases the osmosis effect, whereby those ideals are incorporated into the value system of the child. The long-term effect increases the possibility of a virtuous adult. Perhaps your spouse can accept that the lessons of consistency and commitment taught by the act of regular church attendance, combined with the moral lessons learned in church, can accentuate good parenting.

In your discussions about the children's Christian education, you can encourage your spouse to explore the subject of faith for themselves. Perhaps if they can see this education in action, or hear the lessons taught, they might be inspired to learn more as well.

We can take comfort in the truth that no one goes through life without considering the possibility of a higher power or a God that rules the universe. At some point, everyone must make this decision.

> *For since the creation of the world God's invisible qualities—his eternal power and divine nature—have been clearly seen, being understood from what has been made, so that people are without excuse.*
> — Romans 1:20 NIV

People can fight the concept of religion all they want, but in their heart, they know that God is real. More commonly, they acknowledge the possibility of the existence of God, but may question which god and which religion is the real truth.

It's difficult to prove an experiential God when one hasn't experienced Him for themselves. It's like trying to prove the emotion of romantic love to someone who has never fallen in love. This is when frequent contact with other Christ followers is helpful in encouraging curiosity of the Christian faith. When someone sees positive changes in another's life because of Jesus, they will ponder this faith that we embrace.

If your spouse is openly hostile to church attendance and religious training—you will need to find creative ways to introduce Christianity to your children. You can do this through bedtime Bible stories, songs, or just general discussion when the opportunity presents itself. I am not advising you to openly defy your spouse, but only to educate in those areas where you do not have open resistance. Whenever possible, you want your spouse's agreement as to how to help your children explore the subject of faith.

Co-Parenting in a Secular World

Folly is bound up in the heart of a child, but the rod of discipline will drive it far away.
— Proverbs 22:15 NIV

Christian upbringing isn't going to be the only battle you will face as you co-parent with your unbelieving spouse. The arena of entertainment and expressive language will become front and center, as children grow into adolescents and learn to flex their personal boundaries. What they learn from their peers, they will eventually attempt at home. While you might be concerned at some of the choices your children are making—your spouse might laugh at the same thing, seeing this as a normal developmental stage. How can you impress your Christian ideals on your children when your spouse has differing values?

The discussion of right and wrong happens between most parents. In many homes, the definition of morality is related to the culture that the family is immersed in. If the educational and social environment says that it's perfectly acceptable for teens to date at sixteen; parents will be pressured to cave to that norm. That might not be acceptable in another neighborhood or a different culture.

Setting boundaries, in families where parents have differing moral values, can be challenging. In the unequally yoked marriage, the Christian parent wants to set boundaries and make moral decisions through the guidance of the Holy Spirit, which may be different than the socially-acceptable definition that the spouse understands. Whether it's deciding on an appropriate TV show, or setting policies on dating for teens—conflict is bound to arise.

Entertainment choices happen almost daily, and can be difficult to enforce or agree on. If you feel that certain sexual content, the level of violence portrayed, or the language displayed on the screen is inappropriate—but your spouse doesn't—then you have a conflict that needs to be resolved. Both parents need to understand that children absorb everything on the TV and the internet, interpreting what they hear and see as normal human behavior. Many TV shows exaggerate and make fun of a person's odd personality characteristics. This teaches children to make fun of others who are different from them. Do you or your spouse want your children to grow up with those values?

Sitting down with your spouse and discussing differences of opinion is the best first step. If this doesn't work, sometimes asking your children about their interpretation of what they are watching, and explaining how you understand it, can broaden your child's perspective of moral differences.

For example, I might say something like this: "I don't find this show funny. To me, it comes across as disrespectful to people who are different. I would be sad if my friends treated people like that." Or, "I find language like that distasteful and disrespectful. Can we talk about this?"

Left to their own choices, children will always gravitate to what is easiest and the most fun. They are unable to discern how this content will affect them down the road. They don't understand the osmosis factor. It's our job—as parents—to protect them from things that might negatively affect their perception of themselves, others or of the larger world.

Unfortunately, many parents don't know what's appropriate for a child's age level. Movie and television shows usually have age-appropriate ratings to guide parents in making entertainment decisions for their children. Age restrictions made by other authorities are often the easiest way to end many arguments.

When teaching morality to their children, parents really need to be on the same page. When that isn't possible, it's a good idea to ask yourself, "How important is it?" When you pray about this, ask for guidance in seeing all sides to this divisive problem. Check your own motives and think about the long-term effects before you enter the conflict zone. Our values may be important to us, but honor and respect of the very people we are trying to reach is a greater priority.

> *Train up a child in the way he should go, and when he is old he will not depart from it.*
> — Proverbs 22:6 NKJV

In parenting, the fruit of what you are striving for is rarely seen immediately. It can take two or three decades to reach maturity.

If you plant a fruit-bearing tree, you expect that it will eventually produce fruit. But a tree that not has not been pruned properly, will produce suckers that literally suck the life out of the tree, and prevent good fruit from developing. A pruned tree still produces fruit, but the sweetness of the fruit depends on the strength of the root system and your dedication in nurturing the tree. If you don't follow through consistently, you won't get the fruit that you desire.

Children will learn what you teach them, and they will integrate some type of spiritual values into their lives. What those values look like will depend on which parent had the biggest impact. We must strive to be a positive example of a life glorified by Christ in our homes and our day-to-day lives. If you do the best that you can, God promises the long-term results will be worth all the work that has gone into your efforts.

When we confront our family members about moral dilemmas, there is one piece of information that we need to keep in mind— our non-Christian family members will often accuse us of being religious, self-righteous and hypocritical. We need to be careful about how we approach these conflicts, so that even if they accuse us of those things, they will still respect us for standing up for what we believe is right.

Family Counseling

Many parenting conflicts are about value differences between parents. Entertainment is only one example. Peer friendships, choices in clothing, or dating relationships may be some of the more obvious issues. But even bedtime and homework create conflict. If the home environment is consistently negative or tense, everyone is unhappy. It may be time to seek out a family therapist.

A family counselor can encourage both parents to articulate differing concerns, and assist in incorporating effective and enforceable boundaries. They can help your spouse understand that your belief system benefits the moral and spiritual development of the children. At the same time, they can see your blind spots and help you understand the bigger picture from their perspective. If the children are manipulating your differences to their advantage, a few sessions with a Christian family counselor can help to stop the division in your home, and the pitting of one parent against another.

When children enter their teen years, life becomes even more complicated. The sexual development of teenagers can be a difficult time for parents. This is another touchy subject that needs consensus between you and your spouse. This can be difficult if one spouse has very liberal ideas about teenagers and sexual development, and the other does not.

The subject of delaying sexual gratification is often seen as old-fashioned in our modern world. However, there is plenty of information (in both secular and Christian literature) as to why sexual activity outside of a loving marital relationship is not mentally, physically, or spiritually healthy. If you and your spouse can't agree on some mutual values and how to maintain respectful boundaries during this difficult stage of adolescent development—get help from a qualified family counsellor, so that you can enter this battleground from the same point of view.

Keep in mind that children model what they see. Their primary learning comes from watching you. Your marriage is the model that they will use when they grow up, get married, and have children. A loving relationship between parents with respectful guidelines, good communication, and genuine affection—is the best example. We all want our kids to be more successful than we were, to have better marriages than we had, and to be better parents than we were.

This information may seem logical and generic to you, but if your spiritually-different spouse has a laissez-faire attitude toward parenting in these sensitive areas, the inconsistency in your home will affect your children's future. As you pray for your spouse's spiritual growth, pray also for harmony in your home. Then strive to do everything you can to introduce Christian values into every facet of your child's development. Ensure you do this without strife, as the Holy Spirit gives you guidance.

Finally, remember that there is a spiritual war going on for your children's souls, as well as your spouse's. Be diligent. A good book to help you is *Devil! Get Your Hands Off: 6 Strategies to Snatch Your Kids Out of Deception* by Cathy Coppola. (Amazon: ISBN #1530872081)

CHAPTER TWENTY-FIVE

━━◆━━━━━◆━━

Taking Care of Yourself

Finally, my brethren, be strong in the Lord and in the power of His might. Put on the whole armor of God, that you may be able to stand against the wiles of the devil. For we do not wrestle against flesh and blood, but against principalities, against powers, against the rulers of the darkness of this age, against spiritual hosts of wickedness in the heavenly places. Therefore, take up the whole armor of God, that you may be able to withstand in the evil day, and having done all, to stand.
— Ephesians 6:10–13 NKJV

L iving on different spiritual levels in the unequally yoked marriage is complicated and exhausting. Do you feel that you are always being watched, but never doing the right thing? Are faith differences the primary problem in your marriage—or just symptoms of deeper issues? Maybe you are aware of other problems, but sorting them out or getting help seems impossible.

I wish I could give you a checklist to help you identify things more specifically. Difficult relationships often have more than one problem area that needs help. Unfortunately, faith differences can color so much of our lives that it can be hard to pinpoint what else is inside that tangled ball of stress. In this book, I've attempted to give insight into some of the more common issues. You've probably noticed that I've spent considerable time talking about changing ourselves and being aware of how we impact others.

Wearing a breastplate of righteousness, the belt of truth, and the shoes of peace—directly impacts on our relationships with others. The helmet of salvation and the shield of faith, encourages our relationship with Jesus. The sword of the Spirit, helps to defend us against attacks of the enemy. While all of this helps to strengthen our spiritual walk, putting on our armor isn't as easy as putting on a coat. We also must learn how to use our armor. That takes time, patience, diligence, motivation and vigilance.

Vigilance in conduct builds righteousness, but without the Holy Spirit, we are only building religious walls. Our motives need to be pure and built through love. This love can only come through intimacy with our Heavenly Father. The more time we spend with Him, the stronger our armor becomes. A strong armor helps us to repel the negative forces that threaten to sabotage our lives. How we stand in our trials sends a message to the world of how powerful our God is.

An activated armor gives us the healthy guidance that we need in our relationships with others. It also fortifies our soul and spirit and gives us the strength to get through those tough times.

> *My help comes from the LORD, who made heaven and earth!*
> — Psalm 121:2 NKJV

God is ready to help us when we need Him. He also expects that we do our part. A relationship is a two-way street. If we want to have a healthy relationship with the Lord, we must do our part to encourage it. As He has given to us—we must also declare His love by giving to others.

Everything we have comes from the Lord. We celebrate the gifts that He has given us by taking care of them. That includes our spouse, our family, our friends, and *ourselves*. If we don't take care of our spouse or our family, our relationships will deteriorate and possibly die. If we don't take care of our friends, they will disappear from our lives. If we don't take care of ourselves, we will deteriorate and be unable to accomplish the tasks that God puts before us.

The Body

As Christians, we know that our physical body is only one part of who we are. Taking care of our bodies is an easy thing to understand, because we can see ourselves with physical eyes. We know from personal experience—that when we exercise, eat right and get enough sleep—we feel better. Taking care of our bodies helps us to think clearer and make better decisions. In turn, that helps us to be better marriage partners and better parents.

It's never too late to start living a healthier life. If you don't eat properly, start now. Learn all you can about healthy eating to build up your body and get the maximum benefit from it. If you don't exercise regularly—start now. Strengthen those bones and muscles before they weaken and start to cause pain. If you don't sleep properly—start a proper sleep regimen now. Get a sleep assessment to help you understand where your problems lie. If stress is interfering in the ability of your body and mind to function properly—get some help to get it under control.

Take care of your body so that it can take care of you.

Body, Soul, Spirit

What about the rest of us?

We are after all, spirit, soul and body, created in the image of God (Genesis 1:26–27). We are triune beings. The Bible is clear that there are three distinct parts of who we are.

For the word of God is alive and active. Sharper than any double-edged sword. It penetrates even to dividing soul and spirit, joints and marrow; it judges the thoughts and attitudes of the heart.
— Hebrews 4:12 NIV

God speaks to our soul, spirit, and our body. Since He differentiates between all three levels, we must learn to understand the distinctiveness of each. If we can define health on each level of our being, we can nourish and strengthen each part, according to its needs. We can make ourselves sick by allowing sin or negative influences into our lives—or we can make ourselves healthy by flooding our lives with the light of God's Word, positive influences, wise decision-making, and right-thinking.

The Soul

Our soul is the heart of our being—containing our thoughts, emotions, and our character. It is the unseen part of us that is beyond the obvious physical traits of the body. It is this part of our being that attracts others to us, or repels them from us. Since our soul works in conjunction with our mind to make decisions, it contributes to the health of the body and the mind. When people use the term "emotional well-being," they are talking about the state of our soul.

Our soul absorbs information from everything and everyone that we connect with—whether good or bad. Consequently, it is easily contaminated by sin. Do you remember my explanation of how children learn by osmosis? We don't stop learning that way when we become adults. God teaches us new things as we grow older and more mature. We are learners by nature. We only stop learning when we refuse to change.

Refusing to change, is to fight against the natural state of who God made us to be. This is unhealthy. We must be willing to change in healthy, positive ways, that build us up and make us better people.

An unhealthy soul state has profound implications. For example, negativity is a state of the soul that can contaminate the body, and cause illness and dysfunctional relationships. A negative mindset is not only sinful, it attracts more sin. This is the scary part about sin. Temptation leads us down the wrong path...luring us into destruction. Then, once we commit one sin, we make excuses for it. Then we fall into a destructive sinful pattern. Our souls become contaminated and sick.

Helping our soul heal from destructive patterns requires repentance. The word 'repentance' can be defined by "turning around" by changing your thinking, words or actions.[42] Repentance is a conscious act. When we repent to God, He has mercy on us, cleansing our soul.

The blood of Jesus saved us from eternal destruction when we recognized our need for Him, repented for our sins, and invited Him into our lives. Although this act ensures eternal salvation, it doesn't mean that we can do whatever we want, whenever we want. We still need to willingly repent for any sin that enters our lives and strive to live righteously.

> *What shall we say, then? Shall we go on sinning so that grace may increase? By no means! We are those who have died to sin; how can we live in it any longer?*
> — Romans 6:1–2 NIV

Taking care of our soul and spirit means that we must consciously and deliberately live a lifestyle that honors God and exemplifies the Christian life. If we call ourselves Christians, then we must be seen to be Christ followers. We are to be salt and light to a dark world. Keeping our soul healthy should be just as deliberate as keeping our physical body healthy.

A positive mindset encourages a healthy soul. The Bible says:

---

[42] See www.gotquestions.org/repentance

A happy heart makes the face cheerful, but heartache crushes the spirit.
— Proverbs 15:13 NIV

If our mind is negative, our soul is unhappy, and our spirit is also grieved. Grief disrupts channels of communication, and can prevent us from connecting with others.

Likewise, sin disrupts our ability to hear the voice of God, and to commune intimately with Him. The channels of communication with Him must be kept open. We can't hear His voice if we are continually sinning or ignoring this vital relationship. Our spirit needs to remain open to the Holy Spirit.

Our Spirit

Our spirit is the part of us that communes with God, the angels, and the spirit world outside of our physical awareness. Keeping a healthy soul involves making those decisions that encourage our spirit. The book of Job speaks of the impact of grief on our soul and our spirit:

> *Therefore, I will not restrain my mouth; I will speak in the anguish of my spirit; I will complain in the bitterness of my soul.*
> — Job 7:11 NKJV

This verse refers to the interaction of all parts of our being. If grief (physical) gives into bitterness (soul), our spirit is also anguished. We can counteract this downward spiral, with praise and worship, and intimate time with the Lord. This helps us to develop an attitude of gratitude, even in our darkest hours. Thankfulness, praise and worship—invigorate our spirit, encourage our soul, and give us the physical and emotional strength to carry on.

One of the most difficult lessons that I learned in my life was when I gave in to depression. It grabbed ahold of me and took me into a very dark place for a long time. Climbing out of that deep dark pit took a lot of grit and much prayer. When I threw myself at the Savior's feet, He gently picked me up and helped me to stand again. I was very bruised for a long time, but eventually I healed. To receive my healing, I needed to do my part. That included repentance (to God, others and myself), praise and worship to encourage my spirit to open to the light of Christ, and intimate time with the Lord to feel His healing arms around me.

Intimacy with the Lord opens our spiritual ears to His voice. Without that intimacy, we have difficulty discerning the voice of the Holy Spirit from the voice of the enemy. If we can't tell who is talking to us, setting boundaries against negative influences will be a struggle. We must guard against those things that would take us down the wrong path.

Guard Your Heart

> *Above all else, guard your heart, for everything you do flows from it.*
> — Proverbs 4:23 NIV

Guarding our heart refers to our thought-life and attitudes that form part of our soul. The decisions that we make, help to shape our character, which affects our personality.

Our heart is the decision-maker that determines which direction we are going to take physically or spiritually. Too often, we make spontaneous and unwise decisions with our mind and emotions, that are not healthy for our bodies. Guarding our heart takes on a physical dimension when you consider the necessity of a healthy heart to have a healthy body.

Since we are triune beings, we can interpret verses like this on all three levels. Guard your heart: 1) Take care of your physical heart—exercise, healthy diet, etc.; 2) Take care of your spiritual heart—the soul—guard what enters your mind through thought and the portals of the senses—seeing, hearing, smelling, tasting, touching; and 3) Take care of the heart of your spirit—your relationship with God.

How do you take care of your relationship with God? By building your faith through prayer, fasting, reading, and hearing the Word. Then, by acting on what you learn, and implementing that new knowledge into your life. Finally, positive and frequent contact with your Christian family strengthens your faith through the encouragement and love that we show to one another.

We are not in the world alone. We are connected physically and spiritually to others. The health of those connections depends on us. We must look in the mirror and examine ourselves for unhealthy patterns, and be willing to change. Our reflection to others must be so attractive that it invites others to find Christ.

Life in the unequally yoked marriage is complicated, confusing, and difficult. Every facet of our life is subject to spiritual compromise and deception. Standing up for our beliefs takes courage, discernment, and daily prayer. We need to keep ourselves in a state of spiritual readiness—a safe place of rest in the Holy Spirit away from the front lines of the battleground whenever possible.

Our spiritual and cultural backgrounds shape the way we interact and communicate with one another. Sadly, our attitudes, pride and rebellion often get in the way of God doing His work in our relationships. We need to maintain an attitude of humility and forgiveness, being willing to repent to the Lord, as well as to our spouse and others in our lives. Sharing our faith can often be as simple as keeping an attitude of love.

> *Bear with each other and forgive one another if any of you has a grievance against someone. Forgive as the Lord forgave you. And over all these virtues put on love, which binds them all together in perfect unity. Let the peace of Christ rule in your hearts, since as members of one body you were called to peace. And be thankful.*
> — Colossians 3:13–15 NIV

CHAPTER TWENTY-SIX

---◆━━━━◆---

It's Your Journey

For you created my inmost being; you knit me together in my mother's womb. I praise you because I am fearfully and wonderfully made; your works are wonderful, I know that full well. My frame was not hidden from you when I was made in the secret place, when I was woven together in the depths of the earth. Your eyes saw my unformed body; all the days ordained for me were written in your book before one of them came to be.
— Psalm 139:13–16 NIV

Psalm 139 explains God's unique and creative design for us. The miracle of life is the same—whether we are believers or not. Everyone is conceived with the assistance of the spark of life that comes from the Holy Spirit. Every human being on the planet is written on the palm of the Father's hand and He loves each of us equally (Isaiah 49:16). Yet, the design of each person is unique.

The essence of creativity means differences. We see the evidence of God's creativity all around us, evidenced in nature. Just look at the varieties and colors of flowers, trees, animals, even fish. Even the geology of our earth is complex. A rainbow of colored jewels lie encrusted within multi-hued layers of rock.

God loves diversity and sees all things as beautiful. In the beginning, He observed His creation and "...it was very good!" (Genesis 1:31). Human beings are just as diverse in their appearance and personalities as all other forms of life...and we too, are good!

Despite our awareness that we are diverse creations—we expect that others will think like us, feel like us, and have similar experiences to ours. They don't. Each person is a unique and exquisite creation, exploding with beauty. Each person walks on their own perplexing trail that is contained within the Creator's blueprint. But God does not dictate which pathways we must take. Each person can manipulate those pathways to their own desires. This part of our creation is called "choice."

As we choose the roads most suitable to our liking, we traverse among varied scenery—sometimes alone—but more often alongside others. As we connect with fellow travelers, we compare travel maps. Temporary layovers (called friendships) give us glimpses into others' lives. If we are paying attention, we notice that every person is at a different stage in their expedition. Some are similar, but there are interesting routes with twists and turns on each map that are different from ours.

We experience both pleasant and rocky trails on our journeys. Often our challenges distort our view—putting us in deep valleys, turbulent waters, or breathless snow-capped mountains. Sometimes, the road is bumpy and painful, and we want to scream for it to be over. Often, we need help to get through the most difficult of chasms. The long road cries for a perfect ending that seems to be out-of-our-reach in this lifetime. We look for someone who can share our viewpoints and our burdens.

Our attitudes alter our viewpoints, and our burdens change the colors of our sunrises and sunsets. It's easy to look back and see the valley we climbed through, but not so easy to see around the next mountain.

As we travel, we drag our old baggage with us, and pick up new baggage on each adventure. We carry baggage that's chipped, broken, dented and warped. When we bring that baggage into this adventure we call marriage, we present it to our spouse as a gift. Then we often find out too late that it doesn't match with our partner's bags. We thought it did, until we took the wrapping off. Our present to our spouse isn't a gift of our future, it's a recycled affair of our past.

The journey of marriage begins as a rose-colored experience. There are always surprises after marriage—some good, some not so pleasant. Our success depends on what we've learned before we're joined, how we've integrated that learning into our lives, our ability to problem-solve, and how adaptable we are to change.

Lessons learned come from discovering how to recycle and repurpose pain to give our lives new meaning. These lessons shift our perspectives and shape our relationships. As we search for ways to make our differences fit compatibly, we establish our own rhythm and routine.

When children enter the relationship, a whole new dynamic happens. Once again, the world becomes very complicated and challenging. Our paths broaden as children grow up and leave home. Further changes in our life-journey continue during the next phase of grandchildren, retirement, and aging.

Entering a relationship with the Lord is much like a physical marriage. You never really know what it's going to be like until you make that final commitment. We enter this journey unprepared for all the ups and downs that we will experience. Our travels with Jesus are new explorations into the mountaintops and valleys of life with a Partner that never leaves our side. He romances us with new revelations and comforts us with the ultimate security blanket.

As we engage with our Heavenly Lover more and more, our knowledge increases and our love goes to new depths. Our swim with the Lord is often in a murky ocean with many surprises. That pristine beach is a beautiful promise, but sometimes, it feels more like an illusion. We don't receive all our knowledge at once. When we think we finally have it all it figured out, then—wham! A new piece of information throws us into an entirely new direction. Life is full of surprises!

We have no idea what we are going to look like, think like, or understand when this tour is over. Our spiritual understanding at the end of our life will probably look very different from the spot we are standing on right now. Like the roots of a tree, we are constantly growing, even if we can't see it ourselves.

When we return to the arms of God after our pilgrimage into the destructive ways of the world, we are welcomed with royal robes of love and a crown of purity. We take our place in the royal family only to discover that our earthly family doesn't want to follow us down this path to our eternal home. It's discouraging to realize that some people want to hang onto dented baggage and hideous travel clothes.

We desperately want to shout the exhilarating message of unconditional divine love and eternal life to everyone—especially our most dearly-beloved family members. We want to scream, "I found it, I found it, I found the pearl in the oyster and it's the most beautiful pearl ever!" But the unbeliever can't possibly know the joy, the love, and the intimacy that goes on between a Spirit-filled believer and Jesus Christ. Like a person who has never been in love, you can try to explain it in a million different ways, but it doesn't make any sense until they experience it for themselves.

Just like no two people have the same marriage, no two people grow in their relationship with the Lord at the same speed or depth. When we fall in love with Jesus but our spouse doesn't, our life suddenly becomes unbalanced.

We usually have no preparation for what we are going to face when we bring the presence of our Savior into our marriage. We can introduce this incredible gift to our spouse, but if they reject Jesus, we too feel rejected. It's not much different than giving them a beautiful piece of jewelry only to notice that they refuse to wear it, using the excuse that it's too beautiful and they don't want to lose it. As believers, we too can be afraid to show off our new gift of salvation, fearing what others might think of us.

The offer of the gift of a new birth to our unbelieving spouse is like a difficult pregnancy. The process of growth and awareness may be uncomfortable or difficult. Some births are more painful than others. Some pregnancies produce children with mental and physical difficulties, and other pregnancies produce the perfect child. Some pregnancies, sadly, produce no child.

All the work that we do in our marriage can have either a wonderful ending or a disappointing one. There are no guarantees. The fact is, we don't know what that end will look like. We don't have spiritual ultrasound that can detect the progress that is going on in someone's heart. This is where trust and faith come in.

Just as there are limits to how much a pregnant woman can affect the growth of the child inside her body, we can't change our spouse's spiritual growth. We can nurture it with kindness, love, and intimacy. We can shine our light as brightly as we possibly can. But just as a baby doesn't arrive until it's ready, our spouse won't come to Jesus until they are ready. They must go through the pain of childbirth themselves. Our wishes won't make it happen sooner or easier, but we can be there to celebrate the arrival when it happens.

While you are waiting for that spiritual birth to arrive—take care of your spouse. Love them, cherish them, respect and honor them. Demonstrate the love of Jesus every day. Never hold a grudge. Always forgive. Be the light of Jesus that shines and keeps on shining. Be the gift that keeps on giving. Do the impossible. Love when it feels impossible.

Continue in your own journey with the Lord—regardless of whether your spouse decides to join you. Carry your quiver of spiritual weapons to fight the evil that confronts you, and hold your shield of faith up high to deflect the enemy's arrows. At times, you may feel lonely and burdened with dented baggage, but keep your focus and stay on the path. As a warrior of God, you have the protection of an army of angels. They continually watch over you and if you stumble, they are given the mission to keep you from harm (Psalm 121; Psalm 91).

Afterword

I pray that you have been encouraged by my hard-learned lessons of faith that I have shared in this book. I hope that I have given you some powerful and useful tools, and that your faith has been strengthened in knowing that you are not alone. As sisters and brothers in the body of Christ, we are one. We suffer together. We also need to encourage one another.

Please don't fight this battle alone. There are people who can hold your hand and help you walk this difficult journey. My first command from the Lord before writing this book was that we are to "Pray *with* each other, pray *for* each other, and pray *for* each other's unsaved spouses." We have an incredible mission field, and we face seemingly insurmountable obstacles. Even though we sometimes feel insignificant, we are *not* walking this valley alone. The very fact that you are in this battle and you haven't quit means that you are courageous! God honors your fight, and His warrior angels stand beside, in front of, and behind you...and fight *for* and *with* you.

Above all, stay strong and stand tall! Remember:

> *You are of God, little children, and have overcome them, because He who is in you is greater than he who is in the world.*
> — 1 John 4:4 NKJV

I'm sure you are curious to know how things turned out for my husband and me.

In the year that it took me to write this book, the person that changed the most was me. As I changed into a more loving, giving and forgiving person, I noticed subtle changes in my husband as well. Changes that included a more thoughtful attitude, and a desire to resolve differences. These changes have helped to improve our relationship. Although he does not acknowledge any overt desire for spiritual growth, he watches some Christian movies with me and occasionally attends church with me. He rarely engages in faith-based discussions, and he continues to avoid friendships with Christians. But it's the little things that have changed that give me hope for the future. Your prayers for both of us would mean a lot to me (and hopefully, as well, to him one day).

If you have been encouraged by this book, please recommend it to someone else. If you have questions about anything that I have said here, feel free to email me via my website at mirandajchivers.com.

With love and hope,

Miranda

Thank you for buying my book.

Your thoughtful review on Amazon helps others to find this book. I am extremely grateful for every comment. Thank you so much.

Do you want the free workbook? Click the link on my website: https://mirandajchivers.com

If you want to learn how to hear from God, check out the courses at the Christian Leadership University. Here is the link: www.cluschoolofthespirit.com?affiliates=84

Discover how you can write and self-publish your own book: *Go here: https://xe172.isrefer.com/go/curcust/mchivers*

Appendix

———◆———

Definitions of Abuse

H ere are the technical definitions of the various types of
abuse.[43] If you find yourself in one of these situations, please
get help. Every city, and most towns, in North America have a
shelter where you can get help and stay if you need to. Your local
police or your family doctor will help you to locate a shelter if you
cannot do so yourself. Never put yourself or your children in
harm's way. Silence always encourages more abuse. Speak out to
someone and don't stop speaking until you get help.

The United Nations defines violence against women as:

"Any act of gender-based violence that results in, or is likely to
result in, physical, sexual or psychological harm or suffering to
women, including threats of such acts, coercion or arbitrary
deprivation of liberty, whether occurring in public or in private
life."

This violence can include:

---

[43] Source: http://www.canadianwomen.org/facts-about-violence#WHAT

- Physical abuse: Slapping, choking, or punching her. Using hands or objects as weapons. Threatening her with a knife or gun. Committing murder.
- Sexual abuse: Using threats, intimidation, or physical force to force her into unwanted sexual acts.
- Emotional or verbal abuse: Threatening to kill her (or to kill the children, other family members or pets), threatening to commit suicide, making humiliating or degrading comments about her body or behavior, forcing her to commit degrading acts, isolating her from friends or family, confining her to the house, destroying her possessions, and other actions designed to demean her or to restrict her freedom and independence.
- Financial abuse: Stealing or controlling her money or valuables (particularly concerning to older women). Forcing her to work. Denying her the right to work.
- Spiritual abuse: Using her religious or spiritual beliefs to manipulate, dominate, and control her.
- Criminal harassment/stalking: Following her or watching her in a persistent, malicious, and unwanted manner. Invading her privacy in a way that threatens her personal safety.

Acknowledgements

Thank you to all who helped to make this book possible. To the Holy Spirit, who nudged me to write this book, and gave me the words as I needed them.

To Dr. LaNora Morin and Fountain of Life Christian Fellowship, for encouraging me to dig deep for spiritual riches.

To Dr. Mark Virkler, for teaching me how to hear from God.

To Cathy and Michael Lowdermilk, for being my inspiration.

To my friend Martine, who kept encouraging me to listen to God and not people.

To Victoria and George Bridgeman, who taught me things that no one else could and continually keep me in their prayers.

To my family, who had no idea what I was writing about and do not understand the subject matter of this book. I pray that one day you will understand.

To my husband, who quietly suffered and went without a wife while I struggled through the birthing pains of this project. Even though we walk on different spiritual levels, you still believe in me. Your loyalty to me inspires me in my Christian walk.

To Chandler Bolt and the helpful staff at SPS, without your writing program I would never have been able to accomplish this difficult task.

To my editors, Miranda Regan—for teaching me so much; and Jonathan Puddle—for picking up the pieces. To my copy editor and proofreader Karen Haukedal, who *voluntarily* took on this huge task when my eyes failed. To my Beta-readers—Author Chris Lambert and Author Meredith Swift—your advice and questions were so helpful. Above all, you inspired me with confidence to publish this book. Thank you so much

About the Author

Miranda J. Chivers [B.S.W., R.S.W (ret.), R.R.P.(ret.)] is a retired social worker, entrepreneur, brain injury survivor and PTSD survivor. She was born in rural Manitoba, Canada to Mennonite parents. An inquisitive and tenacious child, she left home at age of sixteen. A life-long fascination with the human condition and a deep desire to find truth compelled her to continue exploring the teachings of Jesus. In her later years, she discovered the love and power in the Trinity.

She married her first husband at the age of nineteen. Together they raised two children. The challenges of raising an autistic and cognitively challenged daughter, a severe financial crisis, and an abandonment of faith, eventually contributed to their divorce. She later remarried an airline pilot, the father of two daughters, the eldest having Down Syndrome.

During Miranda's fifteen-year career in social work, she pioneered a PTSD desensitization program for motor vehicle accident victims. In later years, she and her husband also operated a small cottage resort in the beautiful Georgian Bay Biosphere (Ontario, Canada). During this time, she served on the Board of Directors of the Ontario Association of Social Workers, Huronia Branch. She also served on the Parry Sound Chamber of Commerce Board of Directors, receiving the Business Person of the Year Award in 2002.

In 2001, Miranda suffered a major health crisis which eventually terminated her ability to work at her chosen careers. After the businesses were sold, she continued to look after their two special needs daughters, while attempting to recover. Eventually in 2011, she suffered a complete breakdown.

After the onset of her disability, Miranda devoted herself to studying the Word of God, improving her connection with the Lord, and regaining her health. Miranda and her husband reside in Niagara, Canada. This is her first book.

Ms. Chivers is available to speak to your church or women's groups.

Ms. Chivers can be contacted at www.mirandajchivers.com

Now It's Your Turn

T his book was written with the encouragement and support of the amazing staff at Chandler Bolt's Self-Publishing School. If you have a story that you want the world to hear, consider writing your own book. This school can teach you how.

SELF-PUBLISHING
SCHOOL
NOW IT'S YOUR TURN

Discover the EXACT 3-step blueprint you need to become a bestselling author in 3 months.

Self-Publishing School helped me, and now I want them to help you with this FREE VIDEO SERIES!

Even if you're busy, bad at writing, or don't know where to start, you CAN write a bestseller and build your best life.

With tools and experience across a variety niches and professions,

Self-Publishing School is the only resource you need to take your book to the finish line!

DON'T WAIT

Watch this FREE VIDEO SERIES now, and Say "YES" to becoming a bestseller:

Go here: https://xe172.isrefer.com/go/curcust/mchivers

Urgent Plea!

Thank You For Reading My Book!

I really appreciate all of your feedback, and I love hearing what you have to say.

I need your input to make the next version of this book and my future books even better.

Please leave me a helpful review on Amazon letting me know what you thought of the book.

Thank you so much!

Thank you so much!
~ Miranda J. Chivers

Made in the USA
Las Vegas, NV
30 November 2020

11809015R00184